STUDIES IN GLOBALIZATION AND ECONOMIC TRANSITIONS

Also by Keith Griffin

ALTERNATIVE STATEGIES FOR ECONOMIC DEVELOPMENT
THE DISTRIBUTION OF INCOME IN CHINA (*editor with Zhao Renwei*)
THE ECONOMIC DEVELOPMENT OF BANGLADESH (*editor with E. A. G. Robinson*)
THE ECONOMY OF ETHIOPIA (*editor*)
FINANCING DEVELOPMENT IN LATIN AMERICA (*editor*)
GLOBALIZATION AND THE DEVELOPING WORLD (*with Azizur Rahman Khan*)
GROWTH AND EQUALITY IN RURAL CHINA (*with Ashwani Saith*)
HUMAN DEVELOPMENT AND THE INTERNATIONAL DEVELOPMENT STRATEGY FOR THE 1990s (*editor with John Knight*)
IMPLEMENTING A HUMAN DEVELOPMENT STRATEGY (*with Terry McKinley*)
INSTITUTIONAL REFORM AND ECONOMIC DEVELOPMENT IN THE CHINESE COUNTRYSIDE (*editor*)
INTERNATIONAL INEQUALITY AND NATIONAL POVERTY
LAND CONCENTRATION AND RURAL POVERTY
PLANNING DEVELOPMENT (*with John Enos*)
THE POLITICAL ECONOMY OF AGRARIAN CHANGE
POVERTY AND LANDLESSNESS IN RURAL ASIA (*editor with Azizur Rahman Khan*)
POVERTY AND THE TRANSITION TO A MARKET ECONOMY IN MONGOLIA
THE TRANSITION TO EGALITARIAN DEVELOPMENT (*with Jeffrey James*)
UNDERDEVELOPMENT IN SPANISH AMERICA
WORLD HUNGER AND THE WORLD ECONOMY

Studies in Globalization and Economic Transitions

Keith Griffin
Professor of Economics
University of California, Riverside

First published in Great Britain 1996 by
MACMILLAN PRESS LTD
Houndmills, Basingstoke, Hampshire RG21 6XS
and London
Companies and representatives
throughout the world

A catalogue record for this book is available
from the British Library.

ISBN 0-333-66987-8 (hardcover)
ISBN 0-333-66988-6 (paperback)

 First published in the United States of America 1996 by
ST. MARTIN'S PRESS, INC.,
Scholarly and Reference Division,
175 Fifth Avenue,
New York, N.Y. 10010

ISBN 0-312-16224-3

Library of Congress Cataloging-in-Publication Data
Griffin, Keith B.
Studies in globalization and economic transitions / Keith Griffin.
p.   cm.
Includes bibliographical references and index.
ISBN 0-312-16224-3
1. Economic policy.   2. Social policy.   3. Economic assistance.
4. Economic development.   5. Economic conversion.   6. International
economic relations.   I. Title.
HD87.G75   1996
337—dc20
96-17558
CIP

10   9   8   7   6   5   4   3   2   1
05   04   03   02   01   00   99   98   97   96

Printed and bound in Great Britain by
Antony Rowe Ltd, Chippenham, Wiltshire

To my uncle,
Martin Cherkasky,
whose energy, enthusiasm and commitment
are an inspiration

Contents

List of Figures and Tables

Figures

Tables

Preface

These *Studies in Globalization and Economic Transitions* have benefited much from comments, helpful criticism and advice from friends and colleagues around the world. My greatest debt is to Azizur Rahman Khan, my colleague at the University of California, Riverside (UCR). Aziz not only is the co-author of Chapter 7 and the Appendix (on China), but he was also a member of the team that produced the report on Uzbekistan (from which Chapters 10–12 are drawn), and he commented extensively on the essay on domestic policies in developing countries (Chapter 6). More generally, he has listened for years, and with great patience, when I used him as a sounding-board for many of the ideas that subsequently appeared in a more refined form in these studies and other publications. His words of advice often have helped me avoid error and his suggestions often have stimulated further work.

The essay on foreign aid (Chapter 3), written at the OECD Development Centre in Paris, enjoyed the support of Louis Emmerij, then the President of the Development Centre. Useful comments were received from Jean Bonvin, James Boyce, Giulio Fossi, Laurence Harris, Rachel Meghir, Helmut Reisen, Hartmut Schneider and David Turnham. Phil Martinez was my research assistant on this project. The study of development cooperation (Chapter 4) was originally stimulated by Mahbub ul Haq and is based on work done jointly with Terry McKinley. The version included in this volume was produced for the North-South Institute in Ottawa and was improved thanks to comments from Albert Berry, Roy Culpeper and Frances Stewart.

The essay on regulating world markets (Chapter 5) was written for a conference at Queen Elizabeth House, Oxford, at the request of Frances Stewart, its Director. The published version benefited from the comments of Stephany Griffith-Jones, the principal discussant of the paper at the conference. Some of the ideas in the paper were provoked by the contrary views of Stephen Cullenberg, one of my colleagues at UCR.

Chapter 6 was written as a background study for the International Labour Office in Geneva and was used by them in preparing the *World Employment Survey 1995*. I am grateful to E.L.H. Lee, Samir Radwan and Hamid Tabatabai for helpful comments on an early draft. Stephen Cullenberg commented on Chapter 7 and kindly invited Aziz Khan and myself to present the paper at a conference he organized on 'Whither Marxism?'.

In 1989–91 I was an economic adviser to the government of Bolivia. It was during this period that I first became interested in the effects of the drugs trade on economic development. Most of my work in Bolivia, however, had little to do with the coca economy but was instead concerned with designing a human development strategy for the country. Robert Pollin, Rosemary Thorp, Charles Oman and Stephen Cullenberg were part of my 'Bolivia team' and their comments and advice influenced the views expressed in Chapter 8. Chapter 9 (on Nicaragua) was first presented at a conference in Washington at which John Weeks was the discussant. Our friendly disagreement continued after the conference and the Appendix to Chapter 9 is one of the results.

In 1994 I was invited by Khalid Malik, the UNDP Resident Representative in Tashkent, and Samir Radwan, a senior ILO official in Geneva, to lead a mission to Uzbekistan to prepare a report on social policy during the transition to a market-guided economy. Chapters 10–12 are drawn from that report. I am very grateful to Khalid Malik and Samir Radwan for giving me an opportunity to study the economy of Uzbekistan and to present our findings to the government. I also am grateful to Aziz Khan, Helene Harasty and Deniz Kandiyoti, three of the members of my 'Uzbekistan team', for their comments and suggestions on drafts of these chapters. Our experience in Uzbekistan was memorable and I am pleased that the ILO and UNDP have published the entire report.

Kathy Lowney and Marie Lucille Russo prepared the manuscript for publication in Riverside, California. I am very grateful to them.

KEITH GRIFFIN

List of Abbreviations

AID	Agency for International Development
AIDS	Auto-Immune Deficiency Syndrome
CASID	Canadian Association for the Study of International Development
DAC	Development Assistance Committee
ECOSOC	Economic and Social Council of the United Nations
FAO	Food and Agriculture Organization
FSE	*Fondo Social de Emergencia* (Emergency Social Fund)
GATT	General Agreement on Tariffs and Trade
HDI	human development index
IBRD	International Bank for Reconstruction and Development (World Bank)
IDA	International Development Association
IDS	Institute of Development Studies
IFAD	International Fund for Agricultural Development
ILO	International Labour Organization
IMF	International Monetary Fund
NAFTA	North American Free Trade Agreement
NGOs	non-governmental organizations
ODA	Official Development Assistance
OECD	Organization for Economic Cooperations and Development
OPEC	Organization of Petroleum Exporting Countries
PPP	purchasing power parity
SSB	State Statistical Bureau
TRIPs	trade-related international property rights
UCR	University of California, Riverside
UNDP	United Nations Development Programme
UNESCO	United Nations Educational, Scientific and Cultural Organization
UNFPA	United Nations Fund for Population Affairs
UNICEF	United Nations Children's Fund
UNIDO	United Nations Industrial Development Organization
UNRISD	United Nations Research Institute for Social Development
WHO	World Health Organization

1 Introduction

The world economy is undergoing a major transformation. First, there is a continuing, indeed accelerating, process of globalization. The three-fold division of the world that arose during the Cold War and the era of decolonization is disappearing and national economies are merging into a single and increasingly integrated world economy. In the process, the economic significance of individual states is diminishing. National economic policies are daily becoming less effective, yet our institutions of global economic management are feeble and have failed to adapt to changed circumstances. Next, large numbers of developing countries have introduced policies of structural adjustment in order to respond to the new global economic realities and to become more closely integrated into the global economy. At the same time, the socialist economies have begun to restructure their economies. They have entered into a long and painful process of systemic change, seeking a transition from a centrally planned to a more market-oriented economic regime. As part of this transition they, too, have become more closely integrated into the world economy.

The essays collected in this volume are concerned with these two themes, globalization and economic transitions. Most of them were written between 1990 and 1995; most have been published before, but they have been dispersed among a variety of journals and edited books and there may be some advantage in bringing them together in one place.

Part I contains four essays under the heading of 'Global Prospects and Possibilities'. The first essay (Chapter 2) is the keynote address I presented at the 1994 conference of the Canadian Association for the Study of International Development, held in Calgary. The address is a survey of the terrain and touches upon a number of issues that are explored at greater length in other chapters. The influence of the 'human development approach' is apparent and reflects my close association during several years with the UNDP *Human Development Report*.[1]

The objective of development is specified as human development, not growth of national product, and human development is defined as a process which increases the choices people enjoy and enhances their capabilities. One question that naturally arises from such a formulation is the relationship between development and security. Until recently the word 'security' was used in an international context to mean state security or national security but, following the 1994 *Human Development Report*, I reinterpret it to mean 'human security'. Security in this sense is concerned with the sustainability of people's livelihoods in the face of shocks, with the degree and types of risk that individuals face and with the extent of vulnerability of different groups of people to unanticipated events. There is also an inter-generational dimension, however: namely, maintaining human security over an extended period of time. Security in this second sense provides a link between development processes and the protection of the environment or, more generally, the need to pass on to future generations a stock of physical, human and natural capital that is sufficiently large to ensure that opportunities and choices open to our successors are no less than the ones we enjoy today.

Looking ahead, the outlook for the global economy is moderately encouraging. There is a possibility of accelerated economic growth, stimulated in part by continued liberalization of international trade and factor markets and in part by a reallocation of resources from military expenditure to more productive economic activities. There is also a prospect of diminished global income inequality, led by continued rapid growth of per capita income in several of the populous low income economies of Asia, notably China, India, Pakistan and Indonesia. There is, too, a likelihood that international differentials in human development indicators will continue to narrow. The developing countries have been catching up with the more developed countries in a number of areas – life expectancy, literacy, years of schooling, etc. – and this is likely to continue.

None of this, however, gives grounds for complacency. World poverty remains very serious. Some countries, particularly in sub-Saharan Africa, have experienced declining real incomes over extended periods of time. Most countries which have attempted to restructure their economy have encountered considerable difficulty and the ex-socialist countries, with few exceptions, have found the transition from a planning regime to a market-based system to be exceedingly difficult. Thus there still is much hardship in the world and in some countries hardship is increasing.

It is commonly argued that one of the causes of hardship is rapid population growth. I dissent from this opinion. There is no evidence that population growth rates are increasing. On the contrary, fertility rates and population growth rates are falling in virtually every region of the globe. Moreover, there is little empirical evidence that population growth rates are slowing development or resulting in other undesired consequences, such as increased unemployment of labour or greater income inequality. The anti-Malthusian case seems to me to be strong. That is, there is at best only weak evidence of a causal link running from demographic expansion to increased underdevelopment. There is much stronger evidence that population growth is endogenous and that the chain of causation runs from increased development to reduced population growth.

The population issue thus is really a development issue. It has much to do with the emancipation of women in developing countries, with creating equal opportunities for girls and women to receive an education, with allowing women to enter the paid labour force and with providing economic security to men and women in their old age. Whenever broadly-based human development has occurred, population growth rates have declined.

In Chapter 3 the role of foreign aid in promoting development is discussed. On this issue, too, I am a dissenter. Indeed the essay contains a comprehensive criticism of foreign aid programmes as they have evolved since the late 1940s. The origin of foreign aid is linked to the Cold War, and the motive for aid, I argue, never has been to promote development but rather to secure the political objectives of donor countries. The economic justification for aid has always been suspect – namely, to provide capital and technical skills on the assumption that these were the primary constraints on development – when in fact the major constraint has usually been a lack of human development arising ultimately from poor domestic policies.

Foreign aid has tended to support the status quo. It has been socially and politically conservative; it has been anti-reformist in the sense of helping to maintain the concentration of political power and an unequal distribution of income and wealth while inhibiting institutional changes such as land reform. Aid has tended to strengthen the recipient state and thereby strengthened those who happened to be in power.

Aid has not been channelled systematically to the poorest countries or to poor people within countries. There is no systematic relationship between inflows of foreign aid and faster economic growth. Aid often has acted as a substitute for domestic savings, domestic taxation and exporting. Because of the effects of large inflows of aid on relative prices – notably in appreciating the real exchange rate and in lowering real interest rates – foreign aid has sometimes changed the structure of incentives in an anti-development direction. Aid has often financed increased military expenditure and capital flight rather than domestic investment and, because of this, foreign aid has indirectly been one of the causes of the debt burden of developing countries.

A number of explicit predictions are made about the future of foreign aid in the chapter, almost all of which have turned out to be accurate. Thus there has been a decline in aid flows in real terms in recent years. For example, aid from the OECD countries fell 5 per cent in 1993 and a further 1.8 per cent in 1994. Of the 20 OECD donor countries, 13 gave less aid as a percentage of their GDP in 1994 than they gave on average in 1984–88; one country (France) was unchanged and six countries increased the proportion of GDP allocated to aid. The USA, as predicted, gave less, viz., only 0.15 per cent of GDP in 1994, and continued to be a large recipient of foreign capital. Russia, as predicted, reduced its aid very sharply and in fact became a net recipient. Germany, as predicted, reduced its aid and redirected its resources to the former East Germany in order to speed up the process of national reunification. Japan, contrary to my expectations, reduced its aid ratio too, but as predicted, it has continued to displace the United States as the largest donor.[2] Foreign aid as we have known it in the past is of diminishing significance and the time has arrived to write off the debts of the most heavily indebted developing countries and then bring conventional aid programmes to an end.

Chapter 4, based on work for UNDP,[3] contains proposals for a new framework for development cooperation. The proposed new framework rests on three pillars. First, we need a new mechanism for providing foreign assistance to poor countries to replace the discredited conventional aid programmes. I suggest a pure international tax and transfer mechanism. Resources would be raised through a low and mildly progressive international income tax on the GNP of high income countries. These resources would then be disbursed automatically through a negative income tax. That is, foreign assistance would be distributed to low income countries in inverse proportion to the recipients' per capita income. This mechanism would ensure that the burden of foreign assistance is equitably distributed among the rich countries, that the available funds are distributed among eligible poor countries in accordance with their need and that foreign assistance is insulated from the political, commercial and other interests of rich countries. All of this would increase the likelihood that aid might actually make a contribution to development.

Second, a separate mechanism is needed to facilitate mutually beneficial inter-governmental transactions where there are cases of market failure and externalities. Examples of what I have in mind are environmental programmes in developing countries which are at least in part of benefit to developed countries and programmes to destroy nuclear weapons and reduce the risks of radiation to countries downwind of nuclear facilities. In all such instances it may be advantageous for one country to pay another for services rendered, but we do not at present have an institutional mechanism for negotiating mutually beneficial agreements, monitoring compliance and effecting payments. This form of international cooperation is likely to become increasingly important in future and should be clearly distinguished from foreign aid.

Third, we need to strengthen rule-based systems governing international economic intercourse. If liberalism is to be taken seriously, countries must be discouraged from acting arbitrarily and unilaterally and harming the interests of their trading partners. I propose that a mechanism be created to provide compensation for damages when one country breaks the rules of the game and inflicts economic injury on another. How such a mechanism might work is illustrated in Chapter 4 by the case of restrictions on the international mobility of low-skilled labour, perhaps the most glaring departure from a liberal global economic regime.

A liberal economy is not the same thing as a *laissez faire* economy and in some instances a strong case can be made for regulating some world markets. This argument is considered in Chapter 5.

A number of analysts in developed countries have claimed that trade between rich and poor countries is 'unfair' because the developed countries have 'high' labour standards (e.g., as regards health and safety) while the developing countries have 'low' standards (e.g., as regards child labour). I argue, however, that the 'high' labour standards in developed countries should be seen as a benefit which increases well-being in rich countries and these benefits cannot logically be used as a justification for imposing trade restrictions on imports from developing countries. Indeed high labour standards provide incentives to improve working conditions in dangerous or unhealthy activities or, where this cannot profitably be done, to shift resources to other sectors where conditions are less dangerous or unhealthy. Restrictions against imports that compete with domestic production in dangerous industries would neutralize the incentive to move resources out of such industries and hence would partially offset the potential benefits of the high labour standards. Thus both the developing and the developed country would be harmed.

As regards the 'low' labour standards in developing countries, these are a matter for the countries concerned and should not be used as an excuse by developed countries to impose tariffs and other trade restrictions. If anything, trade restrictions would make matters worse in the developing countries, e.g., by lowering the incomes of households partially dependent on child labour. There may indeed be some labour practices that should be abolished and some minimum standards of behaviour that should be applied universally, but these prohibitions and universal minimum standards should be agreed internationally and embodied in ILO conventions, not imposed unilaterally on developing countries by trade barriers erected in developed countries. There is unfortunately more than a hint of hypocrisy in this debate since it is the United States that has taken the lead in threatening trade sanctions to enforce its view of appropriate labour standards while at the same time it is the United States that has been most unwilling among the developed countries to sign democratically agreed ILO labour conventions.

A second area of controversy centres on the use of trade regulations to achieve environmental objectives. Again, I argue that policies intended to improve a country's environment, by internalizing an environmental externality, confer a potential benefit on the country concerned and it would be illogical and self-defeating to use the enactment of environmental policies as an excuse to restrict imports from developing countries. The situation is more complicated when the environment to be protected straddles national boundaries. Trade restrictions, however, clearly are a second best policy and the optimal solution would be an internationally negotiated agreement with side payments as appropriate, as discussed in Chapter 4.

Running throughout the essay is the view that globalization is eroding the sovereignty of states. Governments can either resist this tendency or they can accommodate themselves to it. There is much to be said for accommodation. Liberalization will bring static and dynamic efficiency gains and create opportunities to improve living standards worldwide. Some market regulation, however, will be required and some sort of tax and transfer mechanism will be necessary to reduce global poverty and ensure that the benefits of globalization are equitably distributed. This, in turn, implies a need for global collective action and improved institutions of global governance.

In Part II the emphasis shifts to studies of national policies during transitions. Chapter 6 is concerned with domestic policies and their effects on employment, the distribution of income and wealth, and poverty. It was written as a background paper for the ILO during the period when *World Employment 1995* was being prepared.[4]

Macroeconomic policy is fundamental. We have become excessively fearful of inflation in the rich countries and this has given a deflation-ary bias to the world economy. It is necessary to reverse this bias and adopt macroeconomic policies that favour growth and employment. Policies should be designed to encourage high rates of physical capital formation (in plant and equipment and infrastructure) and high rates of human capital formation. A set of incentives should be created which encourages an efficient pattern of investment and the desirable degree of labour intensity in production. Factor markets often function inef-ficiently and a case can be made for government intervention to create lending facilities that provide credit to the poor and for governments to mount guaranteed employment schemes. The informal sector is a potential source of dynamism, creativity and private initiative and es-pecially in countries going through a transition from central planning to a market guided economy, small scale informal sector activities can be a major source of growth and job creation.

Some people, notably the elderly and the infirm, are unable to sus-tain their livelihood through employment. The poor among them face great economic insecurity and I argue that the state should and can provide modest pensions, even in the poorest developing countries, so that no one is reduced to destitution and humiliation in their old age. Beyond the modest redistribution of income that would be required to finance a nationwide pension programme, the evidence suggests that those countries, as in East Asia, which have effected a relatively equal distribution of productive assets, have enjoyed not only greater equity but also a faster rate of growth. That is, growth and equality may be complementary rather than conflicting as is so often suggested.[5]

This raises a question about the role and size of the state. There is no doubt that the state has had a bad press in recent years. It is said to be too large, to be inefficient and to do more harm than good (and hence the exhortation to 'get the state off the backs of the people'). As a general proposition these claims are nonsense. Historically the state (local, provincial and central governments combined) has been a major instrument of collective action and an important institution through which human goals have been achieved. The issue is not whether we should have a small and weak state as compared to a large and strong one, but rather what should be the tasks assigned to the state. The view adopted in these studies is that the prime task of the state is to promote human development, directly and indirectly.

It is fashionable nowadays to assign increased responsibilities to non-governmental organizations (NGOs), mass organizations (trade unions, women's organizations, farmers' organizations, etc.) and other institutions of civil society. In some countries governments are abdicating their responsibilities for social policy to NGOs, charitable organizations and the private sector in general. It is hoped, in effect, that an expanding NGO sector will offset a contracting state sector, and that 'a million points of light' will illuminate the darkness following the exit of the state. At the rhetorical level this may be attractive, but I do not believe it is wise policy. The NGOs are not a substitute for government but a complement to government. Their role is advocacy and grass roots mobilization. Their task is to be sceptical of government, to be critical, to challenge conventional ideas and to present new, less conventional ideas that may later form the basis of policy. NGOs can also engage in small scale experimentation, testing ideas and demonstrating what does and does not work. These are vital functions. Moreover they are functions which governments either cannot do or else do rather poorly. But we must not ask NGOs to do more than this, and in particular we must not ask them to replace the state.

Just as in some cases we ask too much of NGOs, in other cases we ask the state to do too much, too fast. This is particularly true in the ex-socialist countries which have embarked on a regime change, switching from central planning to a market guided economy. Advocates of instantaneous and comprehensive reform of the economy and polity, i.e., advocates of 'shock therapy' and a 'big bang', have been influential in Western academic and policy circles and have in fact tended to dominate the discussion. In Chapter 7 and the Appendix (both written with Azizur Rahman Khan) this dominant view is challenged, using evidence from China to support an argument for sequential reform during a period of structural disequilibrium.

I have long been interested in China and have followed the reform process since its inception.[6] The Chinese experience contrasts sharply with that of eastern and central Europe, the former Soviet Union and Mongolia,[7] and much can be learned by studying its reform strategy. The Vietnamese experience also is instructive although the reform process began much later (in 1988–89) and the evidence documenting its success is less abundant.[8] Even so, the favourable outcome in Vietnam is helpful to the debate because it makes it more difficult to dismiss China as a 'special case'.

The Chinese reform strategy was distinctive in four ways. First, the reformers did not liberalize all prices at once. They maintained many price controls and operated a dual price system with free market prices and regulated, planned prices side-by-side. This led to many inefficiencies but it had the great advantage of enabling the authorities to maintain financial stability and to prevent the emergence of very rapid rates of inflation. Second, the reformers placed a high priority on sustaining rapid rates of growth and high levels of investment. The pursuit of static allocative efficiency, which elsewhere led to a fall in output and incomes, was sacrificed to maintain growth. In effect, the authorities chose to grow out of inefficiency by channelling investment resources on the margin into activities which enjoyed high rates of profit.

Third, the Chinese placed no priority on privatizing state enterprises. Instead they concentrated on creating opportunities for new, small scale, labour intensive private enterprises to emerge, in both the rural and urban areas. This strategy was highly successful: it resulted in very rapid growth of output, incomes and employment; it helped to distribute the benefits of reform quite widely, across households and regions; and it resulted in a rapid rise in the share of the private sector in total output and in manufacturing while allowing output in the state enterprises to continue to grow.

Finally, the Chinese took great care to ensure that poverty did not increase during the transition period. The benefits of reform initially were concentrated in the rural areas, where most of the poor are located. The emphasis on sustaining growth and investment meant that average incomes rose very rapidly, thereby ensuring that the benefits of reform were spread widely. The refusal to privatize state enterprises meant that the social services provided by those enterprises (housing, pensions, health services, etc.) remained intact and hence the social safety net in urban areas continued to operate reasonably well. Income inequality did increase as a result of the reforms, but the degree of inequality has been tolerable, at least so far, and inequality in China continues to be moderate compared to other developing countries.

In the Appendix to Chapter 7, in response to a criticism by Laszló Csaba of Hungary, we discuss the case for a reform sequence that puts economic transformation before political democracy. The argument rests on the assumption that in the short term there may be high costs of systemic change whereas the benefits of reform will become realized only after a lag, perhaps a long lag. Liberal political systems, however, tend to adopt policies which concentrate benefits in the near future and postpone costs to the more distant future. As a result, there is a possible dissonance between economic liberalization and political liberalization and the Chinese 'strategy' of first introducing economic reforms and then (hopefully) political reforms may be justified in terms of political economy.

During the period 1989–91 I was an economic adviser in Bolivia.

The study in Chapter 8 is based on work done at that time. Bolivia is of interest to a general audience for two reasons that seemingly are unconnected, namely, the 1985 stabilization programme and its aftermath and its flourishing coca economy.

Bolivia was one of the first countries to undergo 'shock therapy' and the alleged success of its 'new economic policy' of 1985 has been widely cited by those advising Eastern Europe and the Russian Federation after 1989. Bolivia's success in negotiating a transition to a more liberal economy should, however, be heavily qualified. Per capita income began to fall in 1979 and inflation accelerated so that by the middle of the 1980s the country experienced both economic recession and hyperinflation. The stabilization programme that was introduced in 1985 was fairly orthodox: government expenditure was cut back sharply, the budget deficit was brought under control, the availability of credit was curtailed and real interest rates were raised to very high levels. This orthodoxy was tempered by a *de facto* default on the country's external debt payments and by the creation of an emergency employment scheme intended to provide some relief to unemployed miners and urban workers. Even so, economic conditions for the majority of the population deteriorated further: unemployment rose, poverty increased and inequality became even more pronounced.

In response to this distressing state of affairs I advocated the adoption of a human development strategy that placed emphasis on (i) primary and secondary education, particularly in the rural areas; (ii) investment in internal transport, particularly on secondary roads; and (iii) a guaranteed employment scheme that could be used to promote investment in small scale irrigation and labour intensive public works. The purpose was to encourage a resumption of growth and ensure that the benefits of that growth would be widely shared through employment creation and human capital formation.

The situation in Bolivia would have been desperate had it not been for the existence of a thriving coca economy, a sector of the economy that was largely outside the law and which the government (with the forceful support of the United States) tried to suppress. As incomes began to fall, peasant farmers from 1979 onwards migrated from the highlands to the coca producing regions in the Chapare to take advantage of the high prices of coca and cocaine and the income earning opportunities those high prices created. Somewhere between 6.7 and 26.2 per cent of the labour force came to be employed in the coca economy.[9] One careful estimate puts it at about 10 per cent of the labour force.[10] Whatever the correct number might be, Bolivia's peasant coca cultivators were well organized. As LaMond Tullis explains, 'five peasant federations account for all but a small portion of coca production, with each of the federations sporting sophisticated organizational subdivisions . . . that actually function somewhat like local governments. . . . In the 1980s these federations grew to become probably the most powerful political pressure group in the entire country.'[11]

Not only was the sector well organized, it was the largest sector in the economy and the most important source of foreign exchange. It is estimated that the coca economy accounted for 12 per cent of GDP,[12] or perhaps 20 per cent,[13] or as I argue in Chapter 8, possibly even as much as 24 per cent. This illegal, informal but well organized sector sustained the entire economy, and particularly the poor, during Bolivia's period of shock therapy and transition. James Painter notes that 'in the late 1980s Bolivia may have been the country . . . with the highest degree of dependence on the revenue and jobs from the production and trafficking of a narcotic', and he goes on to add that 'the benefits of the coca-cocaine trade helped to ensure the "success" of the stabilization plan initiated in 1985'.[14] That is, the coca economy in Bolivia played the same role as the small scale, labour intensive private sector in China during its transition to a more market-oriented economy.

One great difference is that there was constant pressure from the US government in Bolivia to suppress the coca economy and in effect to destroy the country's safety net, whereas in China the government was careful not to destroy it. Efforts to suppress the coca economy were ineffective – in fact it continued to grow – but repeated failures led only to intensification of efforts and the militarization of anti-coca campaigns. US troops were first used in 1986 on coca search-and-destroy missions; later, yearly coca eradication targets were established; most recently the campaign has become more militarized through forced eradication programmes and the so-called Operation Safe Haven. A range of alternative policies is reviewed in Chapter 8 which include crop substitution in coca growing regions (to provide alternative sources of income to coca growers) and rural development in the altiplano (to reduce the incentive of peasants to migrate from the highlands to the coca growing lowlands). The inescapable conclusion, however, is that neither repression nor alternative development will work and the best policy for Bolivia would be to decriminalize the coca economy. This evidently is a controversial conclusion but I continue to believe it is correct.

In Chapter 9 and the Appendix attention is turned to a different type of transition, namely, the attempt in Nicaragua during the Sandinista period (1979–89) to transform the economy from capitalism to socialism. The currents of history are at present flowing in the opposite direction, and the transition in Nicaragua was a failure, but Nicaragua's experiment was important and we need to understand what went wrong. In the early 1980s, writing in the context of the debate about 'basic needs', I published a book with Jeffrey James on *The Transition to Egalitarian Development* in which some of the issues faced by the government in Nicaragua were addressed.[15] The debate engaged in Chapter 9, which is really a debate with the romantic Left in the United States, gave me an opportunity to review my thinking on socialist transformations.

State power in Nicaragua was used to achieve three major objectives. First, the Sandinistas were determined (rightly in my view) to reallocate resources in favour of the poor, including the provision of basic health services to all and universal primary and secondary education. Second, the government decided that the state should assume responsibility for investment and growth. This proved to be a misguided decision. Private investment collapsed and the state was unable to mobilize sufficient resources to prevent a dramatic fall in total investment and in output and incomes. The attempt by the state simultaneously to raise public consumption (to benefit the poor) and public investment (to accelerate growth and create a socialist society) foundered because no effort was made to increase savings. The result was hyperinflation, not faster growth or a higher standard of living for the population as a whole.

Matters were made worse by the government's policy of turning the terms of trade against the peasantry. This not only alienated some of the Sandinistas' natural allies, it also resulted in a sharp decline in food supplies, which had an unfavourable repercussion on the urban population. The situation was further aggravated by credit policies which discriminated against small producers in both rural and urban areas. That is, many of the government's sector and microeconomic policies had adverse consequences for the poor. Policies on balance were anti-peasant, anti-trader and anti-private, and the predictable results were negative growth of income per head, a collapse of savings, soaring inflation, a decline in exports, a dramatic fall in household consumption and increased hardship for virtually everyone.

All of this occurred in the midst of a war against the Contras. This imposed on the government a third major objective, namely, the need to defeat the Contras in armed conflict. The war, however, was partly endogenous, i.e., it was a consequence of the failure of the government to attain its first two objectives and of the misery that ensued. I do not wish to absolve the US government for financing and inspiring the civil war, but it is important to recognize that there was widespread discontent with the Sandinistas in Nicaragua and the Contras were able to exploit this discontent quite effectively. The transition to socialism failed in Nicaragua as much for domestic reasons as for external ones.

Part III consists of three essays on the transition from central planning to a market guided economy in Uzbekistan, until recently one of the five Central Asian republics of the USSR. In 1994 I was invited by the ILO and UNDP to lead a group of economists and policy analysts and prepare a report for the government on social policy during the economic transition. The chapters reproduced in this volume are taken from that report, which was written in 1995.[16] The attentive reader will notice that many of the themes of earlier chapters find an echo here.

Chapter 10, on development, culture and social policy in Uzbekistan, is didactic in tone and argues that social policy is indistinguishable from development policy, especially when development is interpreted to mean human development. I then outline the rudiments of a human development strategy as it might be applied in Uzbekistan. The most novel feature of the chapter, however, is the discussion of culture, which I define broadly as 'ways of living'.

Human development is primarily concerned with individual human beings, increasing their 'capabilities' and widening their range of choice. The human development approach is therefore rather individualistic. Culture, in contrast, necessarily is concerned with people in groups, i.e., the ways individuals interact with others of their kind and with nature. Robinson Crusoe, marooned on his island and living in isolation, brought his culture with him from England and it is inconceivable that he could have developed a culture on his own without an opportunity to interact with others. Culture thus highlights the 'collective' dimension of human development and casts old issues in a new light.

I had an opportunity to explore the relationship between culture and development as a member of the World Commission on Culture and Development.[17] My work in Uzbekistan overlapped with my work on the Commission and I took advantage of this happy coincidence to raise four cultural issues in the Uzbekistan report, viz., the nationality question (politically sensitive in a new multi-national state), language policy (in a context in which a decision in principle had been taken to switch from the Cyrillic to the Latin script), the revival of Islam (in a region where atheism had previously been the official doctrine) and political culture (where pressure for a more liberal polity was in conflict with an ingrained tendency towards authoritarianism).

Macroeconomic issues are discussed in Chapter 11. Although economic performance in Uzbekistan has not been as bad as in many other countries going through a similar transition, growth rates have been negative, inflation has been several hundred per cent a year and real incomes have declined quite considerably. Evidently it was necessary to reverse these trends. In order to do so, we recommended a strategy with three pillars.

First, it was necessary to stabilize prices through a tight credit policy so that the newly liberalized price mechanism could begin to function efficiently and transmit accurate signals to investors and consumers. Second, special efforts were required to improve the price mechanism in a number of 'strategic' areas. These key markets affect the overall performance of the economy and, unless they function well, there is a danger that the transition process as a whole will yield disappointing results. In Chapter 11 I concentrate on five areas: the market for foreign exchange, the market for finance capital, the wage rate for low skilled labour, the market for water and the market for energy. The third pillar consists of measures to achieve a positive rate of growth and an equitable distribution of income. I recommended that four things are done: (i) create space for small scale private sector activities to emerge; (ii) introduce a temporary pause in the programme to privatize large scale state industrial enterprises; (iii) give higher priority to the transformation and expansion of the rural economy; and (iv) organize a large scale public works programme that would guarantee employment to all those seeking work, and which would accelerate capital formation and growth.

Lastly, in Chapter 12, the issue of social protection in Uzbekistan is considered. Prior to independence, thanks to massive transfers from the USSR, Uzbekistan had an extensive and generous system of social protection. After independence the problem became how to continue to provide the essential elements of a system of social protection in the absence of massive subsidies and in a context of falling output and incomes. What services should be eliminated? Which services should be reduced and become less generous? Which services should be restructured to reflect changing views of the responsibility of the state and the individual?

The problem of social protection in Uzbekistan is insoluble unless general economic conditions improve. Hence the emphasis on accelerating growth, creating employment opportunities and sustaining basic health and education services so that 'residual' distress is manageable in the sense that unbearable claims would not be imposed on the exchequer. The macroeconomic issues discussed in Chapter 11, in other words, are keys to a solution. Once the overall policy framework is put right, one can consider the specifics of social protection policies.

The first specific issue to arise is what to do about poverty. Although incomes in Uzbekistan have fallen, there is no evidence of widespread poverty. The proportion of the population living in poverty is low and the depth of poverty (that is, the shortfall of income below a poverty threshold) also is low. This is encouraging, but the incidence of poverty undoubtedly has increased and hence some public intervention to assist the lowest income households is necessary. We recommended that the government work through the *mahallas*, neighbourhood committees that exist throughout the country. The role of the *mahallas* would be to use local knowledge to identify the poor, to determine the extent of need and then to channel the funds available for relief to the most needy households.

Open unemployment is not a major problem in Uzbekistan, but the country has a gigantic system of 'disguised unemployment compensation'. The system is not of course explicit but has emerged as a consequence of ill considered *ad hoc* policies. In the urban areas, the banks finance the operating deficits of the state enterprises and of the newly privatized enterprises (which are not allowed to shed labour for three years). A significant part of these deficits, however, is due to over-manning, or disguised unemployment, and hence the inflationary expansion of bank credit is really being used to prevent open unemployment from becoming widespread. In the rural areas, agricultural output has declined while employment in agriculture has increased. That is, the average productivity of labour has fallen and agriculture, in effect, has become the residual source of employment. Disguised unemployment in agriculture is perhaps as serious as the disguised unemployment in industry. Rather than continue with the present system of 'disguised unemployment compensation', I suggested that urban and rural enterprises be allowed to dismiss redundant labour and that the funds now used to cover enterprise deficits be reallocated to finance an employment guarantee scheme. In this way open unemployment would be avoided and surplus labour could be used to undertake investment projects on public works schemes.

Uzbekistan has a lavish pension programme which absorbs about 11.4 per cent of the country's GDP. Given the reduced resources available to the government, the present pension system is unsustainable, yet some provision evidently must be made for the social protection of the elderly. We suggested, first, that the age of retirement be raised to 65 for both women and men (at present some women can retire at 45 and some men at 50); second, that all retired persons be granted the same basic pension regardless of the level of previous earnings (the implication being that those who wished to supplement their state pensions would have to do so through private savings); and third, that the basic pension be fully adjusted to offset the effects of inflation. Such a scheme, far less generous than present arrangements, has the virtue that it would provide a minimum degree of economic security for the elderly while being affordable to the government during a period when its revenues are depleted.

These policies to combat poverty, unemployment and the hardships of old age, plus essential programmes to protect women and children, could form the core of social protection during the transition period. Once economic stability is achieved and expansion resumes, the range of social policies could be increased and the level of protection raised.

Notes

1. See the UNDP *Human Development Report*, published annually since 1960 by Oxford University Press, New York. Also see Keith Griffin and Terry McKinley, *Implementing a Human Development Strategy* (London: Macmillan, 1994).
2. The seven largest donor countries (in order: Japan, USA, France, Germany, Britain, the Netherlands and Canada) provide 80 per cent of the official aid from the OECD countries. Between 1984–88 and 1994, foreign aid as a percentage of GDP fell in six out of seven of these countries. In the seventh, France, the aid ratio remained constant.
3. See Keith Griffin and Terry McKinley, *A New Framework for Development Cooperation*, Occasional Paper No. 11, Human Development Report Office (New York: UNDP, 1994).
4. See International Labour Office, *World Employment 1995: An ILO Report* (Geneva: ILO, 1995).
5. For a recent statement of this view see Nancy Birdsall, David Ross and Richard Sabot, 'Inequality and Growth Reconsidered: Lessons from East Asia', *World Bank Economic Review*, Vol. 9, No. 3 (September 1995).
6. On the early agricultural reforms see Keith Griffin (ed.), *Institutional Reform and Economic Development in the Chinese Countryside* (London: Macmillan, 1984). On the effects of economic reforms on rural and urban inequality see Keith Griffin and Zhao Renwei (eds), *The Distribution of Income in China* (London: Macmillan, 1993).

7. See Keith Griffin (ed.), *Poverty and the Transition to a Market Economy in Mongolia* (London: Macmillan, 1995).

8. See, however, George Irwin, 'Vietnam: Will Market Transition Increase Poverty?', The Hague: Institute of Social Studies, mimeo, 18 May 1995.

9. LaMond Tullis, *Unintended Consequences: Illegal Drugs and Drug Policies in Nine Countries* (Boulder, CO. and London: Lynne Rienner, 1995), p. 157 and Table 5.1, p. 158.

10. James Painter, *Bolivia and Coca: A Study in Dependency* (Boulder, CO. and London: Lynne Rienner, 1994), p.140.

11. Tullis, *Unintended Consequences*, p. 72.

12. Painter, *Bolivia and Coca*, p. 140.

13. Tullis, *Unintended Consequences*, p. 100.

14. Painter, *Bolivia and Coca*, p. 140.

15. Keith Griffin and Jeffrey James, *The Transition to Egalitarian Development* (London: Macmillan, 1981).

16. Keith Griffin (ed.), *Social Policy and Economic Transformation in Uzbekistan* (Geneva: ILO, 1996).

17. See World Commission on Culture and Development, *Our Creative Diversity* (Paris: UNESCO, 1995).

Part I

Global Prospects and Possibilities

2 Global Prospects for Development and Human Security*

It is a great honour to be invited to present this keynote address in Calgary. Canada has an admirable record of constructive concern with broad issues of international development and this country has historically been a generous donor of foreign aid. Canada has also been much concerned with measures intended to improve the lot of the poor directly and has been among the few to provide a warm welcome to immigrants from developing countries and elsewhere. This Association deserves much credit for contributing to the global research effort on the problems faced by developing countries and to public education on those problems in this country. The theme of this year's conference – violence, human security and development – is very apposite, for it touches upon hitherto neglected topics which suddenly have come to the forefront of international debate. There are multiple connections between violence, security and development which are being explored in some depth during the conference. My ambition in this presentation is a modest one: to scan a small part of the terrain from the perspective of an economist.

OBJECTIVES

The ultimate objectives of development are easy to list. We are concerned about the reduction of global poverty and raising the standard of living of millions of people whose material well-being is extraordinarily low. We are interested in expanding the range of choice open to people so that they may choose for themselves more satisfying lives and we are concerned to enhance the capabilities of people everywhere

* Keynote address at the annual conference of the Canadian Association of the Study of International Development (CASID), Calgary, 12–14 June 1994, published in the *Canadian Journal of Development Studies*, Vol. XVI, No. 3 (1995).

so that women and men may come closer to fulfilling their potential. Development thus is about putting people first and inevitably this means that ultimately the focus of policy and initiative must be on human development. None of these objectives, however, can be achieved if individuals and groups of people do not enjoy personal and collective security. A concern with security, in turn, raises issues of the degree and types of risks people confront, of the extent of vulnerability of different groups of people to unanticipated events, both man-made and natural, and the relationship of vulnerability to the distribution of income and wealth. Secure development implies that livelihoods are sustainable in the face of shocks – floods, droughts, earthquakes, civil wars. Human security in this first sense is not the same thing as human development, but it is an essential condition for human development. It is not enough that people are secure, but it is necessary that they be secure.

Development should be seen within an historical perspective. That is, development is concerned with the long view, and this implies among other things that we are concerned with maintaining economic security over an extended period of time. Hence the sustainability of the development process and the protection of the environment are central issues in the development debate. This is a second dimension of the notion of sustainability. The foundation of long term growth is a steady increase in the stock of capital broadly defined, i.e., an increase in the total of physical capital, human capital and natural capital. In the short term a country can run down its natural capital – consume part of its capital stock – but in the long run sustainability implies that any reduction in the stock of natural capital be fully offset by an increase in physical and human capital. Seen in this way, there is no conflict between human development and sustainable development. Indeed, sustainable development is essential if long run human development is to occur. The recent emphasis on sustainability in this second sense should therefore be seen as an enrichment and deepening of the concept of development. This view of the process is becoming widely accepted and lies behind the advocacy by the UNDP of what it calls sustainable human development.

Concerns with equity and with the distribution of income and wealth have always been part of the debate on development policy. The introduction of the notion of sustainability, however, casts these old debates in a new light. Sustainability in the first sense, viz., resilience in the face of shocks, has a distributional dimension that frequently is overlooked. When disaster strikes, be it man-made or natural, the distribution of income and wealth affect both who is hurt and how many are hurt. Pain is not distributed evenly or randomly; the poor invariably are harmed more than the non-poor. And the greater is the degree of inequality, the larger the number of people who suffer. Moreover, in the case of man-made disasters such as civil war, distributional conflicts over land and access to resources in general often are at the root of the problem. El Salvador, Guatemala and Nicaragua are vivid examples of the interlinkages that exist between security, the sustainability of development and distributive justice.

Sustainability in the second sense, viz., maintenance of the value of the total stock of human, physical and natural capital, also has a distributional dimension. The need to ensure that the process of development can be continued indefinitely has implications both for intra-generational equity, i.e., the distribution of capabilities among the population alive today, and for inter-generational equity, namely, the resources, opportunities and range of choices that we who are living today pass on to our successors. If the poor have restricted access to resources and employment opportunities, they will have little choice but to exploit intensively the resources to which they do have access, cutting down trees for fuel, lowering the water table to irrigate their crops, depleting stocks of fish in coastal waterways, and so on. This, in turn, will deprive the next generation of resources on which their livelihood depends. An inequitable distribution of resources in the present can lead to an inequitable distribution across generations. Sustainable human development has thus embedded within it the idea of justice as fairness.

The end of the Cold War has created both enormous opportunities and serious problems. New conflicts have emerged, often centred on ethnic differences, which can be understood in part as a struggle of people to redefine their identity and to discover new ways of relating to one another. This has its positive aspects, but there is also a great potential for violence. Whether we like it or not, the institution of the state, as the fundamental unit of political organization, is being threatened simultaneously from above and below. Powerful economic forces of globalization are weakening the ability of the state to regulate its own economy, and we may live to see the day when the traditional state has as much influence in global economic affairs as a single province has in national economic affairs. Working alongside global economic forces, but independent of them, sub-nationalist forces are undermining the state from below and challenging its legitimacy.

The rise of sub-nationalism, the search for new identities, the rediscovery or invention of old identities, the forging of reconfigured relationships among groups of people: such movements are sweeping the globe. They can be found in new states created by a departing colonialism, in the disintegration of the Soviet empire, in central and eastern Europe, even in Canada. The rise of religious fundamentalism, be it Hindu, Muslim or Christian; the upsurge of nationalism among the Kurds, the southern Sudanese, the Kashmiris; even the decision to move away from the Cyrillic alphabet in favour of an older Uigur script in Mongolia: the signs are everywhere that people are moving away from a state-based identity.

Spare a thought for the violence, mass rape, ethnic cleansing and genocide that the world has witnessed in Bosnia. That unhappy land was a microcosm of an idealized world. Bosnia was a state, internationally recognized. It was secular, democratic, multi-ethnic and multi-cultural. It was home to Catholics, Muslims, Eastern Orthodox and non-believers. The pluralism of Bosnia was not unlike the pluralism of the European Union, North America, Russia or India. Indeed Bosnia holds up a mirror to the world, for the inevitable globalization of labour markets means that sooner or later we shall all live in plural societies. Yet in Bosnia the centre did not hold: the polity disintegrated, violence came to rule, human security could not be ensured and development was sent into reverse. Perhaps a pale shadow of the idealized Bosnia can be constructed out of the rubble, but the Bosnia that might have been is gone forever.

Bosnia is a terrible warning of what may happen on a larger scale if we are unable to construct new, post-Cold War structures for global governance and cooperation among peoples. For nearly fifty years our global institutions have been preoccupied with the security of states; indeed the United Nations Organization is an inter-governmental organization, not a supra-national one. The time has come to shift the emphasis from national sovereignty and state security to individual rights and human security. The potential for violence inherent in the present disorder and anarchy is enlarged by the increased military spending that has occurred in a number of developing countries, supported by military assistance from developed countries and subsidies to exports of armaments. Global ideological conflict and a nuclear confrontation between two superpowers have given way to the dismemberment of states and empires, civil war and localized international conflict. The growing number of emergencies has led to an increase in the number of international peace-keeping operations necessary to protect innocent human beings, prevent starvation and encourage the peaceful settlement of conflicts. These activities have diverted resources from economic and social development – they have threatened in some cases to undermine sustainable human development – and yet they have become essential in the absence of reliable mechanisms for guaranteeing human security. It is for this reason that the *Human Development Report* for 1994 devotes considerable attention to the issue of human security.

PROSPECTS

If the politics of the post-Cold War era is rather gloomy, the economics – recessions in Japan and Europe notwithstanding – is more encouraging. The end of the Cold War has been accompanied by more open economic relationships among countries. There is always a danger that must be guarded against that progress towards greater openness will come to a halt and even be turned back, but so far this has not happened. Commodity markets have become more open; capital markets have been liberalized; global competition has increased and more countries have begun to exploit the advantages that come from greater specialization. The next step in creating a genuinely open world economy is to liberalize further international labour markets.

We could be on the threshold of a period of accelerated economic growth. Technological advances and basic knowledge have accumulated at an historically unprecedented rate and yet there is an enormous gap between what is known and the knowledge that is actually used. Closing this gap, creating greater access worldwide to available useful knowledge, is one major source of potential future growth. Another source consists of the further exploitation of possibilities for mutually advantageous global trade, possibilities which have been enhanced by the recently concluded GATT agreements. Still another source of accelerated growth arises from the greater use of market forces in the former centrally planned economies and a continuation of the global trend towards lesser use of administrative procedures to allocate resources.

A large number of developing countries have implemented major adjustment programmes in recent years. We have witnessed in the developing countries a greater orientation towards the use of the market and greater recognition of the benefits that come from competition. International trade has been liberalized, quotas have been replaced by tariffs and tariff levels have been reduced. Production has been restructured and the composition of output altered to increase efficiency in the overall use of resources. State enterprises have been privatized

– sometimes with beneficial results – and the role of the state in promoting development has been re-examined.

More can be done and should be done. People should be given a stronger voice in affairs of greatest concern to them. Governments should become more accountable to those who are governed. The erosion of confidence in public institutions should be addressed, for we have already seen that in many countries the legitimacy of the state itself is being called into question. If the decline of authoritarian regimes and the spread of democracy are to be more than ephemeral phenomena, participation of people in public life must be institutionalized and become a commonplace. Development is partly about choices, but not all choices are made in the market place; many are made in the political arena.

Observers in the developed countries have talked and written at length about restructuring in the developing countries and in the former centrally planned economies. But we in the developed countries, too, need to restructure our economies in order to create conditions favourable to accelerated growth. The GATT agreement creates opportunities for further trade liberalization, but agricultural protection in the developed countries remains high. There are worries in some regions of the world, particularly in Asia, that if growth should falter, protectionist attitudes could be strengthened and the European Union, the North American Free Trade Agreement (NAFTA) and possibly other regional groupings could be transformed into trade restricting institutions. A specific issue of vital importance to Eastern and Central Europe is access to the markets of Western Europe. The developed countries need to restructure their production in order to permit a substantial flow of imports from the Eastern and Central European countries while they try to negotiate the transition to a more market-oriented economy. Aid is no substitute for trade; indeed, in the absence of more liberal trade, foreign aid may do little more than perpetuate an inefficient pattern of resource use. That, in turn, could lead to massive emigration from Eastern Europe.

Despite many obvious problems in the world economy, the current growth outlook can be seen as a glass half full. There has been very rapid growth in East Asia, notably in China with its huge population. There has been rapid growth in Southeast Asia, including Indonesia and its large population. There has been an acceleration of growth in South Asia and most important in the three populous countries of Bangladesh, India and Pakistan. There has also been a recovery of growth in Latin America. Among the developing regions, only Africa and West Asia are conspicuous for continued slow growth.

This is encouraging. Indeed the developing countries are today acting as the engine of global growth. Countries which account for about half the world's population have experienced a significant improvement in their average standard of living. Moreover, those countries account for many of the poorest people in the world. As a result, in recent years the pattern of global growth, contrary to a widely held belief, has helped to reduce inequality in the distribution of world income. For once, the proportionate gains of the poor exceed those of the rich. The narrowing of global income inequalities has been accompanied by a narrowing of differentials in human development indicators and hence, at the world level, polarization among peoples has diminished.

The developing countries, however, account for only little more than 34 per cent of global output (in purchasing power parity terms). That is, nearly two-thirds of the world's output and income are generated in the developed countries and in the former socialist countries of the Soviet Union and Eastern and Central Europe. Seen from the perspective of global production, the current growth outlook is a glass half empty. Western Europe and Japan are in the midst of recession. There has been a sharp decline in output and incomes in Russia and in parts of Eastern and Central Europe. The cyclical recovery in the United States is unusually slow by historical standards. Within the developed countries, incomes have become polarized, unemployment (in Europe) has remained high and in the United States employment creation (of full-time jobs at least) has been disappointing and the real wages of unskilled workers have declined.

POVERTY

Even if, as I have argued, the outlook for development can be seen as a glass half full, mass poverty remains a central economic and social problem of the developing countries. And hence there is an important and inescapable role for the state to provide security for its citizens by insuring vulnerable groups against threats of impoverishment and reducing the hardships of those who already are poor. But what exactly is poverty? What do we mean when we say there are so many poor people or that x per cent of the population is living in poverty? It was once hoped, at least by economists, that poverty could be measured precisely or quantified in a way that left no ambiguity or room for disagreement. Recent thinking, however, has altered our understanding of the nature of poverty and made it more ambiguous rather than less.

Poverty has come to be seen as a social illness; it is not a yes-or-no situation like a medical condition, a broken arm or a ruptured appendix which one either does or does not have. Poverty necessarily is a relative concept not an absolute one, but one must still ask, relative to what?

There are three different ways to define poverty. One way – which can be called income poverty – conceives of poverty as a relationship of a person to a bundle of commodities. In one variant the bundle is disaggregated and specified as a list of 'basic needs' with a threshold or norm established for each basic need, such as a minimum consumption of food, fuel and clothing, a minimum standard for shelter, and so on. 'If for any one of these . . . indicators a household does not meet the selected norm, it is scored as being poor. Poverty is thus a state in which any one of the several basic needs is unsatisfied.'[1] More commonly, the bundle of commodities is aggregated and specified as a minimum living standard or a minimum level of income. Often the minimum level of income – the so-called poverty line – is based on nutritional standards, e.g., that level of income which is sufficient to prevent malnutrition. In effect, then, the minimum income standard is anchored to one basic need, namely food, which implicitly is regarded as more fundamental or more important than other basic needs.

A second way to view poverty is as a relationship of a person to a set of 'capabilities'. This approach regards commodities or income not as ends in themselves but as means which enable people to function or to exercise their capabilities. The ultimate objective is capabilities, not income, e.g., the ability to lead a long life, to function without chronic morbidity, to be capable of reading, writing and performing numerical tasks, to be able to move about from place to place, and so on. Some people will require more resources, commodities or income than others to achieve the same capability. Women, for example, may have special disadvantages in converting income into capabilities. For instance, because of the demands of pregnancy or nursing an infant, they may encounter nutritional disadvantages; because of abandonment or mistreatment by their husbands, they may have special difficulties achieving security. The poor, according to this view, are those whose capabilities fall below minimum acceptable standards. It is quite possible, hence, for one to be capability-poor but not income poor.[2] This view of poverty is consistent with the human development approach alluded to earlier.

There is, however, a third way of looking at poverty, namely, to see it as a relationship between one person and another. Let us call this the social deprivation approach. Income and capabilities undoubtedly are relevant – they are 'intermediating' factors – but the essence of poverty according to this approach lies in relations among people. The poor are those who are socially deprived; they are people whose incomes, capabilities or other characteristics are unacceptably distant from the norms of their community or reference group. To be poor is to fall below the minimum accepted standards of one's society, to live in shame, to be indecent. Poverty here is a social construct which has little to do with physiological requirements (minimum calories, basic needs or minimum incomes) or with capabilities (longevity, mobility, literacy, numeracy and the like). It is quite possible that a person could be regarded by her community as poor – and would regard herself as poor – even though she were not income-poor or capability-poor in the conventional sense. She would be poor because relative to other individuals her capabilities or income are low. Thus, under this conception, poverty is intimately related to inequality. They are not of course the same thing, but the elimination of social deprivation implies reducing inequalities at the lower end of the distribution.

DEMOGRAPHY

Given the employment problems in developed countries that I mentioned earlier, it may come as a surprise when I say that I favour liberalization of the global labour market. Some of you, indeed, may believe that controlling population growth in developing countries is far more important than reducing controls on immigration in developed countries. I beg to differ.

Contrary to those who fear a Malthusian explosion, population growth rates are falling. Human capital is increasing, human development is occurring. True, the number of human beings is rising, but the number is increasing at a declining rate. The phenomenon is worldwide. Perhaps more important for future trends, fertility rates in developing countries have begun to fall in virtually every region and, in the developed countries, fertility rates are so low that an era of zero population growth is visible on the horizon.

Demographic issues sometimes are discussed in isolation from their socio-economic context, yet in all societies population growth is an endogenous variable. In particular, in all societies fertility is influenced or regulated by institutions, custom and convention, laws and social sanctions. There are numerous ways in which a country's birth rate can be affected. Let me mention just a few of the more obvious ones.

Most societies regulate by law the age at which young men and women may marry. Many societies also have rules or conventions governing the remarriage of widows, some going so far as to prohibit it. In some societies it is the custom that a male must be able to establish and maintain an independent household before he is allowed to marry. In others, bride price ensures that a minimum amount of wealth is created or amassed before marriage.

In some societies where the resource endowment will not support a large population, a high proportion of males enter religious institutions and practise celibacy. The Buddhist monasteries of Tibet and Mongolia and the Catholic priesthood are important historical examples. In still other societies, young women, particularly the daughters of the poor, are encouraged to enter convents, as in Catholic Spain.

Practices concerning the length of time mothers breast feed their babies affect the rate of population growth, since lactation produces a natural contraceptive that reduces the likelihood that a woman will become pregnant while she is nursing. Some societies, including Japan, have relied extensively on abortion to control the birth rate; others, including China, have in the past tolerated female infanticide. Today, particularly in Western societies, birth rates are regulated by modern contraceptives, male and female sterilization and surgical or chemically induced abortion.

In times of economic stress, birth rates can adjust very rapidly. In Mongolia, for instance, the transition from a centrally planned to a market guided economy has been accompanied by a precipitous fall in the standard of living. Average incomes per head fell between 25 and 30 per cent between 1989 and 1993 and other indicators of individual and social well-being provide additional evidence of hardship, distress and dislocation: unemployment rose, morbidity rates increased, the number of reported crimes soared and school enrolment rates declined. One response of people to this deterioration in their standard of living was to cut the birth rate, and indeed between 1989 and 1993 the crude birth rate fell from 36.4 per thousand to 21.5, or by nearly 41 per cent in just four years. A similar response to similar circumstances also has been reported in the countries of Central and Eastern Europe.[3]

The ways of regulating fertility (and indeed mortality) evidently vary across space and time. The point I am making, however, is that population growth does not just happen: decisions about individual behaviour, the choices made by couples and pressures exerted by the wider society and economy jointly determine the outcome. Demographic expansion has less to do with biology than with economics and sociology. This is what I mean when I say that population growth is an endogenous variable.

The population issue, I suggest, really should be seen as a development issue. It is closely linked with broad social trends and with the emancipation of women. Human development and fertility rates are strongly and inversely correlated. In countries where infant mortality rates are low, families have less of an incentive to have many children. In countries where literacy rates are high, where women are given equal opportunities to obtain an education, and where women are allowed to seek paid employment, the opportunity cost of childbearing is increased, the ability of women to earn higher incomes is raised, and the number of births per female is lower. In countries where social safety nets exist and provision is made for security in old age, parents are less dependent on their children at the end of their life, and average size of family therefore tends to be smaller.

In the developed countries the most prominent demographic change in recent decades is the change in the age structure. Increased life expectancy combined with low fertility rates is resulting gradually in an ageing of the population and a rise in the ratio of retired persons to active workers. That is, labour of working age is becoming increasingly scarce relative to the population as a whole. An obvious solution to this problem is to import labour from countries where it is abundant and it is here that liberalizing international labour markets, structural change in developed countries and the ageing of the population intersect. The potential gains in well-being from a freer international labour market should in principle be at least as large as the gains from more liberal capital markets and markets for goods and services. The reason for this is that the restrictions in labour markets are much greater than were the restrictions in capital and commodity markets before the latest wave of economic globalization began.

Greater international mobility of labour would raise total output in the developed countries and contribute to an increase in efficiency in the use of the world's resources. It would increase the supply of entrepreneurship, stimulate small business and accelerate innovation. It would raise savings and investment in the developed countries while contributing remittances to the developing countries, thereby helping to accelerate growth in both groups of countries. Faster growth, in turn, would make it easier for the developed countries to restructure their economies and, finally, by importing labour from countries where populations are young, it would alleviate the problems associated with an ageing population.

There are undoubtedly greater limits to international flows of labour than to flows of capital and commodities, but the objective of public policy should be to allow the levels of migration that people seek while simultaneously improving human security and raising the prosperity of people in the developing countries themselves. Similarly, there are problems of integration, tolerance and pluralism both for the migrants and for the host country, but these are issues to be addressed by policy makers, not excuses for inaction.

The benefits of labour market liberalization would of course be greater, the faster is the rate of growth in the developed countries and the lower is the rate of unemployment. Stagnation and unemployment, however, are not arguments against liberalization; they are arguments for government action to restructure production, remove obstacles in rigid internal labour markets and to stimulate investment and an overall expansion. Poor economic performance should not be used as an excuse to erect barriers to migration; it should instead be seen as a signal of the need to adopt policies to increase investment and which permit liberalization and the resulting economic expansion.

CONCLUSION

The end of the Cold War has created an opportunity to rethink the framework for development cooperation. The old framework, centred on bilateral foreign aid supplemented by multilateral assistance, is obsolete. Foreign aid was once used, at least in part, to support the strategic security of states, to achieve diplomatic objectives and to promote particular ideologies. This is no longer necessary, if it ever was, and the focus of cooperation can now shift to promoting the security and well-being of people, particularly the poorest people. That is, the thrust of a new framework for development cooperation should be to reduce global poverty, promote sustainable human development and protect people from severe hardship.

These objectives perhaps can be achieved in part by reforming foreign aid as conventionally understood: improving the allocation among recipient countries, reducing the tied element, overhauling technical assistance, improving the accuracy of targeting, etc. But the implication of my analysis is that in future development cooperation should be seen in a much broader context, including access of developing countries to markets, improved mechanisms for the transfer of technology, greater international mobility of labour, cooperation on environmental issues, and a greater concern for human security. In such a context, foreign aid, although possibly still important, may play a less prominent role.

The global debate on development cooperation is evolving rapidly, partly in response to fresh thinking within the United Nations and partly in response to the writings of academics and the activities of NGOs in developed and developing countries alike. Associations such as this have an important role to play and, judging by the programme for this year's conference, it is clear that Canadians will continue to have a disproportionate influence on the analysis of issues and the design of solutions.

Notes

1. Meghnad Desai, 'Income and Alternative Measures of Well-Being', in David G. Westendorff and Dharam Ghai (eds.), *Monitoring Social Progress in the 1990s* (Aldershot: Avebury, 1993), p. 31.
2. On the capability approach to poverty see Amartya Sen, *Inequality Reexamined* (Cambridge, MA: Harvard University Press, 1992), Ch. 7.
3. UNICEF, *Central and Eastern Europe in Transition: Public Policy and Social Conditions*, Florence, Italy, Regional Monitoring Report No. 1 (November 1993), Ch. III.

3 Foreign Aid after the Cold War*

Foreign aid as it is understood today has its origins in the Cold War. It is largely a product of the ideological confrontation between the United States and the Soviet Union that dominated international politics for forty-five years between 1945 and 1990. It began not as a programme to assist the long-term development of impoverished countries but as a programme to facilitate the short-term economic recovery of Western Europe after the end of the Second World War. The political motivation of what was called the Marshall Plan was to prevent the spread of communism to France and Italy (where the Communist Party was strong), to stabilize conditions in West Germany (and create an attractive alternative to the socio-economic system imposed in East Germany) and to reduce the appeal of socialist policies in the United Kingdom (where the Labour Party enjoyed considerable popularity).

The Marshall Plan was followed by President Truman's Point Four programme (named after the fourth point in his inaugural address), a technical and economic assistance programme for Greece and Turkey, two poor countries bordering on the communist world and thought to be in danger. The third phase was a response to the disintegration of the old European empires and the proliferation of newly independent countries, first in Asia and later in Africa. Freedom from colonial rule led to a contest for the 'hearts and minds' of the people throughout what came to be called the Third World. Foreign aid was one weapon in this contest, not the only weapon and seldom the most powerful one, but nonetheless a significant tool of Western diplomacy.[1]

Particularly difficult problems were posed by the collapse of the Japanese empire, for it was in the territories occupied by Japan prior to and during the Second World War that the confrontation between the First World and the Second became most heated. After the liberation of China by the communists in 1949, the anti-communist nationalist opposition retreated to Taiwan and mounted a political and economic challenge to the mainland. The challenge was supported by large amounts

---

* First published in *Development and Change*, Vol. 22 (October 1991).

of foreign aid. Korea was divided into two countries, a communist north and a capitalist south, and in the early 1950s the Korean War was fought over the issue of reunification. South Korea won the war, thanks to massive military support from the West, and then after the war received large amounts of foreign aid. Similarly in Vietnam, the country was divided into a communist north and a capitalist south, and again a war was fought over the issue of reunification, with North Vietnam ultimately winning in 1975. Throughout the war, however, South Vietnam received huge amounts of military and economic assistance. Indeed, the political purposes of foreign aid are perhaps most clearly revealed in Taiwan, South Korea and South Vietnam.

The early foreign aid programmes, however, were not confined to the fringes of the communist world. The Cuban Revolution of the late 1950s extended the Cold War to the western hemisphere and posed a challenge to the long standing hegemony of the United States in that region. The response was multi-faceted and included the diplomatic isolation of Cuba, sponsorship of a military invasion and an economic embargo. Also included in the package was a foreign aid programme for the rest of Latin America – Kennedy's Alliance for Progress – which attempted to use promises of financial assistance as incentives to induce governments of recipient countries to introduce policy reforms.

Later foreign aid programmes were not always wholly dominated by US–Soviet rivalry but instead reflected narrower regional concerns, as in French aid to Francophone Africa, British aid to Commonwealth countries and Dutch aid to Indonesia. Moreover, although foreign aid was born out of political and ideological rivalry, it has always had an economic dimension, namely, an attempt to create a strong, expanding, global capitalist economy. These qualifications are important, but they must not be allowed to obscure the primacy of politics.

The origins and objectives of foreign aid cannot be understood outside the global political context. Foreign aid is a product of the Cold War, of the division of the globe into First, Second and Third Worlds and of the hostility of the two superpowers. Were it not for the Cold War there would have been no foreign aid programmes worthy of the name, for without the Cold War it would have been impossible to generate the domestic political support in the donor countries necessary to sustain foreign assistance for more than four decades. Other motives apart from ideological confrontation also played a role, not so much in initiating aid programmes as in sustaining them once the general principle had been accepted. Diplomatic considerations clearly were important, e.g., in mobilizing support in the General Assembly of the

Table 3.1   Official development assistance from OECD countries to developing countries, 1950–87 ($billion in 1980 prices)

Years	Assistance	Years	Assistance
1950–55	8.2	1971–75	25.0
1956–60	16.6	1976–80	26.2
1961–65	24.1	1981–85	30.4
1966–70	26.1	1986–87	41.5

Calculated from data in Angus Maddison, *The World Economy in the 20th Century* (Paris: OECD Development Centre, 1989), Table D-11, p. 147.

United Nations and, in the case of France and Britain, in retaining influence in colonial territories after they became independent. Commercial advantage soon became a prominent motive: securing markets, promoting exports, creating a favourable climate for private foreign investment. And of course there were genuine humanitarian motives, e.g., in Scandinavia and one or two other small donor countries. But the conflict between the two superpowers was the *sine qua non*.[2]

Despite the stimulus of the Cold War, foreign aid may already have been running out of steam before the remarkable political developments of 1989. This is particularly true when seen from the perspective of the recipient countries, as is apparent in Table 3.1. Measured in real terms, i.e., the nominal value deflated by a world export unit value index, the average annual amount of official aid from the OECD countries doubled between 1950–55 and 1956–60. In 1980 prices, the yearly flow of aid rose from $8.2 billion in the first half of the 1950s to $16.6 billion in the second half. It increased by another 50 per cent in the next half decade (1961–65) and then remained more or less constant until the 1980s, when falling export prices pushed up the real value of aid. The flow of aid reached a peak in 1972, the year before the first oil crisis, and this peak was not regained until 1983.

Even these figures, unexciting as they are, may overstate changes in the real value of aid. A more appropriate deflator might be a unit value series of manufactured export goods, since the content of aid flows consists largely of manufactures; and the technical assistance component of aid would surely be subject to a higher deflation factor, reflecting the increase in salary and other costs of Western advisers, teachers and technical experts. In addition, account should be taken of servicing and debt repayment of loans from multilateral aid agencies. Many borrowers of World Bank non-IDA funds, for instance, are now receiving very little in net terms. Thus, when viewed properly, real flows of foreign aid to developing countries have not increased all that much since the 1960s. The Cold War may have provided the fuel for foreign aid programmes, but the fuel was not very powerful.

Now that the Cold War is over, two questions are raised. First, as the ideological divisions begin to blur, as globalization proceeds and the three worlds blend into one, what is the outlook for foreign aid to developing countries? Second, if the end of the Cold War were to be accompanied by a significant reduction in foreign aid to poor countries, would this necessarily damage their development prospects? We shall begin by examining the second question, for if foreign aid does not in fact promote development, our joy over the end of the Cold War need not be tempered by sadness over the possible demise of foreign aid.

THE ECONOMIC JUSTIFICATION FOR FOREIGN AID

The fact that the motive for foreign aid is political rather than economic does not necessarily imply that the consequences of aid are not beneficial to economic development. Good things may follow from suspect motives – just as Adam Smith argued that self-interested behaviour can result in collective well-being – but in the case of foreign aid one should not lightly suspend disbelief. The proposition that suspect political motives may lead to desirable economic change may, in this case, turn out to be not only paradoxical but false.

From the 1960s onwards foreign aid has consisted essentially of a flow of resources from the First World to the Third, with the Second World essentially cut out of the loop. True, the major Western donors frequently criticized the communist countries for not contributing more to the aid effort, but in reality First World countries did not welcome competition from aid programmes of Second World countries. The First World was content to see the USSR and the communist countries of Eastern Europe concentrate most of their aid on a limited number of recipients such as Cuba, Vietnam, Mongolia, Afghanistan and Ethiopia.

Some of the Arab countries became major aid donors in a few Islamic countries after the oil price increases of 1973, but Arab aid declined steadily after 1980 when the real price of oil fell. Intra-Third World aid from the Arab countries, China and India is unlikely to be quantitatively significant in the years ahead. In 1987–88, for example, foreign aid from Arab countries was only 6.3 per cent as large as aid from the OECD countries. Aid from the Soviet Union and Eastern Europe in those years was 10.9 per cent as large as OECD aid.

Thus, the economic justification for foreign aid was and continues to be essentially the justification given by the West. It is perhaps no coincidence that Western analysts of foreign aid early came to the conclusion that what the Third World needs to promote its development is what the First World has in abundance. Underdevelopment was characterized by shortages of capital, technology and skills; economic development occurs as a result of increased supplies of capital, technology and skills; and the donor countries are well placed to provide capital (in the form of loans and grants), technology (often in the form of specific projects) and skills (in the form of technical assistance). J. K. Galbraith saw this clearly fifteen years ago. Referring to his period as US Ambassador to India he writes (Galbraith, 1975: v–vi):

> There were, broadly speaking, only two things we could provide to lessen the deprivation [of India] – we could supply capital and, in principle, useful technical knowledge. The causes of poverty were then derived from these possibilities – poverty was seen to be the result of a shortage of capital, an absence of technical skills.[3]

The view that what 'we' have is what 'they' need can be transformed by a sleight of hand into two propositions which clearly are false. First, it has been implied that because of its poverty the only way the Third World can develop, i.e., acquire the needed capital, technology and skills, is by relying on foreign aid from the First World. According to this view, foreign aid acts as the missing 'catalyst' in development, as a 'strategic input' or as the agent which removes 'bottlenecks' and 'binding constraints'. The 'multiplier effects' of foreign aid ensure that its impact on development is grossly disproportionate to its volume. Although the vocabulary of aid – catalysts and multiplier effects – suggests that small contributions sustained for short periods can have large positive consequences, aid has in fact been sustained for long periods and the disproportionality of aid is not its impact but its magnitude. Even technical assistance, a low cost component of the aid package, can be extraordinarily large in comparison to the resources available within the recipient countries. The UNDP, a major provider of technical assistance, now recognizes that 'in many developing countries the amount of technical assistance flowing each year into the salaries and travel of foreign experts exceeds by far the national civil service budget' (UNDP, 1990:5).

Yet it has long been clear that even in the lowest income countries domestic resources are adequate to finance a high rate of accumulation of capital. The potential economic surplus is substantial and actual savings rates can be high. Shortage of capital is not a major obstacle to development and never has been. In 1988, for example, savings accounted for 13 per cent of GDP in the United States (one of the richest countries in the world), whereas they were 38 per cent of GDP in China, 24 per cent in India and 18 per cent in the other low income economies. Savings capacity clearly is not the major problem. The acquisition of technology and skills is in principle even less of a problem for developing countries, as the historical experience of Japan and the other prosperous countries indicates. Aid doctrine has been based on an utterly erroneous diagnosis.

If capital and technology really were the binding constraints on economic development one would expect transnational corporations to invest heavily in developing countries to take advantage of high expected returns to these allegedly scarce factors of production. In fact, however, during the period 1983–88 only 20.1 per cent of total foreign direct investment occurred in developing countries while 79.9 per cent occurred in rich countries (United Nations Commission on Transnational Corporations, 1990:9). Taking all flows into account, it can be argued that the natural tendency in a fully integrated global economy would be for savings to move from poor countries to rich, because rates of return on investment actually tend to be higher in developed economies than in underdeveloped ones (Griffin, 1974). This runs counter to the conventional view which postulates that because of enormous differences in capital–labour ratios, the marginal product of capital in poor countries should be a multiple of that in rich countries and hence there should be a massive flow of foreign capital into poor countries.

The constraining scarcity in developing countries, however, is not physical capital or advanced Western technology, it is the lack of human development as reflected in inadequate general education, insufficient training and a lack of skills in the labour force, poor nutrition and incomplete coverage of the population by primary health services, etc. As a result, returns on human development expenditure in developing countries, e.g., on primary and secondary education, often are higher than the returns on physical investment (Psacharopoulos, 1988; Griffin and Knight, 1990). It is quite misleading to compare capital–labour ratios in developed and underdeveloped economies by dividing the value of the stock of plant and equipment by the number of workers. It is labour power that is relevant, not just the number of bodies. If the denominator of the ratio were corrected by substituting labour power for labourers, capital–labour ratios in rich countries would perhaps not be much higher than in poor countries and differences in the marginal product of capital would decline sharply, if not disappear (Lucas, 1990). Moreover, expenditures on human development generate positive externalities that accrue to the population as a whole; this, too, increases labour power relative to physical capital in the developed economies and, in the absence of compensating international migration, raises the marginal product of capital in rich countries. Thus what the developing countries need above all is a reallocation of domestic resources in favour of human development and not a transfer of capital, technology and advanced skills from the rich countries.

A second false implication of the view that what 'we' have is what 'they' need is that the only thing necessary for development is capital, technology and skills. Aid doctrine has been socially and politically conservative. Because of its origins in the Cold War, it has been against radicalism in all forms and has been instead a supporter of the *status quo.* The relationship between social structure, the concentration of power, the distribution of income and the allocation of domestic resources for development purposes has played almost no part in official doctrines concerning the role of foreign aid. Power enters into the analysis only in the form of purchasing power. Similarly, aid doctrine has tended to ignore, if not be openly hostile to, institutional change. In agriculture, for example, foreign aid has been used to promote technical change (such as the green revolution), but most donors, and certainly the large ones, have been unwilling actively to encourage land reforms in countries where the need is obvious (as in the Philippines) or even to assist the implementation of reforms in countries where they were introduced (Ethiopia, Nicaragua, Mozambique).

True, in some countries aid donors have recognized the need for radical change. Haiti is an example. But for ideological reasons donors have been prepared to continue business as usual even when it became evident that the necessary institutional and political reforms would not be introduced. There has been a marked asymmetry in donor policies: aid has often been discontinued by Western agencies in countries which have introduced radical reforms (Cuba, Chile under Allende, Nicaragua under the Sandinistas, Angola) and such countries have been branded leftist, socialist or communist, while aid has been sustained in countries where reforms are widely acknowledged to be necessary (Zaire, El Salvador, the Philippines, Haiti). Even in Haiti, an extreme case, it is said by enlightened defenders of foreign aid that 'the case for aid withdrawal is far from proven' (Riddell, 1987:262). Surely there is an unanswerable case to reallocate the aid received by Haiti in favour, say, of India, which has a lower average income, is democratic, has achieved some development and receives less aid per head of the population. There seems to be no limit as to how far the aid lobby will go in supporting the *status quo*.

At the end of the day the economic justification for foreign aid has rested on the view that development is essentially a financial and technical matter. It its most extreme form, foreign aid is reduced to filling the 'gap' between the (meagre) savings of a poor country and the (substantial) investment needed to achieve an acceptable or desired rate of growth.[4] This *reductio ad absurdum* is not of course openly articulated, but it underlies much of the economic justification of foreign aid and illustrates just how difficult it has been to reconcile the political motives for aid with an economic rationale.

FOREIGN AID AND THE RATE OF GROWTH

The conventional and seemingly obvious view that foreign aid accelerates growth has long been challenged. Critics have argued that in certain circumstances aid could actually reduce the rate of growth and that in general there is little reason to suppose that aid would have much effect either positively or negatively. Using data from the 1960s, it was shown that the association between capital inflows and the growth of GNP was roughly zero for 15 African and Asian countries and inverse for 12 Latin American countries (Griffin and Enos, 1970). A theory that could account for the results was also presented (Griffin, 1970; Dacy, 1975). The basis for a debate had therefore been launched.

The proposition that aid did not promote growth let alone development was greeted with scepticism and new evidence was presented which seemed to suggest that, after all, aid did help to accelerate the growth of output. Moreover, it was argued by the defenders of the conventional view that where an inverse relationship between aid and growth was found, this was probably because aid tended to be channelled towards countries where growth rates were low (Papanek, 1972).

In the twenty years since the debate was launched much more evidence has become available,[5] and unfortunately for the conventional view the data continue to suggest that aid has not significantly contributed to an acceleration of growth and, in some cases, appears to have retarded it. Econometric analysis of 83 developing countries in the period 1969–77 showed 'a weak and insignificant but *negative* correlation between aid and growth' (Mosley, 1980:82). The results were unaffected by introducing a five-year lag on the aid variable and thus the suggestion that the direction of causation is from slow growth to aid rather than the other way round is in general not plausible. A later study of between 52 and 63 countries covering the period 1960–83 and using more elaborate econometric techniques, disaggregating the data into three periods and five groups of countries (by region and by level of income), concluded that 'aid *in the aggregate* has no demonstrable effect on growth' (Mosley, Hudson and Horrell, 1987:631). The authors go on to add that 'the apparent inability of development aid over more than twenty years to provide a net increment to overall growth in the Third World must give the donor community, as it gives us, cause for grave concern' (Mosley, Hudson and Horrell, 1987:636).

The statistically most elaborate study, based on a multi-equation model, shows that many outcomes are possible, but the general conclusion of the study is unambiguous: 'there is no escaping the implication that reliance on foreign capital [aid, private foreign investment and other sources of external capital] does not offer the solution for high and rapid growth' (Gupta and Islam, 1983:134). This finding is confirmed, albeit reluctantly, by Roger Riddell who, after a thorough analysis of the literature, concludes that 'few, if any studies of aid's long-term impact on a recipient country have ever provided statistical evidence that has been able to show unquestionably that it has had a positive effect at the macro-level' (Riddell, 1987:245).

The statistical evidence, then, for the 1960s, 1970s and early 1980s is not consistent with the hypothesis that aid accelerates growth. The evidence from the 1980s as a whole is even less supportive of the conventional view. In many parts of Africa and Latin America the growth of per capita income was actually negative, yet these were regions which received large amounts of foreign capital in the immediately preceding years. Massive foreign borrowing and grant aid in the 1970s led not to development in the 1980s but to a fall in average incomes. In Asia, on the other hand, growth was sustained, often at a high level, yet in the 1980s many of the rapidly growing countries in Asia received either no aid (Singapore) or very little aid, i.e., less than 1 per cent of GNP (China, India) or only a moderate amount of aid, i.e., little more than 1 per cent of GNP (Thailand, Malaysia). The Philippines is the Asian exception that proves the rule: aid was generous (more than 2 per cent of GNP) while growth was negative and the growth of income per head was sharply negative.

Table 3.2   Official development assistance, 1975–89

| | 1975–79 | 1989 | 1989 |
	(percentage of GNP)		($ billion)
Australia	0.51	0.37	1.0
Austria	0.22	0.23	0.3
Belgium	0.54	0.47	0.7
Canada	0.50	0.44	2.3
Denmark	0.72	1.00	1.0
Finland	0.18	0.63	0.7
France	0.59	0.78	7.5
West Germany	0.39	0.41	5.0
Ireland	0.15	0.17	0.05
Italy	0.11	0.39	3.3
Japan	0.23	0.32	9.0
Netherlands	0.83	0.94	2.1
New Zealand	0.39	0.22	0.09
Norway	0.83	1.02	0.9
Sweden	0.86	0.98	1.8
Switzerland	0.20	0.30	0.6
United Kingdom	0.45	0.31	2.6
United States	0.24	0.15	7.7
Total DAC	0.34	0.33	46.5

Sources: OECD, *Development Co-operation in the 1990s* (Paris: OECD, 1989) and OECD Press Release, 'Financial Resources for Developing Countries: 1989 and Recent Trends', Paris, 14 June 1990.

Cases certainly can be found where a fall in the growth rate precedes an increase in foreign aid and thus slow growth causes aid to flow. Cases can also be found where an exogenous event causes both the rate of growth to fall and the volume of aid to increase. But such cases can no longer be used to dismiss the finding of a persistent zero and even inverse relationship between growth and aid. The data now cover three decades and scores of countries. The phenomenon is a real one: there is a problem to be explained.[6]

None the less, one should keep the problem in perspective: foreign aid is not all that it seems. First, the flow of foreign aid is modest and possibly falling both relative to the GNP of donor countries and absolutely. It has long been a target of the United Nations that official aid should be 0.7 per cent of the GNP of donor countries. Actual aid flows, however, are less than half the target and appear to have fallen marginally from 0.34 per cent in the last half of the 1970s to 0.33 per cent in 1989 (see Table 3.2). Moreover, the absolute volume of aid recently has fallen sharply: it was $1.6 billion less in 1989, the first post-Cold War year, than it was in 1988; in real terms this was a decrease of 2 per cent in just one year.

The amount of foreign aid provided by the United States has fallen dramatically. In 1975–79 aid accounted for 0.24 per cent of US GNP; in 1989 the aid ratio was only 0.15 per cent, the lowest of any DAC donor country and the lowest by far of the major donors. Furthermore, despite its huge economy (the largest in the world) and its high per capita income (the second highest in the world), the United States ceased to be the largest aid donor, being replaced in 1989 by Japan which in that year allocated $1.3 billion more to foreign aid than did the United States. Indeed, were it not for Japan and a few of the smaller donors such as Finland, Denmark and Italy, the aid ratio in 1989 would have been even lower than it was by a substantial margin. Six of the 18 countries in Table 3.2 gave less aid in 1989 (relative to their GNP) than in 1975–79.

Second, there is a danger that as ideological competition subsides with the end of the Cold War, and commercial considerations become even more prominent, the quality of foreign aid may deteriorate. That is, the grant element of aid may decline and the proportion of aid that is untied and freely available for worldwide procurement may also fall. At present the average grant element of official aid is about 90 per cent, but in the case of Japan it is only about 75 per cent. Thus as the proportion of total aid provided by Japan rises, the grant element may fall.

The grant element refers only to the financial terms under which aid is provided. Also important for the quality of aid is the extent to which aid is untied. At present, about 36.5 per cent of all bilateral aid is tied to procurement in the donor country, 17.8 per cent is partially untied in the sense that procurement must be from the donor country or a developing one, and only 45.7 per cent is completely untied (OECD, 1989:209). In other words, well over half of bilateral aid effectively is tied to purchases in the donor country, which presumably are more costly than purchases in the lowest price market. The danger, again, is that as ideological competition diminishes as a motive for aid, commercial considerations may come to dominate humanitarian motives even more than at present, and consequently the quality of aid may deteriorate further.

Third, the geographical distribution of foreign aid is rather arbitrary, as can be seen in Table 3.3. Certainly aid is not allocated across broad regions in accordance with the size of their population. Asia, for example, accounts for 68.7 per cent of the population of developing countries yet receives only a third of official development assistance from the OECD countries. All other regions except Southern Europe receive a higher share of aid than their share of the population. Particularly noteworthy are North Africa and the Middle East (where the aid share is more than twice as large as the population share) and sub-Saharan Africa (where the aid share is nearly three times as large).

Of course, if foreign aid were distributed progressively, so that a disproportionate amount were allocated to those regions with the lowest average incomes, one would not expect aid shares to correspond to population shares. It is readily apparent, however, that aid is not distributed progressively across regions. Considering the six regions in Table 3.3, the largest amount of aid per capita ($244) is given to Oceania, where average income is $1230. The next largest amount ($26) is given to sub-Saharan Africa, where average incomes (at $350) are indeed the lowest. However, the third largest amount of aid per capita ($25) is given to North Africa and the Middle East, where average incomes (at $2500) are the highest of the six regions. Moreover, the difference in the amount of aid received per capita between the richest and poorest regions is only $1.25. Evidently it is political criteria, not poverty, that determine the allocation of official aid.

Even within geographical regions the allocation of aid is based on criteria other than need. In Asia, for instance, per capita income in the region as a whole is $430 and the amount of aid received on average is $5.16. Average incomes in China and India, however, are well below the Asian average, yet the amount of aid they receive also is well below the Asian average, namely, $1.80 and $2.70 respectively. Indonesia on the other hand benefits from being by far the largest recipient of Japanese aid[7] and consequently, although its income slightly exceeds the Asian average, it receives 83 per cent more aid per capita than the Asian average.

In Latin America, El Salvador's income is 39 per cent higher than Bolivia's, yet El Salvador receives 56.6 per cent more aid per head. In sub-Saharan Africa per capita income is about $350 and per capita aid receipts are about $26. Nigeria, with an income close to the average, receives only $0.74 in aid per head. Ethiopia, with an income one-third of the average, receives $19 per capita in aid. Zimbabwe, with an income nearly two-thirds above average, receives more than the average amount of aid. The most extraordinary situation, however, is in the Middle East. Israel, with a per capita income of $6810, is no longer even classified by the World Bank as a developing country, yet

Table 3.3 Geographical distribution of official development assistance, 1987–88

	Per cent of total ODA	Share of population	ODA as per cent of GNP	Per capita income (US$)	ODA per capita (US$)
N. Africa and Mid. East	14.3	5.8	1.0	2500	25.00
Of which: Egypt	4.2	1.3	4.9	710	34.79
Israel	3.2	0.1	4.0	6810	272.40
Sub-Saharan Africa	34.5	11.7	7.5	350	26.25
Of which: Ethiopia	2.1	1.2	16.1	120	19.32
Nigeria	0.2	2.8	0.2	370	0.74
Zimbabwe	0.7	0.2	5.2	580	30.16
Asia	33.4	68.7	1.2	430	5.16
Of which: China	4.4	27.9	0.6	300	1.80
India	5.4	20.8	0.9	300	2.70
Indonesia	3.6	4.4	2.1	450	9.45
Oceania	3.5	0.1	19.8	1230	243.54
Latin America	13.0	10.9	0.7	1830	12.81
Of which: Bolivia	0.9	0.2	8.9	610	54.29
El Salvador	1.1	0.1	10.0	850	85.00
Southern Europe	1.4	2.6	0.3	2010	6.03
Total	100.1*	99.8*	1.4†	740	10.36

* Total does not sum to 100 because of rounding.
† Excludes developing countries which receive no ODA.
Source: OECD/DAC (1989), pp. 240–1.

it received $272 per head of official development assistance in 1987–88, in addition to any military aid it received, most of it from the United States.[8] That is to say, the amount of aid received by Israel was 26 times the average of all aid recipients and more than the per capita income of countries such as Bangladesh, Tanzania and Zambia.

Finally, irrespective of the quality and geographical distribution of aid, the amount of aid available to the developing countries, seen from their perspective, is meagre. Taking all recipient countries into account, foreign aid accounted for only 1.4 per cent of the GNP of developing countries in 1987–88. Thus in general the effect of foreign aid on economic growth, whether positive or negative, is likely to be slight. In Latin America and Southern Europe aid inflows are negligible for most countries; in Asia and in North Africa and the Middle East foreign aid accounts for only 1 per cent of GNP or a little more. Thus in these four regions foreign aid will not be a significant determinant of growth performance, although it may be important in specific countries in these regions. In sub-Saharan Africa and in Oceania aid inflows are sufficiently large to affect macroeconomic behaviour, for good or ill.

FOREIGN AID AND THE COMPOSITION OF EXPENDITURE

An inflow of foreign aid, whether large or small, represents an addition to the total resources available to a country. These additional resources, in turn, make it possible to increase expenditure, and in principle expenditure on anything. Of course, the aid may be 'tied' in various ways, and hence additional expenditures on some types of items may be constrained, but the 'fungibility' of resources is likely to ensure that the constraints on expenditure are not totally binding. In the conventional early literature it was taken for granted that all aid inflows would be used to increase investment expenditure, and that the productivity of new investment would be the same as earlier investment, so that foreign aid would have an unambiguously positive impact on the rate of growth. Indeed, in the simple models designed to illustrate the impact of aid inflows, the growth rate would rise by a/k, where a = the inflow of foreign aid expressed as a per centage of GNP and k = the incremental capital–output ratio.

This approach, however, presupposes that an inflow of foreign aid is equivalent to an increase in investment, i.e., an augmentation of the stock of capital, which in turn will increase output in the next period.

This clearly is wrong. As Joan Robinson said, 'A country which receives an inflow of finance is not receiving a supply of a factor of production called "capital", it is enjoying the possibility of running a surplus of imports or amassing monetary reserves' (Robinson, 1978:220–1). A great deal of wasted time would have been saved had the Robinsonian view prevailed from the beginning. Aid represents an increase in the availability of resources not, as the conventional view would have it, an increase in capital.

Critics of the conventional view argued two things. First, part of the aid flow was likely to finance additional consumption expenditure (and hence reduce the national savings ratio). Second, for a variety of reasons an inflow of aid could well result in a higher incremental capital–output ratio (i.e., a rise in k). The net result of these two effects could be a reduction in the rate of growth of output in the recipient country rather than an increase as commonly supposed.[9] The resulting controversy centred on the first point to the relative neglect of the second. One important study, however, did find a significant 'decline in the general rate of return on capital in the Third World as between the 1960s and the 1970s' and attributed this to 'the multiplication of the number of donors' and a change in the composition of aid financed projects from power and infrastructure to more costly and 'difficult' projects such as integrated rural development (Mosley, Hudson and Horrell, 1987:634–5).

A large number of papers were produced, many using econometric techniques, in which the relationship between savings and aid was explored (Chenery and Eckstein, 1970; Landau, 1971; Weisskopt, 1972; Wasow, 1979; Mosley, 1980; Gersovitz, 1982). Some authors argued that savings were not inversely related to aid and others that it was low savings that caused the aid and not the other way round. Still others suggested that the inverse relationship between capital inflows and domestic savings was simultaneously caused by some exogenous event (Morisset, 1989). But most analysts now agree that aid can be a substitute for local savings and that in fact it often has been. It is now widely recognized, for instance, that after the 1973 oil crisis much of the aid and foreign borrowing in Latin America was used to sustain consumption rather than increase investment. Indeed, it is precisely because investment and hence output did not increase that Latin America encountered such severe debt servicing difficulties. In Bangladesh, the savings ratio fell from 8 per cent of GDP before independence to 2 per cent in the 1980s, much of the decline caused by 'chronic dissaving by the public sector' (Khan and Hossain, 1989:29). An analysis of the post-independence development strategy indicates that 'rather than complementing domestic savings and contributing to raising the rate of investment, foreign assistance has been a substitute for domestic savings' (Khan and Hossain, 1989:177). Similarly in the United States, the ready availability of foreign capital is associated not with an acceleration of investment and growth but with a fall in the rate of savings. The United States has used capital imports to supplement consumption expenditure (or substitute for domestic savings) and in the process has become the world's most indebted country.

These findings of substitutability do not imply that there is no increase in investment, but only that the increase in investment is less than the inflow of foreign capital. Similarly, the findings do not imply that the increase in consumption (or decline in domestic savings) is inevitable, but only that there is a tendency for this to occur. It all depends on government policy in the recipient country. Where government policy is designed to minimize the leakage of foreign aid into unproductive consumption, military expenditure and prestige investment projects, development-enhancing expenditures will rise and growth will accelerate. It has been shown, for example, that in those countries where the ratio of taxes to GNP was rising, an inflow of foreign aid, contrary to the general pattern, resulted in faster growth (Mosley, 1980). But equally, it has been suggested 'that those developing countries which finance recurrent expenditure out of aid are, in many cases, exercising a conscious and deliberate preference for lower levels of taxation than those which would be feasible in the absence of aid' (Mosley, Hudson and Horrell, 1987:625).

The effects of foreign aid on the composition of total expenditure can be more complex than a simple division between consumption and investment suggests. A more refined analysis should take into account the effects of capital inflows on the following:

(a) the level and composition of investment and the degree of capital intensity;
(b) expenditure on human development activities such as education, training and research, primary health care and nutrition programmes;
(c) unproductive or non-growth enhancing consumption;
(d) the amassing of monetary reserves and capital flight;
(e) the level of military expenditure.

The direct (or income) effect of an increase in foreign aid is to raise the level of investment, but by less than the aid inflow. That is, the marginal propensity to invest is less than one. The indirect (or price) effect of an increase in foreign aid is to lower the real rate of interest. This tends to depress the level of domestic savings by temporarily widening interest rate differentials between the recipient country and major international financial centres, and encourages domestic savings to be placed abroad. That is, liberalization of exchange controls and the globalization of capital markets make it easier for savers in developing countries to transfer funds abroad in response to market incentives. In addition, lower real interest rates alter relative factor prices and create incentives to adopt more mechanized techniques of production (or higher capital–labour ratios), with the resulting employment problems that implies. Higher capital–labour ratios in turn are likely to result in a higher incremental capital–output ratio. An inflow of foreign aid also is likely to result in an appreciation of the exchange rate. This will create an incentive to adopt more foreign exchange intensive methods of production and to rely on imported capital equipment. Finally, the composition of investment is likely to be affected directly by donors' preferences and historically donors' preferences have introduced a bias in favour of large, capital intensive, showpiece projects in the public sector with below average rates of return. The result is that the contribution of foreign aid to raising the level of investment and the rate of growth has been modest, if not negligible.

The effects of foreign aid and other inflows of finance capital on interest rates and the rate of exchange are likely to be marginal in most countries. The point is that on the whole capital inflows tilt relative prices in the wrong direction. In some countries, mostly small and very poor ones accounting for a minority of the population of developing countries, the inflows are large in comparison to total financial savings and foreign exchange earnings and the effects are likely to be much more than marginal. For example, of the 42 least developed countries, half in 1987 received official aid equivalent to more than 20 per cent of their GNP, another third received between 10 and 20 per cent and the rest between 5 and 10 per cent. Inflows of this magnitude will affect the price structure and hence the pattern of expenditure. In a number of the least developed countries large inflows of grant aid, soft loans and commercial borrowings have helped to sustain overvalued exchange rates. These overvalued exchange rates were the cause of the so-called foreign exchange gap in the first place and provided an economic justification for large foreign aid programmes, but the continuation of overvaluation, facilitated by aid inflows, has hampered the development of exports and hence the ability of the recipient country to repay foreign multilateral and commercial loans.

Many things that conventionally are classified as consumption might better be reclassified as human development (or expenditure on human capital formation). The rate of return on primary and secondary education is at least as high as the return on physical capital. The return on applied scientific research probably is even higher. Similarly, expenditure on primary health care and nutrition can make a significant long run contribution to development. Insofar as foreign aid permits an expansion of these types of programme beyond what would otherwise occur, the fact that aid often is associated with a decline in savings as conventionally measured is of little significance. Unfortunately, however, there is not much evidence that aid inflows have systematically resulted in greater overall expenditure on human development, or on those types of human development expenditure with the greatest pay-off, although specific instances can of course be found. Typically, foreign aid has facilitated expenditure on urban hospitals rather than rural clinics, on curative medicine rather than preventive public health measures, on scholarships for university students (often abroad and at the post-baccalaureate level) rather than primary schooling, etc.[10] Once again, the result is that the contribution of foreign aid to increasing human development and growth has been modest.

Looking back over the last twenty years or so, the most striking finding is that foreign aid has permitted a rise in unproductive consumption expenditure (which no doubt has raised welfare in the short term), while contributing relatively little to faster growth either through a greater level and efficiency of investment or through human development expenditure. In some cases foreign aid has stimulated unproductive consumption by enabling governments to reduce taxation. The 'Please effect' has worked in reverse (Please, 1967): the reduction in taxation and consequently in public savings has been offset partly by higher private savings but mostly by higher private consumption. In other cases foreign aid has stimulated unproductive consumption by allowing the government to increase its recurrent expenditure, e.g., by hiring more civil servants (sometimes, as in Bolivia and Tanzania, with the donors financing directly the higher salaries of selected civil servants).[11]

There is, then, an economically meaningful negative correlation between aid and savings and the correlation is strong and significant. Even more disturbing is the association in a number of countries between capital inflows in the form of aid and commercial loans from international banks and capital outflows in the form of capital flight. Not all capital flight is caused by the aid inflows: some occurs for political and other reasons, but it has become evident during the last two decades that in countries such as the Philippines the outflow of capital would not and could not have occurred without the inflow (Boyce, 1992). In the French franc zone of West Africa massive capital flight to London and other international financial centres occurred precisely at a time when large amounts of foreign aid (relative to the GNPs of the recipient countries) were made available. A similar pattern can be observed in parts of Latin America. For example, the figures for 1973–87 for the four largest debtor countries in Latin America are instructive.[12] During this period the increase in Argentina in external indebtedness was $48.1 billion while capital flight is estimated to have been $29.5 billion. In Brazil, foreign borrowing increased $96.6 billion while capital flight was $15.6 billion. In Mexico, the external debt increased $95.4 billion while simultaneously there was an outflow of capital of $61 billion. In Venezuela, capital flight ($38.8 billion) actually exceeded foreign borrowing ($29.4 billion).

The main economic causes of capital flight are (i) an overvalued exchange rate, (ii) positive differentials in interest rates on foreign and domestic assets and (iii) an increase in the domestic rate of inflation, which tends to be accompanied by a fall in the real rate of interest. As we have seen, inflows of foreign aid of larger than marginal magnitude tend to result in an appreciation of the exchange rate and in a fall in the real rate of interest. It is for these reasons that foreign aid and commercial borrowing often are associated with increased capital flight. The net effect of aid-induced capital flight is of course to reduce the effectiveness of aid in promoting development in the recipient country.

Another disturbing feature of foreign aid is its association with high military expenditure. This would be cause for concern in any group of countries, but it is especially worrying to discover that among the very poorest countries in the world, above average inflows of official development assistance are associated with above average military expenditure. This is illustrated in Table 3.4.

Consider the 44 countries classified by the UNDP as countries with 'low human development'. In these 44 countries official development assistance is equivalent to 3.6 per cent of GNP and military expenditure accounts for about 3.7 per cent of GNP. That is, aid and military expenditure are virtually identical. Twelve of the 44 countries spend more than average on the military,[13] and among these 12 countries military expenditure accounts for 7.2 per cent of GNP, i.e., nearly twice as much as for the group of low human development countries as a whole. Foreign aid in the high military spending countries, at 16.2 per cent of GNP, is a multiple of the average for the group as a whole,

Table 3.4   Foreign aid and military expenditure compared
(percentage of GNP)

	ODA, 1987	Military expenditure, 1986
12 countries with low human development and high military expenditure	16.2	7.2
All 44 countries with low human development	3.6	3.7
(excluding India)	7.0	3.8

Source: UNDP, *Human Development Report 1990* (New York: Oxford University Press, 1990), Annex Table 18, p. 162, and Annex Table 19, p. 164.

whether or not India is included. One explanation is that among the very poor countries those that systematically receive large amounts of aid do so because they spend unusually large amounts on the military. But an equally plausible explanation is that the availability of large inflows of aid permits those governments that are so inclined to spend large amounts on the military. If this view is correct, a reduction in aid could lead to a reduction in armaments in the developing countries. This, in turn, could lead to a reduction in regional conflicts and to less internal repression. The implications for Iraq and other countries of the Middle East, for example, are obvious.

AID AND DISTRIBUTIVE ISSUES

Let us set to one side the question of the effects of foreign aid on the allocation of resources and consider instead the effects on the distribution of income and the overall incidence of poverty. While it may be true, as argued above, that one must seek the origins of foreign aid programmes in the Cold War, it is also true that many aid programmes are inspired at least in part by humanitarian considerations. Security, diplomacy, commercial advantage and a genuine desire to alleviate poverty and inequality are all part of the mixed motives that characterize contemporary aid programmes. Statesmen may be preoccupied with issues of diplomacy and national security, but the man and woman in the street are likely to judge foreign aid by its ability to reduce world poverty. This is recognized in the aid legislation of some donor countries.

It is stated quite explicitly in the United States Foreign Assistance Act of 1974, for instance, that the first goal of the aid programme is 'the alleviation of the worst physical manifestations of poverty among the world's poor majority'.

It is instructive to compare the performance of the US bilateral aid programme against this clear legislative standard. The US Agency for International Development (AID) is evaluated periodically by outside analysts and their report is published. The latest report, like the earlier ones, consists of an *ex ante* evaluation of AID's activities, project by project and country by country. The evaluation consists of an assessment of the conception of the aid programme – what it is that AID thinks it is doing and how it proposes to go about doing it – and not an *ex post* evaluation of the actual results. Since actual results seldom are as good as planned achievements, one can be reasonably confident that the report does not understate AID's accomplishment.

Considering all types of US bilateral aid, the report concludes that in fiscal year 1989 only 26 per cent was spent in ways that effectively benefit the poor and 29 per cent in fiscal year 1991 (Prosterman and Hanstad, 1990:14). In some countries the situation was even worse. For instance, in El Salvador (the third largest recipient of US aid) and the Philippines (the fifth largest recipient) only 15 per cent of the aid was spent in ways that help the poor. In other words, on average more than 70 per cent of US aid benefits the minority of the population in recipient countries who are not poor and in some countries the proportion rises to 85 per cent.[14] The clear implication of these findings is that US foreign aid programmes, far from reducing inequality in the distribution of income, greatly accentuate inequities in developing countries.

It would be nice to think that the United States is an exception and that the record of other aid programmes is better, but there is no evidence to suggest that in fact other bilateral donors and the multilateral agencies have been more successful in reaching the poor. On the contrary, most of the limited evidence available appears to indicate that most of the benefits of foreign aid are captured by middle and upper income groups.[15] Even projects specifically aimed at low income groups often have great difficulty hitting the target.

For example, an *ex post* evaluation recently was conducted of United Nations rural development projects aimed at the poor. Twenty-five projects were examined in three least developed countries in Africa, namely, Burkina Faso, Burundi and Tanzania. The projects varied in size from less than $200 000 to over $42 million. The most striking general finding was that 'the majority of projects [13 out of 25] did not seem to be really helping to meet an important priority need of the poorest of the poor or of another under-privileged group' (Kabongo and Schumm, 1989:12). In Bolivia, the poorest country in South America, the World Bank undertook a $46.2 million investment programme in three of the poorest regions of the altiplano (Ingavi, Ulla Ulla and Omasuyos-Los Andes). The three projects were a disaster: the planned investment in deep wells was not implemented, the improvement of alpaca and llama herds did not take place, the wool processing factory was left uncompleted, the forestry component was a failure and the health infrastructure reached only 4 per cent of the target group. Only 71.2 per cent of planned expenditure actually was implemented and almost none of this had a lasting impact on the poor (World Bank, Operations Evaluation Department, 1988). If this is true of projects explicitly intended to benefit the poor, it is very unlikely that other aid projects have had much direct beneficial effect on the alleviation of poverty.

Even those who believe that aid has been of benefit to the poor accept that 'donors do not pay enough attention to the poverty impact of their projects' (Cassen, 1986:51) and acknowledge that 'there have been cases where aid has been harmful to the poor' (Cassen, 1986:299). But the issue raised by the critics of foreign aid goes beyond a small number of individual cases and the amount of attention paid by donors to poverty. The issue is about systemic tendencies, i.e., the operation of official aid programmes as a whole on the well-being of the lowest income groups in developing countries. If it is indeed correct, as has been argued, that on the macroeconomic side foreign aid has in general no measurable effect on the rate of growth of per capita income, and on the distributive side that aid increases inequality in the distribution of income, then it follows that aid actually accentuates poverty. This may not occur in all countries or at all times, but it seems likely that it occurs in most countries most of the time.

FOREIGN AID AND THE STATE

A major purpose of foreign aid during the period of the Cold War was political, namely, to support countries whose governments were on the side of the West in the ideological confrontation with the Soviet Union. The effect of any official aid programme, whether bilateral or multilateral, is to strengthen the administration that happens to be in power. Foreign assistance, after all, consists of a transfer of resources from one government (or multilateral agency) to another, and an increase in available resources is highly likely to help perpetuate in power the government of the recipient country, even if that is not the intended purpose of the aid. It is possible to think of exceptions, e.g., aid to the armed forces or police which ultimately subverts a civilian administration, but in general foreign aid helps those who possess power to retain power.

It is for this reason that the political and social effects of foreign assistance are essentially conservative. Aid tends to perpetuate the *status quo* even when, through policy dialogue, donor countries and agencies wish to modify the *status quo* in some non-trivial way. This is as true of Soviet aid to Cuba as it is of US aid to El Salvador. A particular and unfortunately rather common difficulty arises when the *status quo* is the main obstacle to the alleviation of poverty. In such circumstances foreign aid, by strengthening the *status quo*, becomes part of the problem of development rather than part of the solution. More generally, for good or ill, foreign aid enables governments to do what they already were inclined to do, but perhaps to do it more intensively, thoroughly or quickly than would otherwise have been the case.

The objective of governments rarely is to help their poorest citizens. Governments want to help the people who put them in power and keep them in power. In democratic regimes, this means their constituents; in other regimes, the factions, social classes, elites and armed groups that wield political power. Those who receive aid and administer it more often than not regard development in the broadest sense, at best, as a means to some other end, not as an end in itself, the ultimate objective of public policy. We thus come to the conclusion that neither donors nor recipients of official aid typically see aid as an instrument of development. If some development nevertheless occurs, that is a by-product of aid, not its purpose.[16]

As a result of its strong anti-communist orientation, much Western aid, and particularly US aid, was channelled to countries ruled by dictatorship, often of the extreme right, often military in origin. Examples come readily to mind: South Vietnam and Pakistan in Asia, Liberia, Kenya and Zaire in Africa, Guatemala and Haiti in Latin America. Sometimes aid to right-wing dictatorships was directly juxtaposed to left-wing dictatorships receiving aid from the Soviet bloc, e.g., Pakistan *v.* Soviet supported Afghanistan, Somalia *v.* Soviet supported Ethiopia, Honduras *v.* Soviet supported Nicaragua. The juxtaposition of Somalia and Ethiopia is an example of diplomatic musical chairs, since prior to the overthrow of Emperor Haile Selassie of Ethiopia in 1974, the United

States was the dominant supporter in Ethiopia and the Soviet Union in Somalia, but after the Emperor's downfall, the United States and the Soviet Union quickly changed sides, the US becoming the major donor in Somalia and the USSR in Ethiopia.

Foreign aid during the Cold War contributed to the militarization of the Third World. It affected democratic processes by prolonging military rule in many countries, sometimes for years, and in so doing it obstructed the political aspirations of millions of people.

Another political consequence of foreign aid is that it tends to strengthen the state *vis-à-vis* civil society. Foreign aid increases the resources at the disposal of governments. The resources could of course be passed on by governments to private sector enterprises, other nonstate institutions or to individual households, e.g., through loans, tax reductions or direct transfers. More often than not, however, governments use the additional resources to enlarge the state – by increasing recurrent expenditure (civil and military), by increasing public investment in infrastructure and by expanding the number of state enterprises. It would be absurd to claim that foreign aid promotes socialism, but it does promote the state relative to the rest of the economy. As a result, donors now find themselves in the curious position of vociferously advocating the privatization of state enterprises while they themselves inadvertently facilitated the earlier expansion of state enterprises.

In summary, foreign aid during the Cold War had three prominent political effects. First, it tended to strengthen whatever group happened to be in power and even occasionally to create the groups in power. Second, it tended to prolong military rule and weaken democratic procedures. Third, it tended to enlarge the state and increase its power relative to that of civil society. Foreign aid seldom was the decisive influence in recipient countries, but insofar as it had influence, aid tended to perpetuate the *status quo*. That was one of its purposes and in that it often succeeded.

THE FUTURE OF FOREIGN AID

The geo-political context that gave rise to foreign aid programmes after the end of the Second World War no longer exists. The political transformations that occurred in the Soviet Union and in Eastern and Central Europe, beginning in 1989, effectively brought to an end the Cold War and the ideological confrontation that inspired and sustained foreign aid programmes for more than forty years. With the end of the

Cold War the division of the globe into three worlds has ceased to be credible. There is now just one world. Politically, the process of globalization is occurring at a pace that was unimaginable even five years ago. As a result of this process, the Third World as conventionally understood has ceased to exist, or soon will do so.

Foreign aid programmes are bound to change to reflect the new realities of global international relations. While it is never easy to anticipate the future, especially now during the transition to a new order, a number of predictions follow readily from the preceding analysis. First, given the loss of its *raison d'être* and the absence of a politically compelling new justification, it is likely that the transfer of resources from the OECD countries to the rest of the world will decline, gradually at first but then at an accelerating pace as old aid programmes and projects come to an end. The embryonic trend we detected above will become much more pronounced. Political spokesmen in the donor countries have expressly denied that aid to developing countries will be further reduced, but the odds are more than even that aid will decline in the years to come.

Second, the direction of flows of resources is likely to change. The composition of foreign aid programmes will shift, with relatively less going to the former Third World in order to make room for assistance to the USSR (or its successor states) and its former allies in Central and Eastern Europe.[17] The recent cancellation of a large part of the Polish foreign debt is an early indication of things to come. The formation of the European Development Bank in London is another. Aid will flow, as always, not necessarily where it is most needed but where the dictates of national self-interest suggest it will be most productive. Increased demand for capital in the former Second World, combined with an overall reduction in foreign aid, is likely to result in higher global real rates of interest.

Third, Germany will begin to look to its east and this will be reflected in the size and composition of its foreign aid programme. In a sense 'foreign' aid will be a partial misnomer in the case of Germany since after reunification the largest resource transfer will be to the economically more backward part of its own territory, the former German Democratic Republic. Germany can also be expected to take the lead in Europe in providing aid to the Soviet Union, the Czech Republic, Slovakia, Poland, Hungary and possibly a few other European countries. The German aid programme to the developing countries of the former Third World, never very large, will contract, initially as a fraction of GNP and then absolutely in real terms.

Fourth, reflecting its status as a major actor on the world stage and as the second largest economy, Japan will continue to be the largest provider of foreign aid. In absolute terms its lead over the United States will increase. Relative to its own GNP, the aid ratio, still very low, may well continue to rise for the next few years. Japan's aid is likely to remain geographically concentrated on East (China) and Southeast (Indonesia, the Philippines, Thailand and Malaysia) Asia, with a growing interest in South Asia (Bangladesh, India and Pakistan). If Japan's territorial dispute with the Soviet Union over the Kurile Islands can be resolved to Japan's satisfaction, as now seems likely, Japan could join Germany as a major aid donor to the USSR.

Fifth, the United States is a large net recipient of foreign capital and is likely to remain so for the foreseeable future. The end of the Cold War will produce pressures in the United States operating in opposing directions. On the one hand, the disappearance of ideological confrontation will reduce the political inclination to sustain a global aid programme. On the other hand, the attendant reduction in military expenditure – the so-called peace dividend – will in principle increase the economic capacity of the United States to sustain a global foreign aid programme. However, given the resistance of the public to increased taxation, the urgency of addressing pressing social problems at home, the need to invest in economic and social infrastructure and the pressure from the voters to reduce the level of public expenditure, diminished political inclination is likely to count for more than enhanced economic capability. Indeed, the enhanced economic capability – or peace dividend – may turn out to be very modest if President Bush's 'new world order' requires the United States to be the chief policeman, as in the Gulf War.

It thus seems likely that the total amount of US aid will decline, both as a percentage of GNP (a continuation of existing trends) and absolutely in real terms. Geographically, US aid is likely to shift in favour of Latin America. A key question is what will happen to the huge aid programme in Israel. If it declines, as seems possible, this will pave the way for the large offsetting aid programme to Egypt to contract. A general settlement in the Middle East following the Gulf War could lead to a substantial decline in US and other OECD country aid to that region. A US withdrawal to Latin America will leave Japan a free hand in most of Asia and the European Community a free hand in East and Central Europe, the USSR and much of Africa.

Sixth, the Soviet Union and its former allies in Europe can be expected to reduce the amount of foreign aid they provide. In fact the G-7 (Group of Seven: the United States, Canada, Japan, Germany, France, United Kingdom and Italy) has almost made a reduction in Soviet aid to Cuba a political precondition for economic assistance to the Soviet Union from the West.[18] The Second World, never large donors from a global perspective, are nevertheless highly significant for a few recipient countries such as Cuba, Ethiopia and Mongolia. Moreover, although it is difficult to obtain accurate measurements of the size of the Soviet Union's aid effort and its GNP, it is possible that in relative terms 'Soviet foreign aid is about three times as much as West Germany's aid and three and a half times as much as Britain' (*The Economist*, 1990:52). The transformation of the former socialist bloc countries from net donors to net recipients could be one of the more profound consequences of ending the three-fold division of the globe and creating truly one world.[19]

Paradoxically, seventh, the merging of three worlds into one is likely to be accompanied by the greater regionalization of foreign aid. Donor countries and groups – Japan, the United States and the European Community – are likely to become even more closely identified with particular countries, regions and continents than they are at present and there is a possibility that existing spheres of influence will become consolidated and new ones created. Recipient countries may be less able to play one donor country off against another than in the past.

Eighth, the emerging pattern of foreign aid is likely to entail a move further away from multilateralism in favour of bilateral national programmes. This is another respect in which globalization may prove to be less on close examination than it appears to be at first glance. The accentuation of bilateral programmes implies a relative decline (within a declining total) of United Nations aid programmes, especially the programmes of UNDP, the specialized agencies of the UN, the regional development banks and the newer and more imaginative multilateral aid institutions such as IFAD (the International Fund for Agricultural Development). The World Bank probably will begin lending to the Soviet Union and Eastern and Central Europe, or increase its lending where it is already doing so. This will further dilute the emphasis of foreign aid programmes on the developing countries.

Finally, bilateral aid programmes, almost always conducted in the self-interest of the donor countries, are likely to become more explicitly formulated to serve not ideological self-interest but commercial and other interests, such as the control of international trade in narcotic substances and the prevention of further deterioration of the global environment. The proposed aid to Brazil to prevent further contraction of the Amazon forest is perhaps a harbinger of things to come. The aid relationship between donor and recipient countries is likely in future to be marked by greater candour, less hypocrisy, and to take on in part the character of payment for services rendered.

So much for predictions. Let us turn now to the implications.

The world is changing rapidly, most people think for the better. Change, however, usually entails both gainers and losers and it is important to consider what foreign aid after the Cold War is likely to imply for the development prospects of poor countries. Much depends, of course, on the economic strategy the developing countries wish to adopt. No doubt each country will adopt its own set of policies, which may or may not add up to a coherent strategy, but a consensus seems to be emerging within international circles (UN, ECOSOC, 1989; UNDP, 1990; World Bank, 1990) and most importantly from within the former Third World itself (South Commission, 1990) in support of a particular cluster of priorities. This is well summarized in the recently published report of the South Commission where the statement is made that:

> development is a process of self-reliant growth, achieved through the participation of the people acting in their own interests as they see them, and under their own control. Its first objective must be to end poverty, provide productive employment, and satisfy the basic needs of all the people, any surplus being fairly shared. (South Commission, 1990:13)

The emphasis in the quotation is on self-reliance, abolishing poverty, creating employment, satisfying basic needs and creating an equitable society. A number of policy suggestions are made in the report, almost all of them very sensible, but emphasis clearly is placed on human development. Indeed 'the development of human resources has to be a key element of new strategies' (South Commission, 1990:15; 99–108).

One implication of the priorities being recommended by and for developing countries, and hopefully soon to be adopted by their governments, is that they can be implemented without recourse to a large inflow of foreign resources. Self-reliance is more feasible than previously because the recommended strategy relies more on a reallocation of existing resources than on an injection of aid from abroad. This point is not highlighted in the report (in fact, it is nearly invisible), but the South Commission does say that because no significant improvement in the international economic environment for development is likely to occur, 'the development of the South will therefore need to be fuelled by its own resources to a much greater degree than in the past' (South Commission, 1990:79). Thus precisely at a time when foreign aid for developing countries is likely to decline, a report by the South is published calling for greater emphasis on the mobilization of domestic resources and stating bluntly that 'the central message of this Report is that, to get ahead, the South must primarily rely on itself' (South Commission, 1990:211).

This comes as a gush of fresh air after years and years of clamour for more aid. The old habits, however, die hard. The South Commission is 'deeply concerned' that events in the former Second World will lead to 'a probable diversion of both attention and resources from development' and hence the Commission puts in a bid for part of the 'peace dividend' to be 'set aside for agreed international purposes – particularly . . . meeting the basic needs of the South' (South Commission, 1990:220). But above all 'it is essential to reaffirm the need for developed countries to attain the target of 0.7 per cent of GNP for official development assistance' (South Commission, 1990:230).

The 0.7 per cent target was adopted by the United Nations in 1968, i.e., more than 20 years ago. Since then there has been no movement towards the target; if anything, movement has been in the opposite direction. It is not only futile but foolish to continue to insist on a target that is becoming ever more distant: it raises false hopes and distracts attention from more pressing matters. A dose of realism about aid targets would be to everyone's advantage. This is equally true of the target, adopted in 1981, of 0.15 per cent of GNP that donors should allocate to the so-called least developed countries.[20] In 1981 there were 31 least developed countries; today there are 42 and Liberia has been declared by the United Nations Committee for Development Planning, the advisory body on such matters, to be eligible to become the 43rd. In 1981 the donor countries allocated 0.09 per cent of their GNP to the least developed countries and the proportion has remained constant ever since. In other words, because of the substantial growth in the number of eligible recipients and the relative constancy of the amount of aid provided, there has been a considerable dilution of aid flows to the least developed countries.

Undeterred by this disappointing record, the South Commission not only reaffirms the 0.15 per cent target but says 'it is imperative' to raise it 'to 0.20 per cent of donors' GNP by the end of the 1990s' (South Commission, 1990:231). This is not just unrealistic, it is quix-otic. The United States in 1989 allocated only 0.15 per cent of its

GNP to its entire, global foreign aid programme and nearly half of that went to Israel and Egypt, two countries that evidently are not 'least developed'. It can be taken as a fact of international economic relations that the United States is not going to expand the relative size of its aid programme by a third (from 0.15 to 0.20 per cent of its GNP), cancel all aid to countries not on the list of 42 (or 43) and allocate all assistance to the least developed countries simultaneously and within a period of ten years. The United States may be extreme in its lack of generosity to the least developed countries,[21] but one can be quite certain that the donors as a whole will achieve neither the South Commission target of 0.20 nor the United Nations target of 0.15 per cent of GNP. On this point at least, we have reached the end of the road.

The 0.15 target was in any case a side road. Perhaps the main highway also is coming to an end. Perhaps the era of large development aid programmes will fade away as the Cold War becomes little more than an historical memory. This is a distinct possibility. And if it should occur, should the world mourn the passing of aid? It is an ill wind that blows no good. Was development aid the good that was carried along by the ill wind of the Cold War?

It would be churlish to deny the good will, the humanitarian instincts and the sense of solidarity that always formed part of the foreign aid effort. If political expediency fuelled most programmes, it was tempered by a desire to promote development. Unfortunately, however, the record shows that development seldom was in fact promoted by aid. On average, foreign aid seems not to have accelerated the rate of growth. In general, foreign aid went not so much into investment and human development as into unproductive consumption, military expenditure and capital flight. More often than not, foreign aid failed to reduce the great inequalities that characterize so many developing countries. Worse still, after half a century of foreign aid it cannot be demonstrated that aid has actually reduced poverty. The OECD's DAC candidly admitted this six years ago when it wrote that 'the most troubling shortcoming of development aid has been its limited measurable contribution to the reduction . . . of extreme poverty' (OECD, 1985:18). Even the World Bank, the largest of the multilateral development agencies, a far from disinterested advocate of aid and sometimes a champion of the poor, is mildly defensive about its claims. In the latest *World Development Report*, devoted to poverty, it says:

Aid has often been an effective instrument for reducing poverty – but not always. Donors sometimes have other objectives. In 1988 about 41 percent of external assistance was directed to middle- and high-income countries, largely for political reasons. Even when aid has been directed to the poor, the results have sometimes been disappointing – especially in countries in which the overall policy framework has not been conducive to the reduction of poverty. (World Bank, 1990:4)

What a sad commentary! Finally, it cannot be said that for all its economic weaknesses, foreign aid has at least encouraged democratic government. The opposite is closer to the truth: foreign aid has a shameful record of supporting dictatorships and authoritarian regimes.

Those who have long supported aid because they believed it contributed to development have begun to suffer from 'aid fatigue'.[22] Those who supported aid for political reasons, as a weapon in the Cold War, have lost their justification for continuing. The 'aid constituency' gradually is being reduced to businessmen who see foreign aid programmes as a way to increase sales. If aid has indeed come to this, there is no reason to mourn its demise. But before foreign aid can be interred with dignity, the affairs of the deceased should be put in order.

Foreign aid, in combination with commercial bank lending, has imposed an enormous burden on many developing countries. Indeed the World Bank has classified 45 countries as 'severely indebted' and there are a number of others which also have serious debt problems. In 1988 the total external public debt of low- and middle-income developing countries was $911 520 million, of which more than two-thirds was in three regions: sub-Saharan Africa; Europe, the Middle East and North Africa; and Latin America and the Caribbean. In these three regions between 1970 and 1988, external public debt increased from 10.5–13.6 per cent of GNP to 40.6–78.2 per cent and debt service rose from 5.3–13.1 per cent of exports to 16.5–28.1 per cent (World Bank, 1990:225). The South Commission is absolutely correct in saying 'the point must be accepted once and for all that the external debt of the developing countries is not repayable in full, and that its full nominal value will not be repaid' (South Commission, 1990:226).

There are many reasons why the debt burden has become insupportable in so many countries, but a fundamental reason is that a large part of foreign aid and commercial external loans were not used for development purposes but instead were squandered in the ways indicated above. Supporters of foreign aid try hard to separate the ill effects of commercial lending from the assumed beneficial effects of official bilateral and multilateral lending, but the attempt to separate the commercial bankers from the aid donors is disingenuous. In 1973 and again in 1979 when oil prices were increased sharply and huge surpluses emerged in the OPEC countries, the commercial banks were urged by the multilateral and bilateral development agencies to recycle the surpluses by lending as much as possible to developing countries. Similarly, the multilateral development banks were encouraged to increase their lending in order to counteract the feared deflationary impact on the world economy of the OPEC surpluses. Lending did in fact increase dramatically, and for a while the 'success' of recycling was widely celebrated. Roughly speaking, commercial lending was channelled disproportionately to Latin America while multilateral lending was channelled disproportionately to Africa.

When the debt crisis emerged in 1982, triggered by Mexico's inability to service her external debt, lending to developing countries ceased to be regarded as a success. The commercial lenders in particular were blamed for being incautious, for not scrutinizing projects properly and for relying on the taxing power of governments to ensure that sovereign debts would be repaid. Less was said about the reversal of economic policy in the OECD countries, the cuts in public expenditure and the introduction of tight monetary policies, which caused a world recession, a collapse of primary commodity prices, a slowing down in the volume of international trade and a sharp rise in real rates of interest. Massive lending followed by macroeconomic policies in the donor countries which would have made it impossible even in the best circumstances to repay the debt were combined with equally foolish policies in most recipient countries. Development in many countries came to a halt and was thrown into reverse; average incomes fell; poverty increased.

The truth is that the debt burden, not economic development, has become the legacy of forty years of foreign aid. Let us now be realistic, face the facts and write off the debts, completely in the poorest countries and very substantially in the other developing countries. Cancellation of a large part of the external debt of developing countries would be a once-for-all gift from the rich countries to the poor, a form of foreign aid that would help to remedy the errors of the past, and a gift that would cost the donors little in terms of forgone income since they are unlikely to be paid in any event. Debt cancellation would be a last hurrah, a bonfire of the vanities that would bring to an end the era of foreign aid. It could then be said that nothing so became the true spirit of development assistance as the manner of its departure.

A FUTURE FOR OFFICIAL NON-DEVELOPMENT AID

The thrust of my argument is that enough years have passed to be able to assess the effectiveness of ODA and on the whole the assessment turns out to be rather negative. This does not imply that all official aid should be discontinued.

Short-term assistance during emergencies is not being questioned. The case for disaster relief – to overcome suffering caused by earthquakes in the Philippines, floods in Bangladesh, drought in the Sahel, famine in Ethiopia – is evident and compelling. The effectiveness of disaster relief certainly can be increased, but there is no evidence that in general short-term emergency aid has caused harm or, even on balance, done no good. The evidence suggests the opposite, although moral dilemmas can arise when emergency aid is given to a government in the midst of a civil war. Moral dilemmas aside, the response of ordinary people to disasters elsewhere, be they in rich countries or poor, is testimony to the empathy and solidarity which can arise spontaneously when other human beings are suddenly exposed to acute distress.

Next, a convincing case can be made for official assistance to political refugees. The number of refugees scattered throughout the world is large and growing, and hence more rather than less assistance for political refugees would be desirable. Many groups of refugees – Sudanese, Ethiopians, Somalis, Cambodians, Vietnamese, Palestinians, Salvadoreans – are forced to spend long periods in exile and for this reason aid to refugees can be quite different from short-term emergency aid. There is a need not only to help refugees earn a livelihood while they are in exile but also to ease the economic burden on the host community caused by a large influx of impoverished people. Eventually, when refugees are able to return to their own country, foreign aid may be needed to assist resettlement.

Finally, a case can be made for medium-term assistance of five to ten years to Eastern and Central Europe and the Soviet Union. The former Second World does not have a long-term development problem, but it has a severe medium-term restructuring problem. Large injections of foreign finance, over a finite period, if used properly, can be expected to yield high returns. There is no case for prolonged assistance to the Soviet Union or to the countries of Eastern and Central Europe: they are not poor, they have a well educated, highly skilled, experienced and healthy labour force, a reasonably good physical infrastructure and a large (if inefficient and technologically obsolete) manufacturing sector. All they need in order to become relatively prosperous is time and a reasonable amount of external resources to give their economies some flexibility and smooth the way through the transition period. The situation in these countries is more analogous to that in Western Europe after the Second World War than it is to the developing countries of today, and hence a foreign aid programme similar to the Marshall Plan in size and duration could be remarkably successful.

Thus the case for short-term aid during emergencies, medium-term aid to the former Second World and assistance to political refugees for as long as necessary is not under dispute. These forms of foreign aid clearly are desirable. It is long-term foreign assistance intended to alleviate poverty by promoting economic development that has failed and that urgently needs to be reconsidered.

Notes

This paper was written while the author was visiting the OECD Development Centre in Paris. I am grateful to the President of the Development Centre, Louis Emmerij, for creating an intellectual environment where controversial issues can be examined and unconventional views expressed. I am indebted to Phil Martinez for research assistance, and to Louis Emmerij, Jean Bonvin, James Boyce, Giulio Fossi, Laurence Harris, Rachel Meghir, Helmut Reisen, Hartmut Schneider and David Turnham for comments on earlier drafts.

1. A comparison of military expenditure with development expenditure gives some idea of the relative significance of foreign aid. Between 1980 and 1990 world military expenditure was roughly $8030 billion while official development assistance was $360 billion, or only 4.5 per cent as large (Shaw and Wong, 1989:5).

2. In the case of the United States, and probably of several other major donors as well, strategic considerations have remained at the root of aid programmes. (See Lebovic, 1988:115–36.) This essay is concerned only with what the OECD calls official development assistance (ODA), i.e., economic aid intended to promote development. It should be noted, however, that nearly half of what the US government classifies as foreign aid is intended for military purposes.

3. The Galbraithian view has now penetrated some of the multilateral aid agencies. For example, a United Nations report states, 'The development aid system "invented" by the various aid agencies . . . has thought out the causes of poverty as a function of the remedies available to the international community. These remedies were capital, technology and the experts, who, as it were, personified them' (Kabongo and Schumm, 1989:21).

4. The most sophisticated version of the gap analysis is contained in Chenery and Strout (1966).

5. An enormous amount of valuable data is assembled and published annually by the Development Assistance Committee of the OECD. See, for

example, OECD, DAC (1989). The reports of the DAC contain useful discussions of the direction in which the OECD thinks aid ought to go, but the reports are noteworthy for the limited analysis of what actually have been the effects of aid.

6. Econometric studies can never provide a wholly satisfactory explanation. There is always a problem of the quality of data. Beyond that, more fundamentally, crude, one-equation econometric models can be no more than suggestive; they are too simple in their underlying assumptions to be used for precise measurements. Complex, multi-equation models with many independent variables are equally unsatisfactory. The independent variables are likely to be correlated; there are likely to be long and variable lags in the system, especially when indirect effects are taken into account; at least some of the equations are likely to be non-linear and the parameter values are likely to be unstable, e.g., because of policy changes. This is not an argument in favour of ignoring data, but it is an argument in favour of combining econometric evidence with the evidence of more general knowledge and experience and the judgement that comes with them.

7. In 1987–88 Indonesia received 11.9 per cent of Japanese aid. The next largest recipient was China, with 6.6 per cent.

8. Israel is the largest recipient of US aid. In 1987–88 this country of only 4.4 million people received 12 per cent of all US aid. The next largest recipient was Egypt, with 9.4 per cent.

9. I first put these views forward in an article in Spanish with Ricardo Ffrench-Davis in 1964 (see Griffin and Ffrench-Davis, 1964) and repeated the argument in Griffin (1969).

10. There are of course exceptions to these tendencies. France, for example, has sent thousands of secondary school teachers to developing countries in Francophone Africa.

11. In Bolivia the salaries of more than 600 senior and middle level civil servants are paid by donor agencies (UNDP, IBRD, USAID).

12. See Pastor (1990). The data in this article do not take into account interest earnings on the stock of flight capital and hence understate the value of assets held abroad. On this point see Boyce and Zarsky (1988:191–222).

13. In fact there is a thirteenth country, viz., Angola, that spends more than average on the military, but it has been excluded from the analysis because of lack of information about foreign aid receipts.

14. In a classic response to the criticisms voiced in the report, the Assistant Administrator for Program and Policy Coordination, Reginald J. Brown, wrote in a letter to Prosterman that 'A.I.D. missions use *all* of their resources in ways most likely to help the poor majority' (emphasis in the original; Prosterman and Hanstad, 1990:64ff).

15. See, for example, Bornschier, Chase-Dunn and Rubinson (1978).

16. Even such a keen defender of foreign aid as Robert Cassen says only that 'most aid does indeed "work". It succeeds in achieving its developmental objectives (where those are primary)' (Cassen, 1986:11).

17. In OECD (1990:4) it was said that 'Member governments recognize the importance of the fundamental political changes in Central and Eastern Europe and will support the important process of economic reform in

these countries. This support will not diminish their determination to give high priority to their development co-operation with the Third World.' I do not doubt the sincerity of this statement, but I believe that events will lead to a reallocation of aid flows in the direction predicted.

18. In Group of Seven (1990) the G-7 said, 'We also agreed that further Soviet decisions ... to cut support to nations promoting regional conflict will ... improve the prospects for meaningful and sustained economic assistance' (para. 44).
19. *The Economist* believes that 'in the long run, for both donor and recipients, the change [i.e., the reduction in aid] will probably be for the good' (*The Economist*, 1990:54). It is noteworthy that *The Economist* does not express a similar view about Western aid.
20. They are described as so-called least developed countries because although low per capita income is the primary basis for classification, India and China are excluded from the list whereas much richer countries such as Botswana and Mauritania are included.
21. In 1987, the last year for which we have complete data, the US allocated 0.04 per cent of its GNP to the least developed countries. Only New Zealand allocated less (0.03 per cent) and Austria allocated the same proportion. Six countries of the 18 members of the OECD's DAC reached or exceeded the 0.15 per cent target: Denmark, Finland, Italy, the Netherlands, Norway and Sweden.
22. The general public in the United States and the United Kingdom does not strongly support long-term foreign aid programmes although it does support short-term emergency assistance. (For a vigorous statement, from a British point of view, of the case that official aid programmes 'should be stopped forthwith before more damage is done', see Hancock, 1989:189.) Aid programmes have begun to run into political difficulties in Japan and Italy, two countries where the aid ratio has risen. In Germany some disillusionment has become apparent. (See, e.g., a popular book written by a former West German aid official and parliamentarian who describes aid as 'deadly': Erler, 1985.) Even in Canada, the Netherlands, Norway and Sweden – four countries noted for their cosmopolitan values, humane internationalism and generous aid programmes – a recent study indicates that 'humane internationalism in its several forms is clearly disheartened and under siege' (Pratt, 1989:207).

References

Bornschier, V., Chase-Dunn, C. and Rubinson, R. (1978) 'Cross-Sectional Evidence of the Effects of Foreign Investment and Aid on Economic Growth and Inequality: A Survey of Findings and a Reanalysis', *American Journal of Sociology* vol. 84, No. 3, pp. 651–83.

Boyce, James (1992) *The Philippines: The Political Economy of Growth and Impoverishment* (London: Macmillan).

Boyce, James and Zarsky, L. (1988) 'Capital Flight from the Philippines, 1962–1986', *The Journal of Philippine Development*, Vol. 15, No. 2, pp. 191–222.

Cassen, Robert and Associates (1986) *Does Aid Work?* (Oxford: Clarendon Press).

Chenery, Hollis and Eckstein, Peter (1970) 'Development Alternatives for Latin America', *Journal of Political Economy*, Vol. 78, No. 2, pp. 966–1006.

Chenery, Hollis B. and Strout, Alan M. (1966) 'Foreign Assistance and Economic Development', *American Economic Review*, Vol. 56, No. 3, pp. 679–733.

Dacy, D. C. (1975) 'Foreign Aid, Government Consumption, Savings and Growth in Less-Developed Countries', *Economic Journal*, Vol. 85, No. 339, pp. 548–61.

The Economist, 7 April 1990.

Erler, Brigitte (1985) *Todliche Hilfe* (Dreisam-Verlag: Freiburg i. Br).

Galbraith, J.K. (1975) *The Nature of Mass Poverty* (Cambridge, MA: Harvard University Press).

Gersovitz, M. (1982) 'The Estimation of the Two-Gap Model', *Journal of International Economics*, Vol. 12, No. 1, pp. 111–24.

Griffin, Keith (1969) *Underdevelopment in Spanish America* (London: Allen & Unwin).

Griffin, Keith (1970) 'Foreign Capital, Domestic Savings and Economic Development', *Bulletin of the Oxford University Institute of Economics and Statistics*, Vol. 32, No. 2, pp. 98–112.

Griffin, Keith (1974) 'The International Transmission of Inequality', *World Development*, Vol. 2, No. 3, pp. 3–15.

Griffin, Keith and Enos, John (1970) 'Foreign Assistance: Objectives and Consequences', *Economic Development and Cultural Change*, Vol. 18, No. 3, pp. 313–27.

Griffin, Keith and Ffrench-Davis, Ricardo (1964) 'El Capital Extranjero y el Desarrollo', *Revista Economia*, Vol. 22, Nos. 2/3, pp. 11–33.

Griffin, Keith and Knight, John (eds) (1990) *Human Development and the International Development Strategy for the 1990s* (London: Macmillan).

Group of Seven (G–7) (1990) 'Houston Summit Economic Declaration'.

Gupta, K. and Islam, M.A. (1983) *Foreign Capital, Savings and Growth: An International Cross-Section Study* (Dordrecht-Holland: Reidel).

Hancock, Graham (1989) *Lords of Poverty* (London: Macmillan).

Kabongo, Tunsala and Schumm, Siegfried (1989) *Evaluation of Rural Development Activities of the United Nations System in Three African Least Developed Countries* (Geneva: United Nations, Joint Inspection Unit).

Khan, Azizur Rahman and Hossain, Mahabub (1989) *The Strategy of Development in Bangladesh* (London: Macmillan).

Landau, Luis (1971) 'Savings Functions for Latin America' in Chenery, Hollis (ed.) (1971) *Studies in Development Planning* (Cambridge, MA: Harvard University Press).

Lebovic, J.H. (1988) 'National Interests and U.S. Foreign Aid: The Carter and Reagan Years', *Journal of Peace Research*, Vol. 25, pp. 115–36.

Lucas, Jr, Robert E. (1990) 'Why Doesn't Capital Flow from Rich to Poor Countries?' *American Economic Review*, Vol. 80, No. 2, pp. 92–6.

Morisset, Jacques (1989) 'The Impact of Foreign Capital Inflows on Domestic Savings Reexamined: The Case of Argentina', *World Development*, Vol. 17, No. 11, pp. 1709–15.

Mosley, Paul (1980) 'Aid, Savings and Growth Revisited,' *Oxford Bulletin of*

Economics and Statistics, Vol. 42, No. 2, pp. 79–85.

Mosley, Paul, Hudson, H. and Horrell, S. (1987) 'Aid, the Public Sector and the Market in Less Developed Countries', *Economic Journal*, Vol. 97, No. 387, pp. 616–41.

Organization for Economic Cooperation and Development (1985) *Twenty-five Years of Development Co-operation: A Review* (Paris: OECD).

Organization for Economic Cooperation and Development (1990) *Policy Statement in Development Co-operation in the 1990s* (Paris: OECD).

Organization for Economic Cooperation and Development, Development Assistance Committee (1989) *Development Co-operation in the 1990s* (Paris: OECD).

Papanek, Gustav F. (1972) 'The Effect of Aid and Other Resource Transfers on Savings and Growth in Less Developed Countries', *Economic Journal*, Vol. 82, No. 327, pp. 934–50.

Pastor, Jr, Manuel (1990) 'Capital Flight from Latin America', *World Development* Vol. 18, No. 1, pp. 1–18.

Please, Stanley (1967) 'Savings Through Taxation: Mirage or Reality', *Finance and Development*, Vol. 4, No. 1, pp. 24–32.

Pratt, Cranford (ed.) (1989) *Internationalism Under Strain: The North-South Policies of Canada, the Netherlands, Norway and Sweden* (Toronto: University of Toronto Press).

Prosterman, Roy L. and Hanstad, Timothy (1990) *Foreign Aid: An Assessment of the Proposed FY 1991 Program* (Seattle: Rural Development Institute).

Psacharopoulos, George (1988) 'Education and Development: A Review', *World Bank Research Observer*, Vol. 3, No. 1, pp. 99–116.

Riddell, Roger C. (1987) *Foreign Aid Reconsidered* (Baltimore, MA: Johns Hopkins University Press for the Overseas Development Institute).

Robinson, Joan (1978) *Contributions to Modern Economics* (New York: Academic Press).

Shaw, R.P. and Wong, Y. (1989) *Genetic Seeds of Warfare: Evolution, Nationalism and Patriotism* (London: Unwin Hyman).

South Commission (1990) *The Challenge to the South* (Oxford: Oxford University Press).

United Nations Commission on Transnational Corporations (1990) *Recent Developments Related to Transnational Corporations and International Economic Relations* (New York: E/C.10/1990/2).

United Nations Development Programme (1990) *Human Development Report 1990* (New York: Oxford University Press).

United Nations Economic and Social Council (1989) *Report of the Committee for Development Planning on its Twenty-fifth Session* (New York: United Nations).

Wasow, Bernard (1979) 'Saving and Dependence with Externally Financed Growth', *Review of Economics and Statistics*, Vol. 61, No. 2, pp. 150–4.

Weisskopt, T.E. (1972) 'The Impact of Foreign Capital Inflow on Domestic Savings in Underdeveloped Countries', *Journal of International Economics*, Vol. 2, No. 1, pp. 25–38.

World Bank (1990) *World Development Report 1990* (New York: Oxford University Press).

World Bank, Operations Evaluation Department (1988) *Project Performance Audit Report No. 7574* (Washington, DC: World Bank).

4 Globalization and Development Cooperation: A Reformer's Agenda*

Gerry Helleiner's extensive writings on international economic cooperation possess many virtues: generosity of spirit, clarity of thought and exposition, a global perspective and a willingness to challenge the status quo. These virtues are much needed today as the world enters a new era and confronts problems which have long been relatively neglected. Prominent among neglected issues is the framework for development cooperation.[1] The original framework was established in the aftermath of the Second World War and grew to its present size and shape during the decades of the Cold War. The time has come to reconsider the entire structure and perhaps to revamp it. The purpose of this essay is to contribute to such a reconsideration. If it possesses at least some of the virtues of Gerry Helleiner's own writings on this subject, I shall be very pleased.

The reformer's agenda proposed below is based as much as possible on the mutual interests of people rather than of states. In thinking about a framework for development cooperation, I have looked for solutions where everyone gains or, failing that, for solutions where everyone potentially could gain if compensation were paid to the losers. Of course, even if everyone gains there might still be conflicts over the division of gains, but at least such conflicts can in principle be resolved without making anyone absolutely worse off. This approach leads inevitably to giving high priority to policies which accelerate growth or which result in greater efficiency in the use of the world's resources. Often it means extending the market mechanism to new areas (the migration of labour) or devising market-like mechanisms to cope with new problems (global environmental issues, the disposal of nuclear weapons). Growth and liberalization thus are themes which run

*A slightly shortened version of this chapter was published in a Festschrift in honour of Gerry Helleiner: Roy Culpeper, Albert Berry and Frances Stewart (eds), *Global Governance and Development Fifty Years After Bretton Woods* (London: Macmillan, 1996).

throughout this essay. However, it must be recognized that policies which promote mutual interests do not necessarily also promote human development or reduce global poverty or contribute to other desired objectives. Something more is likely to be needed, namely, policies which seek to achieve justice or equity.

It is for this reason that an equally prominent theme is equity: a need to provide a global safety net to combat severe poverty in the poorest countries and the duty of the rich to compensate the poor when discriminatory actions of the former injure those who are weak and vulnerable. These ideas of equity, solidarity, community are a commonplace in nation states and it is proposed to extend them to all people, everywhere. Hunger, disease and misery are becoming no more acceptable 'abroad' than they are at 'home' and, indeed, as our horizons widen, the distinction between home and abroad becomes blurred. It is no longer an oxymoron to speak of a global community. Similarly, just as discrimination within a state is not tolerated, and those who discriminate are liable for damages, so too discrimination by states against others should not be permissible and those who discriminate should be required to pay compensation.

The essay is divided into five sections. In the first section a new framework for development cooperation is outlined. In the second section a new system for financing international transfer payments is presented, based on a progressive income tax on the GNP of rich countries. In the third section, the criterion for allocating transfers is discussed. It is recommended that grants to developing countries be distributed in inverse proportion to their per capita income. The proposed tax and transfer system would thus be the foundation for a global safety net.

The next section contains an outline of a proposal to create a mechanism to facilitate payments by one country to another for services rendered. These services occur outside the market mechanism – they are not part of a network of international commerce – and originate out of a process of bilateral or multilateral negotiation. They are mutually beneficial activities which by their nature cannot be mediated by markets. Examples include payments for environmental services, payments for the control of narcotic drugs and payments for the control of contagious diseases such as AIDS.

The last section contains a proposal to create a mechanism to facilitate compensation for damages when one country inflicts economic injury on another. Compensation can be thought of as fines payable by countries which depart from internationally agreed rules of good conduct. Examples include compensation for trade restrictions on exports from poor countries, restrictions on the international migration of low skilled labour and brain drain. These fines are in a sense voluntary since they can be avoided by refraining from engaging in objectionable behaviour.

A NEW FRAMEWORK FOR DEVELOPMENT COOPERATION

The existing framework for development cooperation between rich countries and poor has centred on a collection of programmes, bilateral and multilateral, loosely classified as 'foreign aid'. These programmes include grants, long term loans at subsidized rates of interest, short term export credits, distributions of surplus commodities, military assistance, technical assistance and much else. The ostensible purpose of these programmes was to promote the economic development of poor countries in the expectation that global poverty would thereby be eliminated. In practice, however, motives were mixed, the donors pursuing diplomatic, military and commercial interests as well as humanitarian ones.

The outcomes also were mixed. Indeed foreign aid has been a great disappointment to those who hoped that the end of the colonial era would usher in a new age of solidarity and cooperation between North and South. Looking back over four and a half decades of international economic assistance to the developing countries, it is clear that expectations of rapid and dramatic progress were too high, the economic analysis was faulty and the political assumptions were simplistic.

It is becoming widely recognized that the economic rationale for foreign aid was built on false premises, namely, that underdevelopment is perpetuated by a lack of savings and access to Western technology.[2] Although this may have been true in the past, savings rates in developing countries today often are higher than in developed ones and, despite the existence of patent and copyright protection, restricted access to technology in an age of instant communications cannot possibly be the major barrier to economic and human development. As regards savings, for example, in 1990 gross domestic savings were 28 per cent of GDP in the World Bank's 'low-income economies', 24 per cent in the 'middle-income economies' and 22 per cent in the 'high-income economies'.[3] That is, savings rates were inversely correlated with per capita income, the opposite of a central premiss of aid programmes.

While there still is much debate about the economic consequences of foreign aid, four stylized facts about aid gradually are coming to be accepted. First, it is evident that foreign aid, contrary to original expectations, has not contributed to a noticeable acceleration of the rate of growth of developing countries. In the case of Africa, by far the poorest continent, growth has ceased even to be a proximate objective of foreign aid, although it may remain an ultimate objective. Instead the immediate objective now is said to be 'structural adjustment'. Yet 'structural adjustment has neither restored growth nor eased poverty in Africa'.[4]

Second, where aid inflows are large in relation to the recipient's national product, relative prices are distorted in an anti-development direction. Large inflows of foreign aid tend to result in an appreciation of the exchange rate, thereby discouraging production for export or production intended to replace goods produced abroad. Large inflows of aid also tend to reduce real rates of interest in the recipient country, thereby discouraging savings, encouraging those who hold financial assets to place their holdings abroad and creating incentives for local investors to adopt techniques of production which are biased against the employment of labour.

Third, the availability of foreign aid has made it easier for the governments of recipient countries to increase unproductive current expenditure, to expand the military and to reduce taxation. Inflows of foreign aid, far from resulting in a rise in productive investment of equal magnitude, as once postulated, have in practice been used to finance higher expenditure on a wide range of activities, some of which contribute to development and some of which do not. Aid has been highly 'fungible' and this has made it possible for those governments that wished to do so to divert aid from its intended purposes to purposes desired by the recipient government. The purposes of recipient governments, as revealed by their actual expenditure programmes, often had little to do with promoting development and eliminating poverty. Fungibility is an inescapable feature of all aid programmes and makes it difficult to tie foreign assistance to particular objectives, policies or expenditure programmes in recipient countries.

Indeed, fourth, there is no evidence apart from the occasional anecdote to suggest that either bilateral or multilateral aid programmes have succeeded in reaching the poor. On the contrary, most of the available evidence indicates that most of the benefits of foreign assistance programmes are captured by middle and upper income groups, i.e., by the elite. Moreover, even when aid-financed projects are aimed directly at the poor, they often miss their target. In the majority of cases, alas, the projects are not even aimed at the poor or at contributing to human development. That is to say, the impact of existing, conventional aid programmes on reducing poverty and inequality in developing countries and on raising the level of human development has been negligible. This, again, is an inescapable fact of present aid programmes. The question is whether one can imagine something rather better.

First, however, what does this imply about the future role of international lending by the World Bank and the other multilateral development banks? A case can be made that international lending by development banks should be wound up and the world should organize resource transfers from rich to poor countries by combining the features of an automatic and progressive income tax in rich countries with an automatic disbursement mechanism in poor countries, in which the resource transfer per head would vary inversely with per capita income or per capita GDP. Under such a scheme there would no longer be a need for the World Bank and the other development banks; they would have reached the end of their useful lives.

Consider the case of the World Bank, the most important of the Bretton Woods institutions. When the World Bank was created it was intended to serve two purposes: to help finance the reconstruction of economies severely damaged during the Second World War and to supplement private capital in financing the long term development of economically backward countries. The first purpose was achieved several decades ago, although some might argue that the needs today in Eastern Europe and Russia are fairly similar to those of Western Europe forty-five years ago. Even if one accepts this argument, however, it is not obvious that the needs of Eastern Europe and Russia should be met by the World Bank since a new institution, the European Bank for Reconstruction and Development, was created specifically to provide capital to the former Soviet bloc countries.

The second purpose, that of supplying capital to the developing countries, no longer is as important as it once was. First, domestic savings rates in developing countries are much higher than they were, say, four decades ago and hence the developing countries are less dependent on foreign aid and foreign capital in general than in previous years. Second, private international capital markets have grown very rapidly and the original justification for publicly supplied international capital (by the World Bank and the regional development banks), namely the poor functioning of global capital markets, no longer applies. In fact, about two-thirds of the capital received by developing countries today originates in the private sector and only a third can be described as foreign aid. True, private foreign capital tends to by-pass the poorest countries, for reasons which are consistent with the logic of markets, but this can best be compensated not by providing subsidized loans from development banks but by giving untied grants to the poorest countries through a scheme such as that described below. Thus the role for international development banks is becoming insignificant and the time may have come to recognize this fact and gradually phase them out.

What about technical assistance? The discussion so far has been concerned with capital flows, but a large volume of resources is transferred to developing countries as technical assistance. By far the largest provider of technical assistance is the UNDP and my observations will therefore centre on its role.

The assistance to developing countries provided by UNDP is in the form of grants and because of this, in terms of net resource transfers, UNDP is one of the largest aid agencies in the world, substantially larger than the regional development banks and broadly comparable in size to the World Bank. It is no exaggeration to say that UNDP is one of the pillars of the current framework for development cooperation. The question is whether it should remain a pillar within a new framework for cooperation.

Until quite recently UNDP did not provide funds directly to developing countries to pay for technical assistance. Instead it operated through the specialized agencies of the United Nations (UNESCO, UNIDO, ILO, WHO, FAO, etc.). In theory the governments of developing countries requested technical assistance from the specialized agencies and the UNDP covered the costs, including a generous contribution to cover the overhead costs of the specialized agencies. In practice, however, technical assistance projects originated in the specialized agencies and the agencies then sold the projects to the recipient countries. Selling activities often were rather intense as the specialized agencies came to depend on UNDP funds as a major source of revenues.

A number of problems arose from this method of supplying technical assistance. First, competition was created among the specialized agencies of the United Nations as each sought to maximize its revenues from UNDP. There was no coordination of technical assistance at the national level or a careful determination of priorities. In principle the Resident Representative of UNDP in each country could have played this role, but in practice each UN agency pursued its own objective. Because of the incentive structure unwittingly created by UNDP, each agency tried to maximize its income rather than assist the development of the recipient countries.

Second, within their area of competence, each specialized agency had a virtual monopoly in providing technical assistance. UNDP was so large that bilateral agencies and non-governmental organizations rarely were able to provide effective competition. The UN agencies had a clear field. The consequence, third, is that the quality of the technical assistance that was provided often was mediocre. The 'experts' sometimes were unsuitable and the value of the advice given to the recipient country often was low. Even worse, finally, because the opportunity cost to the recipient country often was nearly zero, developing countries received technical assistance they neither wanted nor needed. The system was supply-side driven: the agencies supplied the experts, the UNDP paid the bills and the developing countries were the passive recipients.

The results, not surprisingly, were far from satisfactory. UNDP responded by improving the structure of incentives in two important ways. First, each country was assigned a notional budget for technical assistance projects. The effect of this was to introduce an opportunity cost at the country level: if the offer of project A from agency X is accepted, then the offer of project B from agency Y may have to be declined. Countries thus have to choose and think about their priorities.

Second, UNDP broke the monopoly of the specialized agencies in providing technical assistance. Henceforth agreed technical assistance projects are put out to tender and many organizations are encouraged to submit bids, including of course organizations in the private sector. Governments now have a greater choice of supplier; there is more competition and there is reason to hope that the cost of technical assistance projects will fall and the quality increase.

Although governments now are able to exercise wider choice within the area of technical assistance, their national allocation from UNDP still is restricted to technical assistance projects. The logical next step in the reform process would be to remove this restriction and allow governments to use UNDP funds for any developmental purpose, be it technical assistance, investment in human capital, investment in physical capital or investment in natural capital. UNDP would then become a grant giving agency that supplies untied funds to developing countries.

Such a transformation of UNDP would have profound implications for the framework of development cooperation. It would shift the balance of power in favour of developing countries. It would force the specialized agencies to become fully competitive in supplying technical assistance, since not only would they have to compete against other suppliers of technical assistance, but they would also have to show that expenditure on technical assistance yields higher returns than, say, additional expenditure on secondary education. Such a transformation also would reduce dramatically the cost of delivering foreign aid since there would no longer be a need for a huge bureaucracy to administer tens of thousands of small technical assistance projects. Finally, provided UNDP grants were distributed on the basis of need, as reflected in average income per head of a country's population, and provided the governments of recipient countries used the aid wisely, foreign assistance would become more equitable and contribute to a genuine reduction in global poverty.

A NEW BASIS FOR FINANCING AID

There is widespread disappointment, to use the World Bank's words, that 'aid has done much less than might have been hoped to reduce poverty',[5] and this prolonged disappointment has undermined support in the developed countries for foreign aid programmes. The basis for aid will have to be reconstructed if the support for aid is not to wither away.[6] The suggestion of some, including Richard Jolly in this volume [the Festschift for Gerry Helleiner], that foreign aid enjoys widespread support among the public in the industrial countries is wishful thinking, as the sharp fall in 1993 in ODA as a proportion of GNP indicates. Yet the moral case for the people of rich countries to help those in poor countries remains intact.[7] Those who are prosperous do have a moral obligation to assist those who live in poverty and thus there is a prima facie case for a transfer of resources from rich countries to poor. It does not follow from this, however, that there is a moral obligation to support official aid programmes as presently and historically organized. As Roger Riddell, someone who has thought hard about these issues, correctly says, 'the bedrock question about foreign aid' is whether it assists the poor.[8] If it doesn't, and if it can't be reformed so that it does, the moral case for official aid programmes collapses.

Clearly, the time has come to think again. Let us be clear, however, that what needs rethinking is long term foreign assistance intended to alleviate poverty by promoting human development. I am not challenging the need for such things as emergency assistance during famines and periods of economic distress or aid for political refugees.[9]

One issue that needs to be resolved is the amount of aid provided and the way it is financed.[10] At present ODA is financed by what can be described as a system of voluntary taxation of rich countries. In a

rational world one would expect that the burden of aid 'taxation' would
fall most lightly on donor countries with the lowest per capita income
and gradually rise as per capita income increases. That is, one would
expect the 'tax rates' to be progressive. Yet in fact the aid burden is
randomly distributed among donors.

The United Nations aid target of 0.7 per cent of GNP implies a
proportional tax rate. This evidently is inequitable since donor countries with very different levels of average income are none the less
asked to contribute the same proportion of their income as aid. A strictly
proportional aid burden would be less inequitable than the present randomly distributed burden, but it would not correspond to what most
people would regard as fair. The present system in which three very
rich countries (the United States, Japan and Switzerland) contribute
less than the average percentage is utterly indefensible, but it would
be almost as difficult to justify a system that requires, say, Ireland to
pay as much as Switzerland.

When creating a new framework for development cooperation, the
objective should be to end the present system where aid contributions
are voluntary, the aid burden is distributed randomly and inequitably,
and the flows of aid are unpredictable because they are subject to annual appropriations by national parliaments. Instead the world should
move to a system where contributions to the aid effort are obligatory,
the burden is distributed progressively and the annual flows are predictable. In short, what is needed is a progressive international income
tax on rich countries administered by an international authority such
as the United Nations. A reorganized UNDP, for instance, could be
entrusted with this task. Let us call this new organization the XUNDP.[11]
The idea of a progressive international income tax to finance foreign
aid is not new[12] and the time may be ripe to consider it seriously.

The design of such a scheme could be very simple and easy to implement. One scheme to illustrate how it might work is presented below. In this scheme, GDP per capita expressed in purchasing power
parity (PPP) terms is used for the rank ordering of countries while
GDP in current US dollars is used as the tax base. Alternative arrangements could readily be devised, but this one will do for purposes
of illustration. The first issue that must be resolved is what countries
would be liable to an international tax. We suggest that the cut-off
point be a real GDP per capita in 1990 (expressed in US dollars of
PPP) of $10 000. Countries with a real income higher than $10 000
would be liable to the tax; those with an income less than $10 000 per
capita would be exempt. Using this somewhat arbitrary criterion, 31

countries would be liable, ranging from the United States at the top to Ireland at the bottom. The countries are listed in the first column of Table 4.1. I shall refer to these countries as Group A.

The second issue is the rate of taxation. The tax schedule should be progressive in order to take into account differences in real income among the donor countries and it also should be simple in order to avoid disputes over tax liabilities which turn on alternative estimates of a country's GDP. I suggest that there be only three tax rates and that for simplicity the tax base be a country's GDP as conventionally measured, i.e., not adjusted for PPP. Specifically, I suggest that a tax rate of 0.375 per cent be applied in countries with a real GDP per capita (in PPP terms) greater than $16 000. Sixteen countries, from Norway to the United States, fall into this category. Next, a tax rate of 0.25 per cent could be applied in countries with a real income between $12 000 and $16 000. This category includes eight countries, from New Zealand to Italy. Finally, a tax rate of 0.20 per cent could be applied in countries with a real income between $10 001 and $11 999. This category includes seven countries, from Ireland to Spain. The selection of the tax rates is designed to produce a gross flow of revenue roughly comparable to the amount of ODA provided at the beginning of this decade. This choice of the level of taxation should be politically feasible. Moreover, given the scepticism about the effectiveness of aid expressed above, it seems sensible to see how things work out under the new system before proposing a higher level of resource transfer.

Application of these rates of taxation implies that some countries would contribute less foreign aid than they do at present, notably the Nordic countries, France and the Netherlands. Others would contribute more than they do at present, notably the United States and Austria. Still others would join the club of donors for the first time, e.g., Singapore, Hong Kong and the Bahamas. Those countries which wished to contribute more to the aid effort than required by their tax obligation would of course be free to do so. They could either make voluntary contributions to the international development fund (XUNDP) or they could supplement the multilateral programme with their own bilateral programme.

The scheme described in Table 4.1 produces a tax yield of nearly $56.8 billion, excluding Brunei for which data are not available. This is slightly more than the $55.6 billion contributed by the OECD countries in 1990 and $2 billion more than the amount contributed in 1993. Moreover, all of the aid under this scheme would be in the form of grants and none of the grants would be tied in any way.[13] Hence the

Table 4.1 An international system of progressive taxation to finance foreign aid

Country	Real GDP per capita, 1990 ($PPP)	Tax rate (% of GDP)	GDP, 1990 (US$ millions)	Tax yield (US$ millions)
USA	21 449	0.375	5 392 200	20 220.75
Switzerland	20 874	0.375	224 850	843.19
Luxembourg	19 244	0.375	10 889	40.83
Canada	19 232	0.375	570 150	2 138.06
Germany	18 213	0.375	1 488 210	5 580.79
Japan	17 616	0.375	2 942 890	11 035.84
France	17 405	0.375	1 190 780	4 465.43
Sweden	17 014	0.375	228 110	855.41
Denmark	16 781	0.375	130 960	491.10
UAE	16 753	0.375	28 270	106.01
Austria	16 504	0.375	157 380	590.18
Iceland	16 496	0.375	5 457	20.46
Finland	16 446	0.375	137 250	514.69
Belgium	16 381	0.375	192 390	721.46
Australia	16 051	0.375	296 300	1 111.13
Norway	16 028	0.375	105 830	396.86
Italy	15 890	0.250	1 090 750	2 726.88
Singapore	15 880	0.250	34 600	86.50
UK	15 804	0.250	975 150	2 437.88
Netherlands	15 695	0.250	279 150	697.88
Hong Kong	15 595	0.250	59 670	149.18
Kuwait	15 178	0.250	23 540	58.85
Brunei Darussalam	14 000	0.250	n.a.	n.a.
New Zealand	13 481	0.250	42 760	106.90
Spain	11 723	0.200	491 240	982.48

Qatar	11 400	0.200	6 963	13.93
Bahamas	11 235	0.200	2 912	5.82
Saudi Arabia	10 989	0.200	80 890	161.78
Israel	10 840	0.200	53 200	106.40
Bahrain	10 706	0.200	3 435	6.87
Ireland	10 589	0.200	42 500	85.00

Sources: UNDP, *Human Development Report 1993* (New York: Oxford University Press, 1993); World Bank, *World Development Report 1992* (New York: Oxford University Press, 1992).

real value to the recipients of aid under an international tax financed scheme undoubtedly would be considerably higher than the value of the present mixture of loans, export credits, surplus commodities, etc.

Under the suggested scheme, foreign aid would represent 0.35 per cent of the GDP of donor countries as conventionally measured. This can be compared with the actual situation in 1992 and 1993 when foreign aid accounted for 0.33 and 0.29 per cent, respectively, of the GNP in the OECD countries.

DISBURSEMENTS UNDER A NEGATIVE INTERNATIONAL INCOME TAX

Once the question is resolved of how to finance foreign aid under a new framework for development cooperation, attention can be turned to a second issue, namely, the criteria of eligibility to receive development assistance. If foreign aid is to enjoy the support of the public in donor countries, the criteria used to select recipient countries must be clear and fair. That is far from the situation at present. Indeed we now have an extreme case where Ireland is an aid donor and Israel a large aid recipient, yet Israel's per capita income is higher than Ireland's. Such a situation obviously could not be allowed to continue if aid were to be financed through a system of international taxation administered by the United Nations.[14] Indeed in the tax scheme described in Table 4.1, Israel becomes a donor country.

What is needed is an internationally agreed cut-off point so that only those countries below the critical point would be eligible for foreign assistance. The dividing line could be either absolute or relative. Either criterion would permit the composition of eligible countries to change, some graduating and ceasing to be eligible when their incomes rise above a certain level and others becoming eligible as their circumstances deteriorate. One possibility, described in Table 4.2, would be to make a real per capita income (in PPP terms) of, say, $1500 in 1990 the cut-off point. This corresponds to the average income in Honduras, Zimbabwe and Nicaragua and implies that 51 developing countries would be eligible for aid. The countries are listed in Table 4.2. I shall refer to these as the Group C countries. (The Group B countries are those whose income is so low that they are not liable to international aid taxation but whose income is so high that they are not eligible to receive foreign aid.)

The total population of the 51 countries eligible under this criterion (the Group C countries) is just over 1.5 billion persons. If the entire international development fund of $56.8 billion were divided equally among the eligible recipients, the average aid allocation per person would be about $37.87. It would, however, be more equitable to allocate more than the average to the poorest countries and less than average to those who are not quite so poor. To illustrate how this might work, in Table 4.2 the eligible recipients are divided into two groups. The poorest 27 countries, with a real (PPP) income per head of less than $900, are allocated $50 per head of foreign aid. This group of countries, from Zaire to Bangladesh, contains 385.4 million people and merits special assistance. The second group contains 24 countries with a real income per capita between $900 and $1500. This group, from the Gambia to Nicaragua, contains nearly 1182 million people. The aid allocation to this group is $30 per head.

Such a system of grants, a negative international income tax, could become a powerful mechanism for ameliorating and ultimately eliminating world poverty. Much would depend, however, on the policies of the governments of recipient countries. Under the global transfer programme recommended, aid would be concentrated where it is most needed. The amount of aid per head of the population would be large enough to have a significant impact on the well-being of people. And the amount of aid received, expressed as a percentage of GDP, would make it possible, if it is used wisely, to accelerate markedly the rate of growth in the recipient countries. The two largest countries in our group of 51, Bangladesh and India, would benefit enormously under our aid disbursement scheme. Bangladesh, for instance, currently receives aid equivalent to about 9.5 per cent of its GDP; under the negative income tax described in Table 4.2, aid inflows would be equivalent to 23.3 per cent of its GDP, and all of the aid would of course be in the form of grants. Aid to India is only about 0.6 per cent of its GDP; under our scheme it would rise to 10 per cent. Some countries would lose, e.g., Zambia and Ghana, because their entitlements under a negative income tax would be less than the amount of foreign aid they now receive. And of course those countries that now receive aid but are not included in our group of the 51 poorest countries would cease to receive foreign aid under our scheme. Countries such as Argentina, Malaysia, Tunisia and Botswana would not be eligible for assistance from the international development fund. The limited resources available for international transfer payments would be channelled to countries with the lowest real incomes.

86

Table 4.2 Aid allocations under a negative international income tax

Country	Real GDP per capita, 1990 ($PPP)	Population (millions)	GDP, 1990 (US$ millions)	Aid allocation per capita (US$)	Total aid allocation (US$ millions)
Zaire	367	37.3	7 540	50	1 865
Ethiopia	369	51.2	5 490	50	2 560
Guinea	501	5.7	2 820	50	285
Uganda	524	16.3	2 820	50	815
Chad	559	5.7	1 100	50	285
Mali	572	8.5	2 450	50	425
Tanzania	572	24.5	2 060	50	1 225
Sao Tomé and Principe	600	0.1	47	50	5
Burkina Faso	618	9.0	3 060	50	450
Burundi	625	5.4	1 000	50	270
Malawi	640	8.5	1 660	50	425
Niger	645	7.7	2 520	50	385
Rwanda	657	7.1	2 130	50	355
Myanmar	659	41.6	n.a.	50	2 080
Equatorial Guinea	700	0.4	138	50	20
Madagascar	704	11.7	2 750	50	585
Afghanistan	714	n.a.	n.a.	50	n.a.
Comoros	721	0.5	228	50	25
Togo	734	3.6	1 620	50	180
Zambia	744	8.1	3 120	50	405
Central African Republic	768	3.0	1 220	50	150
Bhutan	800	1.4	280	50	70
Somalia	836	7.8	890	50	390
Angola	840	10.0	7 700	50	500
Guinea-Bissau	841	1.0	176	50	50
Liberia	857	2.6	n.a.	50	130
Bangladesh	872	106.7	22 880	50	5 335
Gambia	913	0.9	228	30	27

Nepal	920	18.9	2 890	30	567
Haiti	933	6.5	2 760	30	195
Sudan	949	25.1	n.a.	30	753
Djibouti	1 000	0.4	n.a.	30	12
Ghana	1 016	14.9	6 270	30	447
Benin	1 043	4.7	1 810	30	141
Mauritania	1 057	2.0	950	30	60
Kenya	1 058	24.2	7 540	30	726
India	1 072	849.5	254 540	30	25 485
Mozambique	1 072	15.7	1 320	30	471
Sierra Leone	1 086	4.1	840	30	123
Cambodia	1 100	8.5	n.a.	30	255
Laos	1 100	4.1	870	30	123
Vietnam	1 100	66.3	n.a.	30	1 989
Maldives	1 200	0.2	96	30	7
Nigeria	1 215	96.2	34 760	30	2 886
Senegal	1 248	7.4	5 840	30	222
Côte d'Ivoire	1 324	11.9	7 610	30	357
Namibia	1 400	1.4	1 961*	30	43
Guyana	1 464	0.8	263	30	24
Honduras	1 470	5.1	2 360	30	153
Zimbabwe	1 484	9.8	5 310	30	294
Nicaragua	1 497	3.7	6 950*	30	110

* Refers to 1991.

Sources: UNDP, *Human Development Report 1993* (New York: Oxford University Press, 1993); World Bank, *World Development Report 1992* (New York: Oxford University Press, 1992).

PAYMENT FOR SERVICES RENDERED

The purpose of the international development fund described in the previous two sections is humanitarian, namely, to reduce the most acute forms of poverty. In effect, foreign aid would act as a global safety net. Contributions to the fund would be an international obligation of all states with per capita incomes above a threshold level; resources would be raised automatically and disbursed automatically to countries with a per capita income below an agreed threshold level.

The size of the international development fund envisaged would be comparable to the current level of ODA. However, the number of countries contributing to the fund would be larger than the number of official donors today, the fund would be administered by a multilateral institution (the XUNDP), the number of countries eligible to receive assistance from the fund would be smaller than the number receiving ODA today and all disbursements from the fund would be in the form of grants. The burden of aid would thus be spread fairly and the benefits of assistance would be concentrated where they are most needed.

Quite apart from resource transfers to provide a global safety net, there is potentially a large number of inter-governmental transactions that would be of mutual interest to the contracting parties. Where these transactions involve more than two countries, it may be advantageous to all concerned if the same multilateral institution that administers the international development fund also assumes responsibility for collecting and disbursing these funds and monitoring contract compliance. In effect this would become a second window of operations for the XUNDP, the new international development institution.

The purpose of the second window is to maintain a clear separation between foreign assistance proper and payments to countries for services rendered. There is a category of transactions, mostly between rich countries and poor, where the motivation is not humanitarian interests but self-interest. These transactions are perfectly legitimate, in fact beneficial; they are of a market type but are not mediated by markets; and they are likely to increase in future. But they are not foreign aid and should not be confused with foreign aid; they are payments for services rendered.

Examples include (i) environmental programmes in developing countries which are partly or even primarily of benefit to developed countries; (ii) programmes to destroy nuclear weapons and reduce the risks of radiation to countries downwind of nuclear facilities; (iii) programmes in developing countries to reduce the supply of narcotic drugs exported to developed countries, such as crop substitution projects; and (iv) public health measures in developing countries designed to prevent the spread of the AIDS epidemic or other communicable diseases. One might also include (v) financial support for programmes to convert armaments factories to civilian purposes as a way of reducing exports of military equipment and thereby contributing to global peace; (vi) programmes to control international terrorism and transnational crime; and possibly (vii) measures to improve the health and economic and social position of women as ways to reduce the rate of growth of the world's population. One should also consider (viii) negotiations over the joint financing and management of natural resources which cross national boundaries, such as coastal fisheries and river systems, and perhaps ultimately (ix) the management of the global commons, i.e., Antarctica, the oceans and outer space. If one looks ahead there are many possibilities, although it would be sensible to begin modestly and allow the machinery for negotiation to evolve naturally in the light of experience.

The central point is that if the developed countries wish the remaining tropical forests to be preserved in order to prevent global warming and maintain biodiversity, then it is reasonable that they should bear part of the costs of preservation. Their portion of the costs should reflect the portion of benefits that accrue to them. Similarly, if the developed countries wish to discourage the use of CFCs in developing countries in order to reduce the rate of depletion of the ozone layer in the upper atmosphere, then they should compensate the developing countries for net social benefits forgone, either by making cash payments or by providing substitute technology or by helping to finance the development of alternative technologies. Economic and technological globalization generate 'externalities' and 'free rider' problems, particularly but not exclusively for the environment. As a result, no one has an incentive to contribute to the solution although it is in the interests of all that a solution be found. The purpose of the second window of the XUNDP is to provide a mechanism whereby mutually beneficial transactions can be arranged, the transfer of funds facilitated and the results monitored.

The end of the Cold War creates an unprecedented opportunity to transform swords into ploughshares. Unfortunately, however, this is a costly process. Nuclear weapons must be disarmed, industries dependent in part on exports of arms must be converted to other purposes or else shut down and their workers found employment elsewhere, and nuclear power plants (a by-product of the nuclear weapons research industry) must either be made safe or alternative sources of energy supplied. It is in the interest of the world as a whole that these tasks be accomplished as quickly as possible, yet it is unrealistic to assume that Russia and the other newly independent former republics of the Soviet Union that possess nuclear weapons, armaments factories and nuclear power stations can finance the reconversion out of their own resources. Some foreign assistance will be necessary. Foreign payments to finance a reconversion programme, however, should not be regarded as foreign aid. Instead they should be treated as payments for benefits received or services rendered and the disbursement of funds should be linked to fulfilment of an internationally agreed contract or compact.

The same principles apply in other areas of mutual interest between developed and developing countries. For example, just as it makes sense for the entry visas of international passengers to be checked at the point of departure rather than at the point of arrival, so too it pays developed countries to support public health programmes in developing countries and thereby prevent the spread to them of communicable diseases. It is cheaper to vaccinate the entire population of developing countries against smallpox than it is to police permanently the borders of developed countries; it is cheaper to clean up the water supply in cholera-prone countries than to prevent contaminated food from being loaded on to aircraft. The old saying that an ounce of prevention is worth a pound of cure applies well to some aspects of international relations between rich and poor countries. Of course, in many cases the developing countries should be spending money on such things as public health measures and clean water supplies regardless of possible external benefits. It is in the self-interest of their people to do so. We are here concerned only with those cases where consideration of external benefits makes the difference in the overall evaluation of a project or programme, i.e., where there is a mutual interest in cost sharing.

Where there are externalities of the type mentioned, it pays for countries to cooperate. The question then arises as to how much should be paid. In principle the answer is straightforward although in practice quantification is unlikely to be easy. Let us assume the cost of a programme (C) is borne entirely by the country concerned. Some of the benefits also accrue to the country concerned (Bc) and some to the rest of the world (Br). The minimum payment from the rest of the world that would make the project just worthwhile to the country concerned is $C - Bc$, i.e., the difference between total costs and the benefits received by the country. If $C - Bc$ is negative, the country's benefits exceed its costs and no additional payments would be necessary.

The maximum payment the rest of the world could consider is Br, the value of the benefits received. If Br > $(C - Bc)$, there is room for negotiation and bargaining over the 'price': total benefits to the country and the rest of the world combined are greater than total costs, and there is some scope to haggle over the distribution of the net benefits. Whatever the outcome of the haggling, however, the payment from the rest of the world to the developing country should be regarded as a price paid for a mutually agreed transaction and not as a form of foreign aid.

The second window of our proposed international development fund would be open to all countries whether members of Group A, B or C. The fund would have an important role to play in identifying mutually beneficial transactions, quantifying benefits and costs, assigning benefits to the countries comprising the rest of the world, negotiating an agreement among all the parties concerned, handling payments and supervising adherence to the agreement. By acting as a disinterested intermediary, the second window could also help to ensure that no one party to a negotiation is able to exploit excessively its bargaining strength to the relative disadvantage of its partners. There is much to be done. The amount of 'business' transacted in this way is difficult to forecast, but once the 'market' is established the volume of transactions is likely to be considerable. One aspect of the growing interdependence of peoples and countries is an increase in the number of potentially beneficial transactions that do not take place because there is neither a market mechanism to allocate benefits and costs among parties to the transaction nor a government possessing a global jurisdiction with powers to tax and spend that can 'internalize' externalities. The mechanism proposed here would remedy this deficiency and make it easier for everyone to share in global opportunities by creating a flexible negotiating framework for mutually beneficial economic cooperation.

COMPENSATION FOR DAMAGES

The point of origin for a new framework for international economic cooperation is a liberal, market-oriented global economic regime. The rules of the game of such a regime should permit the unimpeded flow worldwide of goods and services, technology, capital and labour. Departures from this regime can on occasion be justified, but departures from the regime should not be arbitrary and no country should be allowed to ignore the rules with impunity. The rules, after all, are intended to make it possible for everyone to share in global opportunities.

Under a liberal regime this implies that commodity markets, capital markets and labour markets should be allowed to operate freely. We take it as given, as a fact of life, that globalization is occurring and is irreversible. The issue is how to make globalization humane and more efficient.

The intellectual basis for a liberal economy is the demonstration that apart from exceptional circumstances both parties to a transaction benefit. The benefits may be unequally distributed, but both parties gain. In the market for goods and services, both the vendor and the purchaser gain. In the capital market, both the lender and the borrower expect to be better off as a result of the transaction. And in the labour market, both those seeking employment and those hiring workers benefit when jobs are filled. It follows from this that when one party refuses to engage in potentially beneficial transactions with another, he harms both himself and his potential trading partner.

One would perhaps not be unduly concerned if an economic agent (a firm or an individual) were to inflict harm upon itself by failing to engage in beneficial economic activity. One might react with pity, puzzlement or irritation, but one is unlikely to respond by offering charity. The old adage that there is no compensation for self-inflicted injury would apply. When one agent injures another, however, our attitudes are likely to change. Indeed in many countries discrimination against workers (on the basis of race, religion or gender) is illegal, as is discrimination against particular groups of borrowers or businesses owned or managed by particular groups of persons. The injured party may take the offender to court and claim substantial damages. There is a remedy in law.

This same principle that applies at the national level can be said to apply at the international level. Indeed normative sanctions already exist: governments that adopt beggar-thy-neighbour policies and thereby impoverish other countries encounter strong disapproval and condemnation by the international community. There are, however, few provisions in international law to stop such behaviour or to provide compensation to the injured victims. National sovereignty is given precedence over law and justice. As a result, those countries which are damaged by others have few ways to seek redress. They can threaten retaliation, but actual retaliation merely adds to their injuries. They can attempt to negotiate a treaty, but there is no guarantee negotiation will be successful: the offending country, for political reasons of its own, may prefer to continue to inflict injury on itself and others. Or they can attempt to seek relief by appealing to international agreements such as the GATT, but such agreements are narrow in coverage and their provisions for enforcement are weak.

The time may have come to review the situation and consider whether, within a new framework for economic cooperation, and perhaps within the structure of the new World Trade Organization, some provision can be made to compensate countries for damages inflicted upon them by other countries. In the discussion below it is assumed that compensation would be payable only in cases where rich countries injure the very poorest countries, i.e., when Group A countries inflict damage on Group C countries. Obvious cases for consideration are trade restrictions on exports from developing countries and restrictions on the international migration of low skilled labour. For purposes of illustration, let us consider the case of restrictions on the international mobility of low skilled labour, a topic currently under debate.

International Migration of Low Skilled Labour

The international labour market is segmented. Professional, technical and highly skilled labour is relatively free to move, but the mobility of low skilled labour is severely restricted by immigration controls, not only in the Group A countries but in many other countries as well, and this deprives millions of poor people of an opportunity to improve their livelihood.

Both the sending and receiving countries benefit from a free global labour market. The receiving countries are able to augment their human capital, increase the level of output and incomes and accelerate the rate of growth. The economic boom in Western Europe in the 1960s and the explosive growth in the oil producing states of the Middle East were made possible by large flows of immigrant labour. Contrary to popular perceptions, immigration stimulates expansion and prosperity rather than depresses it. The main economic disadvantage is that large inflows of low skilled labour dampen wages at the bottom of the scale and this tends to increase inequality in the national distribution of income, while of course reducing it internationally.

Some of these points can be illustrated by a simple diagram. In Figure 4.1 we assume the initial supply of low skilled labour is OC. Given the demand for labour represented by the marginal product curve (MPL), this results in a wage rate of w_0 and total output of $OABC$. This output is divided between the low skilled workers (Ow_0BC) and the rest of society (w_0AB). Assume the supply curve of labour shifts to S' because of immigration. The additional amount of labour (CF) increases

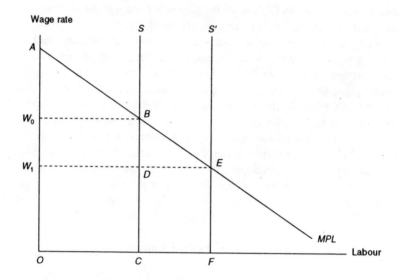

Figure 4.1 Impact effects of immigration

total output by *CBEF*, of which *CDEF* is received by the immigrant workers. The rest, the triangle *DBE*, accrues to the rest of (the non-immigrant) society. That is, the income of the non-immigrants rises by *DBE*, and if part of this additional income is invested, the level of income should increase further.

Within the receiving country, however, the wage rate for low skilled labour falls from w_0 to w_1. There is a redistribution of income from the low skilled to the rest of the population (highly skilled labour, professional and managerial workers, property owners) of $w_1 w_0 BD$. Since in a market economy the remuneration of the low skilled will be less than the average, the initial effect of immigration will be to transfer income from the poor to the rich within the receiving country. That is, unless suitable policy measures are adopted by the government, the distribution of income will become more unequal. This explains why many workers in developed countries are hostile to large scale immigration. Potentially, however, everyone in the receiving country could be better off and hence policy makers should concentrate not on keeping foreign workers out but on introducing policies which ensure that income is equitably distributed.

The analysis so far, moreover, has considered only the immediate impact effects of migration. The dynamic effects lead to additional gains

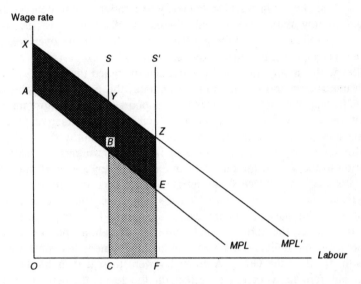

Figure 4.2 Dynamic effects of immigration

for both the migrants and the local population. These dynamic effects arise from investments in human and physical capital that are made possible by the original increase in total income. The local population is likely to save and invest part of their additional income (*DBE*) and this will increase the stock of capital, raise the productivity of labour and, in our figure, shift the marginal product of labour curve to the right. More important, migrants are known for their entrepreneurial propensities, their thriftiness and the emphasis they place on education and training. That is, a relatively high proportion of the migrants' additional income (*CDEF*) is likely to be channelled into human and physical capital formation and this will shift the marginal product curve even further to the right.

This situation is described in Figure 4.2. The shift of the marginal product curve to *MPL'* raises total output to *OXZF*. This represents an increase over the original output by an amount equal to *ABCFZX* (the total area shaded). This additional output has two components: an increase arising from the impact effect of migration equal to *CBEF* (the light shading) and an additional increase arising from the dynamic effects of migration on investment and growth equal to *AEZX* (the dark shading). These dynamic effects, because of the operation of compound growth rates, are likely to be more important than the impact effects and will quickly counteract the tendency of immigration to depress the wages of low skilled labour and worsen the distribution of income. These dynamic effects of immigration on growth often are overlooked.

Our analysis assumes all workers are able to find employment. Some challenge this assumption and it is frequently argued that in periods of high unemployment, immigration accentuates the problem of joblessness. In fact there is little evidence to support this since most immigrants enter low wage occupations which are not attractive to the indigenous population and few become openly unemployed.

Moreover, in practice the inflow of immigrant workers is small in relation to the size of the total labour force and hence even if migrant workers were to displace some indigenous workers and add to unemployment, the quantitative effect on the aggregate rate of unemployment would be marginal. In any case, the solution to unemployment is not to restrict the international mobility of labour but to adopt macroeconomic policies which encourage employment, investment and growth. If all of the Group A countries were to seal their borders to keep out foreign workers, the effect on the level of unemployment would be approximately zero. In some cases, in fact, unemployment might actually increase, e.g., if a less fluid labour market were to reduce incentives to invest.

It is now obvious, moreover, that it simply isn't possible to stop the migration of labour. If immigration is declared illegal, workers will continue to migrate, probably in slightly reduced numbers, but they will enter the recipient countries as undocumented, illegal workers, vulnerable to exploitation (particularly if they are women) and with few, if any, rights.[15] As long as global income differentials are as great as they are, the incentive to migrate will remain strong, and policies to reduce immigration will in most cases be only partially successful.[16] Wise policy makers in receiving countries will not attempt to prevent the flows of labour but to accommodate them.

The stock of migrants actually is very small. Only 1 or 2 per cent of the world's population, say 50 to 100 million people, live outside their country of origin.[17] Moreover, most migrants do not live in the rich Group A countries; they live in other developing countries, i.e., the Group B and C countries. Rough calculations suggest that only 21 per cent of the world's migrants live in developed countries. This includes 13 per cent of the international refugee population and 23 per cent of the non-refugee migrant population. It is ironical and more than a little sad that the greatest barriers to the international flow of labour and the loudest complaints about immigration are found in the developed countries, whereas in fact most of the immigrants are located in developing countries. Those who live in comfort seem least inclined to share global opportunities with those who do not, even when their lack of generosity also harms themselves.

The benefits to the sending countries are considerable. Not only do the migrant workers benefit directly from the higher incomes earned abroad, but those left behind also benefit from remittances sent home. Remittances, in fact, are between $66 billion and $70 billion a year, i.e., significantly larger than the $54.8 billion of ODA received by developing countries in 1993. If restrictions on the international migration of low skilled labour were reduced, there is no doubt that remittances would increase sharply, further reducing the need for, and relative significance of, aid.

Obstacles to the mobility of labour erected in the developed countries harm the developing countries. The extent of the damage depends on two things. First, it depends on the difference between what the migrant would earn in the rest of the world if she were free to migrate (W_r) and what she earns in her country of origin (W_c). The expression $W_r - W_c$ measures the gain in real income received by the average migrant worker.

Second, the amount of damage depends on the extent to which barriers to immigration actually succeed in reducing the flow of migration. Let us call ΔM a measure of labour market repression. It represents the amount by which the number of migrants would increase each year if global labour markets were liberalized. Total damage inflicted on the sending countries is thus $\Delta M \, (W_r - W_c)$.

For purposes of illustration, let us assume that only damages suffered as a result of a loss of potential migration from Group C to Group A countries would qualify for compensation. Let us also assume that if global labour markets were free, the annual flow of labour from Group C to Group A countries would increase by one million workers. Lastly, let us assume that on average migration would raise the incomes of migrant workers by $3000. Under these assumptions, the amount of compensation payable annually by the Group A countries would be $3 billion. The international agency administering the compensation scheme, the XUNDP, would have to estimate the extent of repressed migration and the appropriate income differentials and devise formulas for raising funds from the Group A countries and for distributing the compensation among the Group C countries. These tasks are difficult but the problems posed should not be insuperable. The important points of principle that should be established are that discrimination against workers whether in the national or the international labour market is no longer acceptable and that those who discriminate are liable for damages. Once these principles are accepted, it should be possible to design a feasible scheme for compensation.

CONCLUSIONS

The Cold War changed the world and the end of the Cold War changed the world again: 1995 is very different from 1945. The framework for development cooperation, however, has changed hardly at all since the collapse of the Berlin Wall in 1989. It has been argued in this essay that there is much to be gained from constructing a new framework. Instead of the present *mélange* of bilateral and multilateral aid agencies, development banks that supply capital in the form of loans and UNDP and the specialized United Nations agencies that supply technical assistance, it has been suggested that a single institution be created (the XUNDP) with three distinct functions or windows.

The first function would be to create a global safety net by transferring resources, in the form of grants, from rich countries to the very poorest countries. This global safety net would replace the present system of long term foreign aid whether administered by bilateral or multilateral institutions. The global safety net would be financed through a progressive income tax on the GNPs of rich countries. Funds would be allocated automatically to eligible recipient countries through a negative income tax designed in such a way that the poorer is a country, the larger is the transfer per head of its population.

The second window of the XUNDP would be responsible for correcting global market failures. It would do this by creating an institutional framework to facilitate the negotiation of inter-governmental transactions that are of mutual interest but which fall outside normal market exchange. An archetype would be agreements to protect the global environment, e.g., by preserving tropical forests, but there are many other examples of global market failure and hence many opportunities for self-interested agreements to bring about widespread gains. The task of the second window would be to ensure that the costs and benefits are equitably distributed: that is, that those who gain pay for services rendered by others.

The third window of the XUNDP is intended to ensure that the rules of a liberal global economy are adhered to by all participants. Its main task, however, is to prevent rich countries from discriminating against poor ones and to provide a remedy when rich countries violate the rules of the game and injure poor countries. When injury is inflicted the rich countries would be liable for damages and the poor countries would be entitled to compensation. The assessment of damages and the distribution of compensation payments would be the responsibility of the XUNDP.

One institution would thus be charged with three functions necessary to create and preserve a liberal global economic order. The third window would enforce the rules and ensure that compensation is paid when the rules are broken and the poor are injured. The second window would correct the most important transnational and global market failures and thereby ensure that a liberal global economy results in an efficient use of the world's resources. The first window would create a global safety net by redistributing income from rich to poor countries. It would thereby help to ensure that a liberal global economic order is reasonably equitable. These three functions taken together could go a long way towards promoting efficiency and equity within a market-oriented global economic system.

There is, however, another function, not discussed in this essay, which urgently needs to be covered, namely the response to shocks to the system, political or economic, and the emergencies such shocks create. Essentially what is needed is a global insurance fund to cope with the effects of disasters: floods, droughts, famines, civil war, refugees and the like. No country is immune to shocks and only the richest have adequate domestic resources to meet the needs of people affected by shocks. Moreover, in extreme cases, as in ex-Yugoslavia and the former USSR, even relatively prosperous societies have required external assistance to confront major emergencies. Thus in addition to the three functions which are the subject of this essay, a complete reform of international economic institutions should include provision for insurance against large shocks to the system.

Taken together, the proposed reforms would form the core of a system of global governance. They would not constitute a 'world government' but they would help to impose some order on the present anarchy. Sceptics and self-styled realists may object that the reforms infringe on national sovereignty and therefore are utopian and unlikely to be acceptable. The critics may well turn out to be right, at least in the short run, but national sovereignty was never more than a moderately convenient myth and globalization increasingly has made it an untenable myth. Sooner or later the illusion of the national sovereignty of territorial states will have to be abandoned and, when that turning point

comes, what is now impracticable will become essential and yester-
day's utopians will become the new realists.

Notes

1. This essay has its origin in research done with Terry McKinley for the
   UNDP. The original report – Keith Griffin and Terry McKinley, *A New
   Framework for Development Cooperation*, processed, pp. 119, September
   1993 – was a background document used in the preparation of the UNDP,
   Human Development Report 1994. A slightly revised version of the lengthy
   original report will also be published by UNDP in its Occasional Papers
   series. This essay is a condensed version of parts of the original report. I
   am grateful to Mahbub ul Haq of UNDP for permission to use the original material in this way. And I am grateful to Terry McKinley and Azizur
   Rahman Khan for collaborating with me over a number of years on topics
   closely related to the subject of this essay.
2. See, e.g., Keith Griffin, 'Foreign Aid After the Cold War', *Development
   and Change*, Vol. 22 (1991), pp. 645–85.
3. World Bank, *World Development Report 1992* (New York: Oxford University Press, 1992), Table 9, pp. 234–5.
4. 'Nothing To Lose But Your Chains', *The Economist*, 1 May 1993, p. 44.
5. World Bank, *World Development Report 1990* (New York: Oxford University Press, 1990), p. 127.
6. ODA from the OECD countries fell in nominal terms by 10 per cent in
   1993. The ratio of ODA to GNP fell from 0.33 per cent in 1992 to 0.29
   per cent in 1993, the lowest figure since 1973 and well below the UN
   target of 0.7 per cent. Aid from the United States fell by 25 per cent in
   1993 and was only 0.14 per cent of the country's GDP, the lowest figure
   for any donor country.
7. See Roger C. Riddell, *Foreign Aid Reconsidered* (Baltimore, MD: Johns
   Hopkins University Press for the Overseas Development Institute, 1987),
   Part I, Chapters 1–7.
8. Ibid., p. 217.
9. Short term emergency assistance and aid for political refugees urgently
   needs re-examination in order to increase its effectiveness. I believe it
   should be independently funded and administered separately from the transfer
   scheme discussed below. Emergency assistance should be available to all
   countries needing it regardless of the level of per capita income and should
   be seen as a form of global insurance against disasters. The use to which
   the funds are put, however, should be much more closely linked to long
   term development objectives than has so far been customary. (In 1992
   about 45 per cent of all UN assistance was for emergency relief and help
   to refugees.)
10. See Keith Griffin and Azizur Rahman Khan, *Globalization and the Devel-
    oping World* (Geneva: United Nations Research Institute for Social De-
    velopment, or UNRISD, 1992), pp. 33–6.

11. Throughout this essay the recommended reforms are channelled through a single institution, called the XUNDP, with a variety of 'windows'. Some might prefer several new institutions, each responsible for a single function corresponding to a window of the XUNDP. The choice of three institutions or one is largely a matter of detail.

12. See, e.g., the Report of the Independent Commission on International Development Issues (Brandt Report), *North-South: A Programme for Survival* (London: Pan Books, 1980), Ch. 15. Also see Arjun Sengupta, 'Aid and Development Policy in the 1990s', UNDP, mimeo, 5 January 1993. The academic literature on the subject includes Paul Rosenstein-Rodan, 'International Aid for Underdeveloped Countries', *Review of Economics and Statistics*, Vol. 43 (1963); Irving Kravis and Michael Davenport, 'Political Arithmetic of International Burden Sharing', *Journal of Political Economy*, Vol. 71 (1963); Griffin and Khan, *Globalization*, pp. 33–6. A progressive international income tax was endorsed in the UNDP, *Human Development Report 1992* (New York: Oxford University Press, 1992), p. 79.

13. Note that no strings are attached to the aid flows; no requirements are imposed on the recipient countries; there are no rewards for good behaviour or punishments for bad. This is a deliberate attempt to counteract what Tony Killick has called 'the explosion of conditionality' that has occurred in recent years. There is no evidence that conditionality has improved the effectiveness of aid or helped to reduce global poverty, and the time has come to abandon the mixture of self-serving and paternalistic conditions which rich countries attempt to impose on poor ones.

14. Countries would of course remain free to raise resources through national taxation and to transfer those resources to other countries. There would be nothing to prevent the United States from continuing to give money to Israel, but such a resource transfer would not count as foreign aid and would not reduce the obligation of the United States or Israel to carry their fair share of the international aid burden.

15. The greatest exploitation and discrimination experienced by poor would-be migrant workers is not the racial and ethnic or social discrimination they often encounter in the country of immigration but the discrimination they encounter by not being free to migrate in the first place.

16. I take it for granted that international migration of labour is happening and will continue to happen whether we like it or not. This is as true of Haitian boat people as of Mexican farm workers. The issue is whether developed countries can adjust to the facts of international life and make the global economy more humane or whether we will continue to attempt to resist the inevitable and in the process add to the miseries of the poor.

17. UNFPA, *The State of World Population 1993* (New York, 1993), p. 7.

5 Regulating World Markets in a Liberal Global Economy*

There is an apparent paradox in the title of this essay: regulating markets would appear to be incompatible with a liberal global economy, yet we shall argue that the global economy is not quite as liberal as is sometimes claimed, that illiberal regulation of markets persists and in some cases ought to be removed, whereas in other cases efficiency and equity might increase if there were greater regulation of the global economy within a broadly liberal framework. A liberal economy is not the same thing as a *laissez faire* economy and a degree of market regulation is indeed compatible with a liberal global system. The question is not whether liberalization always is desirable but what are the circumstances under which economic performance would be enhanced by deregulation and, conversely, under what circumstances would intervention in market processes be beneficial.

The institutions intended to regulate the global economy – the International Monetary Fund (IMF), the GATT and the World Bank – are about 50 years old. Apart from the transformation of GATT into the World Trade Organization, the formal structure of governance has remained essentially unchanged for half a century. Of course the shape of the global economy has been influenced as much by the actions of individual states, and groups of states, as by the formal structure of global governance. This 'informal structure of governance' has changed radically in the last 50 years, partly because the policies of individual governments have changed and partly because states have come together and formed 'clubs' to pursue common interests. The most prominent clubs are the European Union and NAFTA, but many other groupings exist for the purpose of affecting flows of commodities, capital, technology and labour across international boundaries.

---

* Presented at the 40th anniversary conference at Queen Elizabeth House, Oxford, 5–8 July 1995. The subject of this conference was 'The Third World after the Cold War – Ideology, Economic Development and Politics'.

At the end of the Second World War in 1945 the international economy was highly fragmented; the closely integrated global economy that we observe today is a very recent phenomenon. Think back 50 years or so. Western Europe and Japan had just embarked on recovery from a devastating war. Food was rationed; wartime controls were still in place; international financial regulations were extraordinarily tight; currencies were inconvertible. The socialist bloc centred on the Soviet Union had entered a period of consolidation of its territorial gains in Eastern and Central Europe; China in 1949 had just become a communist country. The socialist countries were rapidly becoming isolated from the rest of the world: there was little trade, less movement of capital and virtually no legal movement of labour.

The situation in the developing countries was not much better. Latin America had experienced a catastrophic decline in its terms of trade during the Great Depression of the 1930s and then a disruption of its international commerce during the Second World War, when supplies of imports were curtailed. The response was to turn inward and virtually all countries in the region adopted, more or less spontaneously, a strategy of import substituting industrialization behind a panoply of controls: high tariffs, quotas, multiple exchange rates, capital restrictions, etc. Asia, beginning with the independence of India and Pakistan in 1947, had embarked on a long process of decolonization, a process which reached its culmination with the end of the war in Vietnam in 1975. Economic policy in non-socialist Asia tended to be inward-oriented, government intervention – often organized within the framework of five-year plans – was pervasive and government policy was heavily biased in favour of industrial production for the domestic market. Economic liberalization began in East Asia in the 1960s, but it was not until the 1980s that Asia as a whole became closely integrated into the world economy. Fifty years ago virtually the entire continent of Africa was under colonial domination. The colonial territories were divided among the British, French, Belgian and Portuguese empires and production and trade within each colony were tightly regulated to meet the needs of the metropolitan country. Decolonization in Africa did not begin until the 1960s, and even after independence few countries in Africa apart from Botswana adopted liberal economic policies.

The situation today is totally different. Tariff barriers in the advanced economies have been reduced to remarkably low levels. Most quotas on trade have been eliminated. Currency restrictions have disappeared and exchange rates are largely determined by market forces. Long term capital movements have been freed. The Soviet Union has collapsed, the Cold War has ended, and the countries that formed part of the Soviet trading bloc – including the former republics of the Soviet Union – are seeking integration into the global trading system. China, too, has embarked on fundamental economic reforms; indeed China was the first socialist country to make a serious attempt to create a market guided economy. Japan, followed by the rest of East Asia and then by most of Southeast Asia, has pursued an outward-oriented, liberal economic strategy for some time. The countries of South Asia, including India, have begun to liberalize their economies. Latin America has abandoned import substituting industrialization and has become much more closely integrated into the world economy. And even in Africa, economic restructuring has reduced the bias against exports and increased the exposure of countries to global economic forces. The result of all these changes at the global level has been increased interdependence in trade and a dramatic rise in the ratio of global exports to global GDP, from 12 per cent in 1965 to 21 per cent in 1992.

The end of the Cold War thus has accentuated a process of globalization that began fifty years ago. The process is not yet complete, but the end is in sight. Also in sight is the triumph of a liberal ideology, namely, a vision that markets should regulate the economy, that the role of the state should be modest and non-intervensionist and that parliamentary democracy should regulate the polity. All three features of the liberal vision are contested but, at least for the time being, no other ideology has been able to mount a major challenge to liberalism. The 'magic of the market' has triumphed over central planning; private initiative and privatization of state owned enterprises enjoy more support than a strong state in the service of development; and multiparty democratic procedures are favoured over single-party authoritarian regimes. Practice does not always conform to theory, but there can be little doubt that the ideology of liberalism, its appeal to personal freedom in the economic and political spheres, and its scepticism of cooperative action and collective decision making, is in the ascendancy.

REGULATING FREER TRADE

The world economy is characterized by freer trade, not free trade, and it would be a mistake to assume that completely unregulated trade would be in the general interest. Let us consider briefly three cases which account for a significant proportion of total world trade. First, there is drug trafficking. The export and import of narcotic substances is illegal – almost all countries have totally banned trade in cocaine, heroin, marijuana and related products – yet trade in narcotics is flourishing. Because the trade is illicit, it is not recorded in official trade statistics, and hence there is considerable uncertainty about the monetary value of international commerce in drugs. It is estimated, however, that the traffic in drugs is about $500 billion a year.[1] If true, this would make drugs by far the most valuable commodity traded internationally. The trade, although banned, is not *de facto* regulated. Most people, however, would agree that regulation of the drugs industry in some form would be highly desirable. The trouble is that there is little agreement on the form regulation should take, and on the optimal point or points of intervention. Should one try to regulate the production of drugs, or trade in drugs or the consumption of drugs? The answer isn't obvious, but I believe a case can be made for recognizing that 'regulation' by declaring the industry illegal has not worked and that a better alternative might be to decriminalize the production, trade and consumption of drugs and then regulate the market in more conventional ways, i.e., by using tariffs, export taxes, and sales taxes and by reducing demand through public health campaigns, as has been done in the case of tobacco.

Second, there is trade in petroleum and related products. It is widely accepted in principle that the oil industry generates negative externalities both at the point of production (e.g., by oil refineries) and at the point of consumption (e.g., by automobile emissions). These externalities create a case for market regulation, e.g., taxes designed to bring private costs into line with social costs, the imposition of emission standards, requirements to use lead-free gasoline, etc. International trade in petroleum products also generates negative externalities, notably when petroleum is transported by sea in single-hulled ships. Spillages can occur when petroleum is loaded and unloaded onto tankers and when accidents occur during storms or in fog or through negligence of the captain and crew. The social costs of these spillages – in terms of damage to the fishing industry and tourism and the loss of wildlife – greatly exceed the cost to the shipper and the petroleum companies. There is thus a case for market regulation, e.g., a requirement that petroleum be transported in double-hulled ships, automatic imposition of massive fines and penalties when spillages occur, etc. Exports of fuels, of which petroleum and petroleum products are the most important, are about $330 billion a year. That is, oil is the most valuable legal product traded internationally and thus this example certainly is not trivial.

Third, consider the trade in conventional arms. Much of this trade is legal and consists of exports from about a dozen large supplier countries to over a hundred customer countries. Some of the trade in weapons is illegal and consists of private arms traders engaged in smuggling weapons to a wide range of customers (states, opposition groups, terrorists, criminals). Some trade is legal but undisclosed. As a result, the published figures on exports of non-nuclear weapons understate the extent of the trade. Even so, official estimates indicate that exports of armaments were over $18 billion in 1992 (down from $40 billion in 1988). To put this in perspective, exports of arms in 1992 were equivalent to the combined GDPs of the nine poorest countries in the world. Few would advocate free trade in weapons; the case for regulating world markets in armaments is at least as strong as the case for regulating the market in drugs or petroleum.

Unregulated trade in these three products is not in the general interest. Taken together, the three products account for at least 20 per cent of world exports, and perhaps the true figure is closer to 25 per cent. There is thus a strong prima facie case for regulating world markets within a liberal global economy. The case would be strengthened further were we to examine other products where considerations of health (e.g., exports of fresh meat and fish) and safety (e.g., exports of children's toys) are important. Liberalism thus does not imply *laissez faire*. The delicate issue in each instance is to determine when intervention would be in the public interest and what is the best form of intervention.

During the last 15 years (1980–95) international trade has grown much more slowly than in the preceding 35 years (1945–80). Indeed, between 1980 and 1987 the value of world trade grew more slowly than world GDP. The relative stagnation of trade was accompanied by, and probably caused, a drift towards protectionism, and particularly to increasing use of non-tariff barriers, 'anti-dumping' measures[2] and subsidies to domestic industries. There was also a drift towards unilateralism and this weakened confidence in GATT and the multilateral trading system. Resort to unilateralism was especially evident in the United States, which found itself in a series of trade disputes with Japan, the European Union, Brazil, China and India. The Uruguay Round of multilateral trade negotiations, begun in 1986 and completed in 1993, was intended to address these problems.

From the point of view of the developing countries, there were a number of significant results of the Uruguay Round. First, tariffs in the developed countries on imports of industrial products from developing countries should fall from 6.8 to 4.5 per cent on average.[3] Second, non-tariff barriers such as 'voluntary' export restraints and 'anti-dumping' safeguards should be reduced quite considerably in scope and duration.[4] However, third, the most important non-tariff barrier for developing countries, namely the multi-fibre agreement, will not be fully integrated into the liberal multilateral trading system for 10 years, i.e., not until 2005. Fourth, trade in agricultural products was brought into the GATT negotiations for the first time. Non-tariff barriers are to be replaced by tariffs and the level of total trade protection in agricultural products is to be reduced by 36 per cent over six years in the developed countries and by 24 per cent over ten years in the developing countries. Domestic support for agriculture is to be reduced simultaneously by 20 per cent in the developed countries and by 13.3 per cent in the developing countries. There was also agreement to reduce export subsidies to the agricultural sector. World trade in textiles and agricultural products should therefore become more liberal, but the full benefits to the developing countries will not be felt for a decade.

Fifth, for the first time trade in services became subject to multilateral negotiations. This is potentially important to a number of developing countries since services are growing rapidly and already account for more than 20 per cent of international trade. Moreover, many services are labour intensive and hence developing countries may be able to create a comparative advantage in several branches of the services sector. The agreements reached in the Uruguay Round, however, are very modest. In principle virtually all services are covered by the most favoured nation obligation, including tourism, construction, banking and financial services, air transport, telecommunications and general consultancies, but in practice many exemptions will be allowed for up to ten years. The Uruguay Round should be seen as only the first step in a series of negotiations that gradually will liberalize trade in services. Meanwhile, trade in services will continue to be heavily regulated, to the disadvantage of those participating in the global economy.

The global deflation of the 1980s and the resulting stagnation of international commerce, referred to above, had a severely depressing impact on primary commodity prices and on the terms of trade of those developing countries which are highly dependent on exports of primary commodities. In effect the cost of the anti-inflation policies pursued in the developed countries fell disproportionately on the developing countries. Between 1980 and 1991, for instance, a weighted price index of 33 primary commodities fell by almost 50 per cent.[5] Given that over half of the exports of developing countries consist of primary commodities, as compared to only 17 per cent in the OECD countries, the losses inflicted on countries where the poorest people of the world are concentrated were quite considerable. Indeed it is estimated that between 1980 and 1989–91 the annual terms of trade loss in developing countries due to the decline in real prices of primary commodities was between \$50 and \$55 billion.[6] Some have concluded from this experience, and similar experiences in earlier periods of history, that primary commodity markets should be regulated and prices stabilized. My own view, in contrast, is that commodity markets should remain (or in a few cases such as sugar, become) unregulated and that instead emphasis should be placed on avoiding global deflation and sustaining growth. This is likely to require strengthening our institutions of global governance.

LABOUR STANDARDS AND ENVIRONMENTAL PROTECTION

There is much controversy about the desirability of regulating global trade in order to enforce labour standards and protect the environment. The argument often is made that if the developed countries have higher labour standards (e.g., as regards health and safety) or more stringent environmental regulations (e.g., as regards air and water pollution), producers in the developed countries will incur higher costs and be less able to compete against producers located in developing countries. International trade, it is claimed, will be 'unfair', the 'playing field' will not be 'level' and the interests of workers and the population as a whole in the developed countries will be harmed. It is therefore asserted that trade regulations – import prohibitions, tariffs or non-tariff barriers – should be imposed on products originating in countries with 'low' standards.

These arguments are almost entirely fallacious and there is no case for discriminating against trade from developing countries on grounds of labour and environmental standards. Imagine, for example, that a developed country passes legislation requiring producers located within its boundaries to adopt certain measures to reduce occupational injuries or lower the incidence of job-related illnesses. From the point of view of the producer, costs will rise, but from the point of view of society as a whole, all that will have happened is that costs will be shifted either from the taxpayer (e.g., if there is a tax-financed national health service) or the individual worker (if workers are individually responsible for financing their medical care). The legislation will force producers to 'internalize' costs so that private and social costs coincide, but the legislation will not increase costs. The country, far from being worse off, actually is better off, since firms now have an incentive to adjust techniques of production and their output mix to reflect true costs. Trade restrictions against developing countries of the type commonly proposed would offset these incentives and harm not only the developing country but the developed one as well.

Consider next a 'low' labour standard that has excited much comment, namely, the export by a developing country of products produced by prison labour. The objection is not that those serving jail sentences should be banned from engaging in productive activities and acquiring skills but that the products of their labour should be sold in competition with similar products produced by workers abroad. In this extreme case prison labour may receive no money wage and hence the products produced clearly have a competitive advantage in the global market. Is this a legitimate cause for complaint? Unless one is a mercantilist, the answer is no. The source of low costs (inexpensive raw materials, superior technology, cheap transport, relatively low wages) is irrelevant to the importing country; all that matters as far as economic gains are concerned is that it is less expensive to import the product than to use domestic resources to produce it at home. Indeed, the cheaper is the import, the better. (The sun, which supplies light and heat free of cost, is an ideal trading partner.)

Similar arguments apply to products produced by child labour. In strictly economic terms, developed, importing countries have no legitimate complaint against those developing countries which depend on the low cost of child labour to earn foreign exchange. Indeed, imposing tariffs on products produced with the help of child labour deprives the exporting country of its comparative advantage, lowers average incomes and probably increases child poverty. If there are convincing moral objections to child labour, or to certain forms of child labour, then those forms of child labour should be abolished in all sectors of the economy (not just in the export sector) and the prohibitions should be embodied in an international labour convention negotiated through the international agency created for this purpose, namely, the International Labour Organization.[7] Trade regulations are not the appropriate instrument of control.

Thus neither 'high' labour standards in developed countries nor 'low' labour standards in developing countries can be used to justify measures to regulate international commerce. The same is true of national measures to protect the environment. Suppose, for example, a developed country introduces measures (e.g., taxes on emissions or technical norms) to reduce pollution. These controls evidently increase costs which in turn lead to changes in technology, the level of demand and the composition of output. Higher costs, however, do not constitute a competitive disadvantage; they are necessary in order to internalize the environmental externality. That is, higher costs are the mechanism by which the desired benefit of reduced pollution is obtained. Having obtained the benefit by raising private costs to approximate social costs, it would be perverse to neutralize the change in relative costs by imposing an import tax on similar goods produced in developing countries where environmental standards (for good reason or bad) are thought to be lower. The purpose of environmental controls is to protect the country's environment, not to discourage the consumption of goods produced abroad.

A more complex case arises when the environment to be protected transcends national boundaries. Suppose the technology used to catch a commercially valuable species of fish in the deep ocean (a global commons) also endangers another species which it is desired to protect in order to preserve biological diversity. Let us call this harmful method of fishing β-technology. Assume now that one country, and only one country, namely country A, passes legislation requiring its fishing fleet to use a less harmful technology (which we shall call α-technology). The advantage of α-technology is that it poses no threat to the endangered species; the disadvantage is that it increases the cost of catching the commercially valuable species.

Would country A under these circumstances be justified in imposing trade restrictions (tariffs or import prohibitions) on imports of fish from countries using the β-technology? The answer is that this would be an inferior method for achieving the desired result of protecting an endangered species. An import control would merely divert trade away from country A to the home markets of countries using the β-technology and to other export markets. Depending on the size of country A's market for fish, a unilaterally imposed control probably would provide little incentive to other countries to switch to the α-technology and it would have little effect on the total size of the deep ocean catch of both the commercial and the endangered species. Trade controls, in other words, would be ineffective.

Environmental protection in this case could be achieved by creating property rights in the global commons, e.g., by giving an international authority responsibility for managing the deep ocean, protecting endangered species (biodiversity) as well as preventing unsustainable exploitation of commercial species (overfishing). Alternatively, those countries with actual or potential interests in deep ocean fishing could come to an agreement that all would use the α-technology in order to protect the environment, and then devise a mechanism for enforcing the agreement. Unilateral action by country A would be a third-best solution.

TURNING KNOWLEDGE INTO A COMMODITY

Countries and enterprises have always attempted to restrict flows of knowledge and technology to their competitors. Ancient China tried to protect its industrial secrets, e.g., porcelain and silk weaving, and centuries later during the first industrial revolution, Britain tried to prevent its technology from spreading to the rest of the world and undermining its competitive advantage. National copyright and patent legislation was intended to give writers and inventors monopoly rights to their products for a fixed period of time. The coverage of the legislation eventually was extended to virtually all of the industrial countries by international copyright and patent conventions.

None the less, historically knowledge did in fact flow and encountered relatively few artificial barriers. Industrial secrets were hard to protect, technologies were relatively simple, and apprentice workers, craftsmen and engineers could transfer technology from one firm to another and one country to another merely by changing jobs. It was not until the twentieth century that patents in the industrial countries became effective, and even then their effectiveness was reduced by the limited scope of the legislation and the ease of circumventing it. The development of continental Western Europe, North America and Japan was not inhibited by a high price of knowledge.

This situation is now changing rapidly, however. Global competition has become more intense, new products and new processes have become increasingly technology intensive, and the cost of producing new technology is high and apparently rising. The response in the developed countries, where most of the new technology is created, has been to transform knowledge into a commodity to which property rights can be attached. From an economic perspective, this creates a dilemma. On the one hand, existing knowledge ought to be a free good available to everyone, since knowledge has no opportunity cost; it is not 'used up' by those who use it in the production process or consume it directly. On the other hand, new knowledge is costly to produce and unless there are appropriate incentives – monetary rewards – private profit seeking enterprises and individuals will not devote sufficient resources to research and development. Historically this dilemma has been resolved in several ways: by publicly funding research in universities and specialized research institutions, by making one-off payments (prizes and bounties) to successful inventors, and by providing patent protection.

The historical pattern, however, has changed in recent years. First, the proportion of research that is publicly financed out of tax revenues has declined. A smaller fraction of the new knowledge and technology that is produced is available in the public domain free of charge. Second, even knowledge that is produced in publicly funded universities is increasingly being patented and payment is demanded for the right to apply new discoveries. Third, the scope of patent legislation has been extended enormously to cover what once was considered basic knowledge, for which ownership rights could not be assigned. For example, new seeds developed in the laboratories of the industrial countries can now be patented even when they are based on genetic material obtained from developing countries (which cannot be patented).

The result is that developing countries will find it harder than in the past to obtain useful knowledge for productive purposes. The cost of industrialization will rise, in part because of increased royalty payments to enterprises and individuals abroad and in part because of increased prices of products produced under licence.[8] The rise of 'intellectual property' as a new type of commodity which is widely traded will, moreover, increase inequality in the global distribution of income and, everything else being equal, accentuate global poverty. This new form of market regulation is likely, in my judgement, on balance to make matters worse. The Uruguay Round, for the first time, extends GATT principles, notably most favoured nation treatment, to 'trade related intellectual property rights' (TRIPs). The Berne Convention on copyrights is strengthened and extended to cover computer programs; industrial designs are protected; member countries are required to pass domestic laws protecting the intellectual property rights of foreigners as well as those of their own citizens; and settlement of disputes over TRIPs is brought under the GATT dispute settlement procedures. Provision is made for a transition period – one year for developed economies, five years for developing countries and socialist economies in transition to a market-guided system, and 11 years for the least developed countries – after which intellectual property rights will be treated in the same way as trade in goods and services.

THE FREEDOM OF PRIVATE CAPITAL MOVEMENTS AND FOREIGN AID

A prominent characteristic of our liberal global economy is the freedom of capital to move from one country to another in search of profits. Private profit-seeking agents – enterprises, banks, financial managers investing in equity and bond markets – now are able to transfer savings generated in one location and invest them in another location, perhaps halfway round the globe. In fact most savings are invested in the country where they originate and cross-border movements of capital are of only marginal importance when seen from a global perspective. None the less, many analysts had expected that liberalization of global capital markets would contribute significantly to economic development in poor countries and to a reduction in global inequalities. This was to occur through movements of capital in the form of direct investment by transnational corporations, loans by international commercial banks and the operations of financial portfolio managers which, in effect, would transfer savings from the rich, capital-abundant countries to the poor, capital-scarce countries.

These expectations, however, have been dashed. Most global movements of capital consist of one rich country investing in another. There is little net movement of private capital from rich countries to poor. Consider the geographical distribution of the world stock of foreign direct investment. In 1988 about 78.7 per cent of all foreign direct investment was located in the developed countries and only 21.3 per cent in the developing countries.[9] That is, there was 3.7 times as much foreign direct investment in the rich countries as in the poor. Great as is this disproportion, the inequality in the distribution of the stock of foreign capital becomes even larger when one takes into account the fact that most people in the world live in developing countries. In per capita terms, there is nearly 17 times as much foreign capital in the developed countries compared to the developing ones.

If one considers recent flows the picture is no more encouraging. In the eleven years between 1983 and 1993 there was an average annual net inflow of capital into the developing countries in the form of direct investment of only $6.5 billion. This was supplemented by net inflows of private grants of $4.7 billion and of stock transactions, short term borrowing and domestic outflows (i.e., capital flight) of $2.0 billion. Offsetting these positive flows, however, was a large negative net outflow of $19.6 billion under the heading of medium and long term borrowing. The overall result was thus an average annual net transfer

Table 5.1   Average annual net transfer of private financial resources to developing countries, 1983–93

Means of transfer	US$ billions
Direct investment	6.5
Medium and long term borrowing	−19.6
Net stock transactions, short term borrowing and domestic outflows	2.0
Private grants	4.7
Total	−6.5

Source: United Nations, *World Economic and Social Survey 1994* (New York, 1994), Table A.27, p. 288.

of private financial resources from the developing countries to the rich countries. The outflow was $6.5 billion a year (see Table 5.1). Private capital, in other words, has done very little, either historically or contemporaneously, to bring about a more equal distribution of resources in the global economy.

Although the outcome is disappointing to those who hoped a more liberal global economy would lead to a rapid reduction in poverty and inequality, there is no persuasive case for regulating the world capital market in order to redirect long term flows of private capital through taxes, subsidies and controls. There is no evidence that the markets are inefficient or that there is a clear case of market failure.[10] It just so happens that efficient markets in this instance lead to inequitable results. The correct policy response, it seems to me, should be to let the market operate freely and organize a parallel system of capital transfers to address directly the issue of global inequalities. In a sense, this is what some have hoped foreign aid programmes would do.

In practice, however, foreign aid has done this only to a modest extent. The net transfer of official flows was $18.3 billion a year on average between 1983 and 1993.[11] Moreover, the trend was downward. For example, the net flow was $30.6 billion in 1983 and only $14.8 billion in 1993. The net flow of official aid *per head of the population of recipient countries* fell even more sharply because of population growth. Conventional foreign aid programmes are becoming increasingly insignificant.

The overall position can be obtained by aggregating the net flows of private and official capital and the use of foreign exchange reserves. This provides the best estimate of total net transfers of resources. Using this measure, it transpires that the resource transfer to developing countries

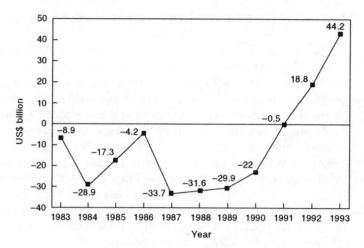

Figure 5.1   Net transfers of financial resources to developing countries

was negative in nine out of the eleven years between 1983 and 1993, becoming positive only in the last two years of the series. The average outflow from the developing countries was $10.2 billion a year (see Figure 5.1).

Foreign aid programmes of the conventional type evidently have not been sufficiently large to ensure that there is a persistent net flow of resources to developing countries as a group. In addition, conventional aid programmes can be criticized for their failure to channel resources to the countries which are most in need (as measured by per capita GNP) and, within countries, for their failure to address poverty directly and to reduce inequalities of income, wealth and life chances.[12] There is a case, therefore, for a radical reform of official aid programmes. One possibility, which I have discussed elsewhere, would be to introduce a progressive global tax on the per capita GNP of rich countries to generate funds for redistribution in the form of grants to poor countries. The funds would be distributed to countries where average income was below a designated level and in inverse proportion to their per capita GNP. This would ensure that those with the lowest incomes would receive the largest amount of aid per capita.[13]

The details of a new aid scheme are not terribly important. The essential point is that liberalized global capital markets are unlikely by themselves to result in a large net transfer of resources to developing countries and consequently there is a case for 'intervention' (but not market 'regulation') in favour of the poorest countries.

REGULATING FLOWS OF HUMAN CAPITAL

Do arguments in support of unregulated flows of finance capital apply equally well to global flows of human capital? The answer is 'not necessarily'.[14] It has long been recognized that the emigration from developing countries of professional, technical and highly skilled persons can result in a serious loss of human capital to the sending country. The developed countries have been the major recipients of this human capital, their immigration laws generally being biased in favour of those who possess valuable skills or finance capital that can be invested in the country of immigration. From the point of view of the developed countries, the numbers are relatively small, but from the point of view of the developing countries the numbers can be very large. In Africa, for instance, it is estimated that one-third of its highly-educated labour has gone abroad in recent decades.[15]

The receiving countries benefit from this so-called brain drain in various ways, but most of all because they obtain trained people without having had to invest in their education. The sending countries lose in three ways. First, highly skilled persons generate positive externalities that accrue to the rest of the population. For instance, the value of a doctor to a developing country exceeds the personal salary he receives. Second, an exodus of technical and professional people creates a shortage of the skills they possess. This drives up the wages and salaries of those skilled persons left behind relative to the incomes of the less skilled. As a result, the distribution of income becomes more unequal, to the relative and absolute disadvantage of the less skilled.

Third, to the extent that tertiary education is financed by taxpayers, the highly skilled were subsidized as students by the society at large. Brain drain in effect prevents taxpayers from reaping a return on their investment and deprives them of the human capital they helped to create. One way to correct for this would be to require the beneficiaries to repay the subsidy prior to emigration. Another way would be to eliminate the subsidy, i.e., to charge students the full cost of tertiary education. Yet another possibility would be to introduce a two-tiered system of tuition charges under which those paying the higher (full) tuition cost would be free to emigrate while those paying the lower (subsidized) tuition cost would be required to engage in national service for a specified period of time.[16]

If international cooperation could be secured, a tidier solution would be possible which would be consistent with the liberal objective that people everywhere should be free to live and work where they please.

A simple, workable scheme could be built around three principles. First, countries of immigration would compensate countries of emigration for their loss of human capital but only in the case of those migrating from the very poorest countries (e.g., those countries classified as 'least developed') to the very richest (e.g., the OECD countries). Second, compensation would be payable only in the case of persons whose tertiary education was subsidized by taxpayers of the sending country. Third, the compensation payable by the receiving to the sending country would be x per cent (say, one-half) of the income tax liability of the migrant for y number of years, where y is the number of years of subsidized tertiary education minus the number of years spent working in the sending country after completion of tertiary education.

This is a simple, even crude, formula and it almost certainly fails to provide full compensation to the taxpayers of the poorest countries for their loss of human capital, but at least it acknowledges explicitly that some compensation should be paid by rich countries to the poorest of the developing countries for the damage caused by brain drain and it does so in a way that is consistent with unregulated markets in a liberal global economy.

DEREGULATING THE GLOBAL MARKET FOR LOW SKILLED LABOUR

In contrast to the market for highly skilled professional and technical labour, the global market for low skilled labour is highly regulated. That is, the mobility of low skilled labour is severely restricted by immigration controls and this deprives millions of poor people of an opportunity to improve their livelihood. Partly because of these controls, the stock of migrants actually is very small. Only 1 or 2 per cent of the world's population, say 50 to 100 million people, live outside their country of origin.[17] Moreover, most migrants do not live in the rich countries; the majority live in other developing countries. Rough calculations suggest that only 21 per cent of the world's migrants reside in developed countries. This includes 13 per cent of the international refugee population and 23 per cent of the non-refugee migrant population. It is ironical and more than a little sad that the greatest barriers to the international flow of low skilled labour and the loudest complaints about immigration are found in the developed countries whereas in fact most of the immigrants are located in developing countries.

The benefits of a more liberal global labour market to the sending countries are considerable. Not only do the migrant workers benefit directly from higher incomes earned abroad, but those left behind also benefit from remittances sent home. Remittances, in fact, are between $66 billion and $70 billion a year, i.e., significantly larger than official flows of aid. If restrictions on the international migration of low skilled labour were reduced, there is no doubt that remittances would increase sharply, further reducing the relative significance of aid.

The receiving countries also would benefit from a freer global labour market. The countries of immigration would be able to augment their human capital, increase the level of output, incomes and investment and accelerate their rate of growth.[18] Historically, the development of the United States, Canada, Australia and Argentina was made possible by large inflows of migrant labour. More recently, the economic boom in Western Europe in the 1960s and the explosive growth in the oil producing states of the Middle East in the 1970s and early 1980s were made possible by immigration. Contrary to popular perceptions, immigration stimulates expansion and prosperity rather than depresses it. The main economic disadvantage is that large inflows of low skilled labour dampen wages at the bottom of the scale and this tends to increase inequality in the national distribution of income, while of course reducing inequality internationally.

Notice, however, that freer trade has a similar effect to liberalization of the market for low skilled labour. An expansion of international trade by the rich countries leads to an increase in the relative price of high skilled labour, the abundant factor of production, and to a fall in the price of low skilled labour, the scarce factor of production. The distribution of income therefore becomes more unequal. Freer trade, however, also leads to a rise in the level of income and thereby provides the resources from which the losers, namely low skilled workers, can in principle be compensated.

The same is true of the case of immigration. Everyone in the receiving country potentially could be better off if controls on immigration were relaxed. Policy makers in rich countries should therefore concentrate not on keeping foreign workers out but on introducing policies which ensure that income and opportunities are equitably distributed. The world as a whole would benefit significantly if the global market for low skilled labour were deregulated.

REGULATION IN WHOSE INTERESTS?

The world is a messy place and there is no single, simple solution that would make it less messy. There are instances where regulation of global markets should be diminished (e.g., trade in clothing and textiles); there are other cases where market regulation should increase (e.g., ocean transport of petroleum); there are yet other cases where unregulated global markets are on balance desirable (e.g., global capital movements) but where mechanisms to compensate for their undesirable distributive effects should be created or strengthened (e.g., foreign aid). Generalization, thus, is not possible; each case has to be considered on its merits.

There are, however, three headings under which most of the issues surrounding disputes about regulating global markets can be grouped. These headings are national sovereignty, efficiency and equity.

Globalization is eroding national sovereignty. Improvements in transport and communications have shortened distances, saved time, reduced transaction costs and destroyed the natural protection that once insulated national economies from one another. It no longer is possible for countries to pursue independent economic policies and to ignore economic forces operating at a global level. Integrated capital markets have made it more difficult for countries to control interest rates and the exchange rate; the high ratio of trade to national product has made it more difficult for countries to avoid importing inflation or deflation; integrated commodity markets have made it easier for traders to circumvent controls on international trade and to engage in widespread smuggling; and as the large numbers of international refugees and illegal immigrants testify, political and economic forces operating through the global labour market are beginning to overwhelm national efforts to regulate flows of labour across national borders. Indeed, borders have become porous and in a few countries almost meaningless.

States can either accommodate or try to resist these global economic forces. There is always a temptation to resist them, to preserve state power and to affirm national sovereignty. Illegal migrants can be imprisoned; coca cultivators can have their crops destroyed; local industries which encounter international competition can be protected; and export industries can be promoted by threatening unilateral trade sanctions against other countries whose policies are thought to be objectionable. It is unlikely, however, that resistance can succeed for the tide of globalization is too strong to be turned back by the feeble instruments available to governments acting alone. Moreover, even if the tide could be turned back, it is not clear whose interests would be served. The preservation of state power or national sovereignty is not necessarily a desirable objective and if higher objectives – freedom, increased human well-being, enhanced capabilities – could be attained by relinquishing some national sovereignty, the sacrifice would be worthwhile.

Accommodation, indeed, seems the wiser course of action. This implies supra-national cooperation at either the regional level (as in the European Union) or at the global level, and probably both. Unilateral action, slowly but surely, is likely to give way to global collective action. This, in turn, will require strengthening, reforming and in some cases constructing global institutions which are democratic and can act in the global collective interest. The regulation of world markets would then become a matter for global negotiation. Policy intervention in this context would not necessarily take the form of regulating international trade, but where appropriate (as in environmental externalities) would be directed to regulating production or consumption.

The sacrifice of national sovereignty should make it possible to increase international efficiency. Global negotiations (as in the GATT rounds and in future under the aegis of the World Trade Organization) reduce barriers to trade in goods and services and thereby increase global efficiency and global incomes. As we have seen, there is more to be done in liberalizing trade in services, agricultural products, textiles and clothing, but much has already been achieved and in future the largest gains in efficiency are likely to arise outside the trade sphere narrowly defined. There is a need to rethink provisions regulating intellectual property rights; international environmental regulations are sure to become more important; measures to permit greater international mobility of labour deserve urgent consideration; and there is a need to strengthen further the enforcement procedures of international agreements and to supplement enforcement procedures with compensation mechanisms for victims of countries which depart from the rules of a liberal economic order.

Resource transfers that occur outside markets, e.g., flows of foreign aid and compensation payments, accrue almost entirely to countries rather than to individuals or groups of persons. National governments, for as far ahead as one can see, are likely to retain their role of intermediary between multilateral and bilateral contributors and the ultimate recipient. It is therefore important on grounds of equity that extra-market transfers be channelled as much as possible from rich countries to poor, and that 'leakages' to non-poor countries be avoided.

The global resources likely to be available for redistribution through aid programmes are bound to be meagre and there is always a temptation to divert flows in response to pressing but perhaps temporary needs, e.g., a debt crisis in Latin America, transitional problems in Eastern and Central Europe, regional conflicts in the Middle East. Emergency situations obviously demand a response from the global community, but they require special funding separate from systematic, organized transfers to poor countries intended to redress global poverty and inequality. That is, the need to regulate extra-market transfers probably is greater than the need to regulate global markets.

Notes

1. UNDP, *Human Development Report 1994* (New York: Oxford University Press, 1994), p. 37. For an annotated bibliography of research on drugs see LaMond Tullis, *Handbook of Research on the Illicit Drug Traffic* (New York: Greenwood Press, 1991).
2. For an illuminating analysis of anti-dumping measures see J. Michael Finger (ed.), *Antidumping: How It Works and Who Gets Hurt* (Ann Arbor: University of Michigan Press, 1993).
3. United Nations, *World Economic and Social Survey 1994* (New York, 1994), p. 80.
4. Anti-dumping actions, however, are subject to a less stringent standard of review than other agreements reached during the Uruguay Round. There is thus a danger of 'a reinforcement of the ability of users of anti-dumping legislation to harass and limit trade.' (United Nations Conference on Trade and Development, *Trade and Development Report*, Geneva, 1994, p. 135.)
5. Frances Stewart, 'Globalization, Poverty and International Action', paper presented at the UNDP Roundtable on 'Change: Social Conflict or Harmony?', Stockholm, 22–4 July 1994, p. 4.
6. Alfred Maizels, 'Commodity Markets, Institutional Support Measures and Challenges for Developing Countries', paper presented at the Colloquium in Honour of Gerald K. Helleiner, North-South Institute, Ottawa, 22–4 June 1994.
7. For a perceptive critique of responses to child labour see Ben White, 'Children, Work and "Child Labour": Changing Responses to the Employment of Children', *Development and Change*, Vol. 25, No. 4 (October 1994).
8. United Nations Conference on Trade and Development, p. 155.
9. Keith Griffin and Azizur Rahman Khan, *Globalization and the Developing World* (Geneva: UNRISD, 1992), Table 3.1, p. 29.
10. There may be a case, however, for developing countries to regulate short term flows of speculative capital. The volatility of 'hot' money is high and in small countries short term speculative inflows responding to sharp fluctuations in real rates of interest can be very disruptive, causing macro-

economic imbalances, an appreciation of the exchange rate and, during the period of capital outflow, possibly precipitating a financial crisis.

11. United Nations, *World Economic and Social Survey*, Table A.27, p. 288.
12. See, e.g., Chapter 3.
13. Chapter 4.
14. This section is taken from Keith Griffin and Terry McKinley, *A New Framework for Development Cooperation* (UNDP, Human Development Report Office, Occasional Paper No. 11, 1994).
15. UNFPA, *The State of World Population 1993* (New York, 1993), p. 23.
16. See Griffin and Khan, *Globalization*, pp. 54–6.
17. UNFPA, *The State of World Population*, p. 7.
18. For a more complete discussion see Chapter 4.

Part II

National Policies during Transitions

6 Domestic Policies in Developing Countries and their Effects on Employment, Income Inequality and Poverty*

The world of the 1990s is very different from the world of the 1950s when issues of employment, income inequality and poverty in developing countries first attracted the attention of policy makers. The world at mid-century was not closely integrated. Western Europe was still recovering from the effects of the Second World War and many of the wartime controls were still in place. The socialist bloc had entered a period of consolidation and was largely isolated from the capitalist economies. Latin America, having suffered the economic consequences of the deep depression of the 1930s and the disruption of international commerce during the 1940s, had turned inward and adopted an import substituting strategy of industrialization. Asia was in the early stages of decolonization and the construction of national economies in newly independent countries. Africa still had a decade to wait before the European empires that dominated the continent collapsed and at last allowed Africans to regain some control over their destiny. Japan, like Western Europe, was slowly recovering from the Second World War and its period of explosive growth and massive penetration of world markets was still over the horizon just out of sight. The United States, by far the strongest economy, was the champion of free trade and the free movement of capital.

Today globalization has triumphed. The world economy is more closely integrated than ever before: the European and Soviet empires have disappeared; the economic hegemony of the United States has been replaced by a multi-polar constellation of forces; the market rapidly is superseding government controls and planning as mechanisms for

---

* This chapter was prepared for the International Labour Office as a background document for the *World Employment Report 1995* (Geneva: ILO, 1995).

allocating resources; and liberal ideas about economic management and social policy have acquired a near monopoly in intellectual circles. Thus the context in which employment, income inequality and poverty are discussed has changed beyond recognition.

Globalization has had three consequences which deserve emphasis.[1] First, it has created opportunities for material betterment. By enlarging national markets to encompass the global economy, it has expanded the dimensions of the market enormously, encouraged greater specialization and division of labour and thereby created conditions which facilitate a growth of incomes and output. The effects of globalization go far beyond the potential benefits arising from a reallocation of resources and the exploitation of static comparative advantage. The benefits include the creation of new markets, the transfer of technology across national borders and the creation of new technologies, the movement of finance capital on a huge scale and the stimulation of investment, the international migration of professional, technical and highly skilled labour and even the emergence in embryo of a global market in low skilled labour. That is, much more is at stake than a simple change in the composition of output in response to a change in relative prices.

Second, globalization has unleashed economic forces which tend to increase inequality in the global distribution of income. One reason for this is that the reduction of trade restrictions has been uneven. Tariffs and other barriers to trade have, on average, fallen quite sharply, but trade liberalization has proceeded more rapidly for goods and services of interest to the industrialized countries than for goods of interest to the developing countries. Restrictions on imports of clothing, textiles, footwear and agricultural products, for instance, all of which are important exports from developing countries, remain high even after the recently completed Uruguay Round of the GATT negotiations.

Another reason why globalization has tended to result in greater inequality is that flows of capital consist largely of one rich country investing in another and net flows of savings often are from poor countries to rich. That is, capital tends to be attracted to the already industrialized and to the rapidly industrializing countries, where the returns on investment are relatively high, and to by-pass the poorest countries, where profit rates tend to be relatively low. This concentration of capital at the global level helps to perpetuate existing inequalities in productivity, incomes and material well-being.[2]

The same thing tends to happen to human capital. Because of discrimination in the international market for labour, there is much greater mobility at the top end of the skill distribution than at the bottom. Moreover, the human capital embodied in technical, professional and managerial workers tends to flow from poor countries to rich, thereby accentuating global inequalities in the distribution of human capital. That is, 'brain drain' is one of the mechanisms responsible for the international transmission of inequality.

Yet another mechanism arises from the transformation of knowledge into a marketable commodity. Until recently, most knowledge was treated as a public good available to all at zero cost, but the spread of market relations worldwide has been accompanied by the creation of 'intellectual property rights' which confer ownership on those who possess knowledge and information. Knowledge thus becomes a private income earning asset that can be sold or rented to the highest bidder. There has been an enormous increase in the scope or coverage of copyright and patent protection as well as the length of time for which protection is granted, and the recently completed GATT negotiations have contributed to this process. Unfortunately, the transformation of knowledge into a commodity has harmed the interests of developing countries since they are large net importers, potentially and actually, of knowledge from the rest of the world. The attempt of the developed countries to create a monopoly of productive knowledge and advanced technology, and then to exploit that monopoly, can only accentuate existing inequalities at the global level.

A third consequence of globalization is that it has weakened the ability of individual states to manage their economies. At the macroeconomic level, the mobility of finance capital has reduced government control over interest rates and the exchange rate; the flexibility of transnational corporations has reduced the ability of government to affect the level of investment and its geographical location; and the international mobility of technical and highly skilled labour has reduced the ability of government to impose progressive income and wealth taxes and to sustain high levels of public expenditure.

At the microeconomic level, globalization has made it harder for governments to regulate productive activities, to protect the vulnerable and to improve the livelihoods of low income groups. International factor mobility has reduced the power of the state: it has increased the costs of government intervention in the economy and has diminished the effectiveness of intervention, whether intervention is intended to prevent firms from damaging the environment, improve health and safety conditions at the workplace, abolish child labour, raise minimum wages or increase security of employment by regulating the circumstances under which workers may be dismissed. The reason for this is that government interventions, say, to raise minimum wages or improve working conditions, almost always increase the cost of employing labour and shift the distribution of factor incomes against profits and in favour of wages. Globalization, by increasing the mobility of firms, has made it easier for transnational enterprises to escape these consequences by moving to countries where the costs of employment are relatively low. The other side of the coin is that the international mobility of capital has made it more difficult for governments to implement an interventionist labour policy of the conventional type. It follows from this not that governments should cease to intervene, but that the form of intervention needs to be reconsidered and that asset redistribution, as argued below, should be given greater priority. Globalization has changed the game and it no longer makes sense to play by the old rules.

GROWTH AND EMPLOYMENT

One fundamental respect in which the world of the 1990s differs from that of the 1950s is in the objective of macroeconomic policy. After the miseries of the Great Depression and the Second World War, governments in the industrial countries adopted growth and full employment as primary goals of economic policy. Indeed the founders of the United Nations, in Article 55 of the United Nations Charter, proclaimed that 'the United Nations shall promote . . . full employment'. Thus full employment became a universal objective as early as 1945.

High levels of employment in the developed countries and rapid economic growth were in fact achieved until 1973 when the first 'shock' of a sharp rise in oil prices led to a reversal of policy. In the two decades and more since the first oil shock, the reduction of inflation has been the primary objective of economic policy: employment and growth have been sacrificed to achieve price stability. The adoption more or less simultaneously in a number of major countries of anti-inflation policies introduced a pronounced deflationary bias to the entire world economy.

The policies worked in their own terms. Inflation in the OECD countries fell from a peak of 12.5 per cent a year in 1974 to just over 3 per cent in 1993. The cost, however, was high: growth rates declined, there were lengthening periods of recession and unemployment rates in the OECD countries more than doubled from 3.9 per cent in 1974 to 8.5 per cent in 1993. Inequality increased, real wages of low skilled labour declined (especially in the United States) and the number of people living in poverty rose to levels unknown since the depression of the 1930s. Many persons unable to find work withdrew from the labour force in despair.

Although the costs were high, many policy makers thought the benefits were higher still. This was stated explicitly in 1991 by Norman Lamont, a British chancellor of the exchequer, who asserted that unemployment was 'a price worth paying to secure low inflation'.[3] National deflationary policies in the industrial countries are reinforced by the deflationary framework of our global economic institutions.[4] Standard IMF policies impose expenditure reduction policies on countries in deficit with no offsetting obligation on countries with large balance of payments surpluses to pursue expansionist policies. The World Bank's structural adjustment programmes, while ostensibly concerned with expenditure switching policies, in fact entail large contractions in public expenditure, including public investment and expenditure on human capital formation. The management of the global debt crisis has imposed most of the burden of adjustment on the African and Latin American debtor countries, forcing them to tighten their belts and endure a 'lost decade' of negative growth of per capita income. This contrasts with earlier periods when creditor countries wrote off debts rather than force (rich) debtor countries to suffer severe hardship. Examples include the writing-off of British debt after the First World War and the writing-off of 70 per cent of the West German debt after the Second World War. Even the Maastricht Treaty, it has been claimed, envisages a deflationary framework for the European Union, with its emphasis on price stability and neglect of measures to encourage employment and economic growth.[5]

The deflationary policies of the developed countries combined with the deflationary framework of our global economic institutions have resulted in a collapse of primary commodity prices. Slow growth in the OECD countries has been translated into a sharp deterioration in the terms of trade of developing countries and a decline in real incomes of hundreds of millions of ordinary working people, above all in sub-Saharan Africa and large parts of Latin America and the Caribbean.[6]

An expansion of economic activity in the OECD countries – particularly in Japan, Germany and the United States – would help to reduce unemployment and poverty in the developed countries as well as permit an acceleration of growth in the developing countries and in the former socialist countries. There has been much talk of 'jobless growth', with the suggestion that growth is occurring but that faster growth no longer results in employment creation. The truth, however, is that what we are experiencing is more akin to 'jobless non-growth' or, more precisely, to a deceleration in the rate of growth. It is misleading to suggest that unemployment remains high *despite* faster growth when the fact is that unemployment remains high *because of slower growth*.[7]

The believers in 'jobless growth' implicitly assume that there has been a decline over time in the employment elasticity of output. An alternative way of expressing this is to claim that there has been an acceleration in the trend rate of growth of the productivity of labour and hence, for any given rate of growth of output, the growth of employment will be slower than in the past. The trouble with this view is that apart from hyperbole about the 'information revolution', there is no evidence that productivity growth has accelerated.[8] Indeed, if anything, it may have fallen. In some countries, notably the United States, slow growth of output and of productivity has resulted in declining real wages in the manufacturing sector since 1973.

Indeed an acceleration of growth is a necessary condition for lower unemployment, more secure livelihoods, reduced poverty and greater equality in the distribution of income. Policy makers in the OECD countries are at last giving higher priority to employment creation and growth, at least in their policy statements. In the United States, for instance, the Clinton administration has made faster growth the centrepiece of its economic strategy, although the expansion programme was rejected by the Congress.[9] Some measures to stimulate the economy have been taken in Japan, although they have so far been rather timid. Germany remains in recession and is no longer the engine of growth of the European Union. Growth has picked up in the United Kingdom, unemployment rates have begun to fall slightly from levels unprecedented since the Second World War and the current chancellor of the exchequer, Kenneth Clarke, declared in May 1994 that 'unemployment must be the main preoccupation of economic policy-makers in the 1990s',[10] thereby reversing the priorities of his predecessor. Jacques Delors, the outgoing President of the European Commission, has advanced an ambitious plan to reduce unemployment in the European Union by more than half by the year 2000.

It undoubtedly is in the interests of the developing countries that growth should accelerate in the OECD countries, but it would be a mistake for the developing countries to assume that their own growth totally depends on what happens in the rich countries. Indeed one of the most gratifying developments in recent years has been the ability of many very poor countries to accelerate their rates of growth despite the low and falling growth rates in the OECD countries. Sub-Saharan Africa has of course performed poorly, but growth has remained rapid in China and accelerated in India, and largely because of this, total output and average incomes have been rising more rapidly in the low income countries than in the OECD countries. As a result, the distribution of income at the global level recently has become more equal, contrary to what many believe.[11]

PHYSICAL CAPITAL FORMATION

Those developing countries which have adopted policies to encourage a high rate of investment have succeeded in attaining rapid growth and those countries which have enjoyed rapid growth, in turn, have succeeded in creating employment opportunities, reducing the rate of unemployment and raising the real wages of low skilled labour. They have also succeeded in creating income earning opportunities and promoting more secure livelihoods for those not engaged in wage employment. Almost always this has been accompanied by some reduction in poverty and occasionally it has also been possible to avoid a sharp increase in inequality.[12] Growth, thus, is necessary for a rapid decline in poverty although it is not sufficient: the weight of evidence from the last two decades indicates that the trickle-down hypothesis continues to be invalid. It does not follow from this, however, that the pace of expansion is of little significance.

Physical capital formation, in turn, remains a necessary condition for rapid economic growth and the growth success of the low income countries is due to the fact that they have allocated a larger share of their GDP to investment than have the OECD countries. In 1991, for example, the rate of investment in the low income countries was 27 per cent of GDP – with rates of 36 per cent in China, 35 per cent in Indonesia and 20 per cent in India – as compared to 21 per cent in the OECD countries on average.

It is not enough, however, to have a high rate of investment; it is just as important to allocate investment efficiently so that each unit of investment adds as much as possible to net income. It is here that many developing countries compare unfavourably with the developed ones and there clearly is scope for policy initiatives to raise the productivity of investment. If this were done, rates of growth would be even higher than they are at present and, more important, the impact on employment, poverty alleviation and reduced inequality would be highly beneficial.

There are two areas where substantial improvement is possible. First, public sector investment often is poorly allocated. It is excessively capital intensive and hence creates less employment than it could; it is excessively concentrated in major cities and hence accentuates rural–urban and regional inequalities; and it often is directed to projects with low rates of return and hence produces less income than it should. These problems could be corrected if governments systematically applied social cost-benefit analysis when appraising public sector investment programmes.

Second, private sector investment also is poorly allocated. The reason for this is the underdevelopment of capital markets in developing countries and the high degree of concentration of the banking system. The problem is partly a matter of inappropriate pricing, namely, low real rates of interest charged for borrowing finance capital, and partly a matter of the sectoral allocation of credit. The pricing issue will be touched upon below; the allocation of credit will be commented upon here.

Economic analysts have devoted much attention to the various ways labour markets may fail to function perfectly in developing countries, but the imperfections in the capital market are much more pervasive and far more important for the overall functioning of the economy. Most people, in fact, have no access to formal sector credit and large sectors of the economy are starved of finance. Small urban businesses have much difficulty obtaining credit; agriculture and livestock are undersupplied and small farmers obtain virtually no credit from banks; fishermen and rural artisans cannot obtain loans from commercial banks; the informal sector as a whole has little access to credit; new enterprises in any sector are rarely able to obtain start-up capital. Most people in developing countries either are self-financed or use the informal credit market supplied by money lenders, traders, landlords, friends and relatives. Most formal sector credit, in effect, is reserved for large, well established, urban enterprises. The consequence of this huge capital market imperfection is that many potentially highly profitable private sector enterprises fail to get established and many small but established enterprises are unable to grow rapidly for lack of capital.

There is, then, an opportunity for policy makers to improve the functioning of the capital market: by institutional innovation, by improved regulation of the banking sector, by supporting credit programmes targeted at specific groups such as women, informal sector entrepreneurs and small farmers and by increasing the supply of 'venture capital'. An improvement in the allocation of capital within the private sector could contribute much to employment generation, to creating more income earning opportunities for the self-employed and to a reduction in the incidence of poverty.

The emphasis should be on encouraging new private sector enterprises to emerge (preferably those which are small in scale and labour intensive) and on enabling small private sector enterprises to expand, innovate and penetrate new markets (including export markets). Far too much attention has been devoted to privatization, i.e., the transfer of ownership of existing enterprises from the public to the private sector. Privatization may on balance be desirable or it may not – that is something to be decided in each country on a case by case basis – but as far as accelerating growth, creating employment, reducing poverty and improving the distribution of income are concerned, privatization is a low priority policy intervention.[13]

HUMAN CAPITAL FORMATION

The most successful developing countries not only have had a high rate of physical capital formation, they have also given priority to human capital formation. Indeed the importance of investing in people – and particularly in women – is now widely recognized and has led to a reformulation of development policy under the label of a human development strategy.[14] There are at least three reasons why expenditure on human development deserves very high priority.

First, human development is a goal in its own right. Greater longevity, reduced morbidity, improved nutrition, widespread literacy, access to the stock of the world's knowledge: these are some of the marks of a civilized society, they are ultimately what development is about and, at the individual level, they constitute an expansion of people's 'capabilities'.[15]

Second, human development expenditures also are a means and can be regarded as somewhat analogous to physical capital formation. Investment in human capital – particularly on basic education, primary health care, nutrition and population programmes – can enjoy rates of return which are at least as high as the returns on conventional investments. Indeed one of the characteristics of the highly successful East Asian economies is the priority given to human capital formation.[16] The emphasis on human development in countries such as Japan, China,

South Korea and Taiwan not only contributed to rapid growth but also to an employment intensive pattern of growth, the combination of which resulted in an exceptionally fast increase in the real wages of working people and a dramatic decline in poverty.

Moreover, expenditures on human development often are complementary to expenditures on physical capital. Where this occurs, increased investment in human capital can help to raise the productivity of investment in physical capital and thereby provide an additional stimulus to growth.

Third, investments in human capital – especially when concentrated on the areas mentioned in the last paragraph but one – tend to result in a more equitable distribution of wealth and hence in greater equality in the distribution of income. A human development strategy is an effective way to redistribute assets in favour of the poor and has the added political advantage that the asset redistribution occurs not by transferring ownership of part of the existing stock of wealth but by redirecting the flow of public expenditure to a broad range of human development activities. That is, policies which focus on human development, if carefully designed, can simultaneously accelerate growth, increase employment and income earning opportunities for the self-employed, reduce poverty, improve the distribution of wealth and income, and enhance people's capabilities. There are few sets of policies of which this can be said and they should be exploited to the full.

THE LABOUR INTENSITY OF PRODUCTION

So far in this chapter there has been little discussion of prices. This has been deliberate: in the last decade or two a disproportionate emphasis has been placed on 'getting prices right' and improving static allocative efficiency to the neglect of 'structural' issues such as physical and human capital formation, the distribution of productive assets and incomes and the aggregate rate of growth. Prices evidently are important, but they are not the only thing that is important and their role should be kept in perspective.

Having said this, one must also say straight away that relative factor prices do have a strong influence on the degree of mechanization, the labour intensity of production and the amount of employment created per unit of investment. Quite apart from the sectoral allocation of credit by the commercial banking system, discussed above, there is the question of the real rate of interest charged by banks to borrowers. If finance capital is 'cheap' relative to the cost of employing labour –

either because real interest rates are well below the opportunity cost of capital or real wage rates are above the opportunity cost of labour – methods of production will be excessively mechanized (i.e., the capital-labour ratio will be above the optimum), employment per unit of output will be below the optimum and, most important from the point of view of long run growth, the number of new jobs created as a result of investment activities will be smaller than would otherwise be the case.

Note that relative factor price distortions can arise either from a malfunctioning of the labour market or of the market for credit. Whereas once it was thought that labour market imperfections were at the root of relative factor price distortions – i.e., that formal sector workers received too high a wage – today it is quite widely accepted that the problem arises in the capital market, and specifically that real interest rates are too low.[17] Indeed in many countries real interest rates frequently have been negative, i.e., the nominal rate of interest has been less than the rate of inflation, and consequently borrowers have received massive subsidies. Credit has been allocated not by price but by rationing.[18]

The problem has been recognized by many governments and some progress has been made, but it is still the case in many developing countries that interest rate policy is strongly biased against the employment of labour. As a result, poverty is accentuated, the share of wages in value added in formal sector enterprises is reduced and the distribution of income between wages and profits is worsened and, to the extent that low interest rates lower the volume of savings, the rate of growth of output is reduced. Thus policy makers primarily concerned with labour issues cannot afford to ignore interest rate policies.

If interest rates in the commercial banking system often are too low, however, they often are too high in the informal credit markets, assuming credit is available at all. The result is that capital–labour ratios outside the formal sector are too low and the productivity of labour is depressed. People may be employed, but their average incomes may leave them in poverty. There is thus a strong case on efficiency and equity grounds for lending to the poor, not by providing subsidized credit but by increasing the quantity of credit available at moderately high real rates of interest.

It was once thought that high transaction costs, absence of collateral and high risks of default precluded lending programmes for the very poor. The enormous success of the Grameen Bank in Bangladesh, however, which devised highly innovative credit schemes in rural areas, particularly among poor women, has shown that these problems can be overcome. The example of the Grameen Bank is spreading to other countries, e.g., Bolivia and Indonesia, but the surface has only been scratched and many unexploited opportunities exist to create employment and reduce poverty by reallocating finance capital in favour of the poor.

A second key price that affects the labour intensity of production is the exchange rate. A great many developing countries have in recent years adopted a more open economy strategy of development, eliminating import quotas and reducing tariffs while simultaneously increasing incentives to export. This change in domestic policy is very much to be welcomed. Sustained success of an open economy strategy, however, requires careful management of the exchange rate. The objective of policy should be a constant real rate of exchange and this implies that the nominal exchange rate should be adjusted systematically to compensate for differences in the domestic rate of inflation and that of the rest of the world.

A more open economy is likely to result in a change in the composition of output which favours labour. A switch from import substituting industrialization, which tends to be relatively capital intensive, to a more export-oriented strategy, which tends to be relatively labour intensive, is likely to increase the demand for labour and hence result in a combination of more employment and higher real wages. That, in turn, should reduce poverty and improve the distribution of income.

These benefits, however, depend upon the ability of the economy to respond to the change in relative commodity prices arising from greater openness. Exposure to the global economy creates a potential for gain; whether potential gains are translated into an actual increase in income and employment depends on the extent to which the economy is able to alter the pattern of production, and the speed of response. If an economy is unable to shift resources to the export sector, or if the speed of response is very slow, the advantages of an open economy will be much diminished. A change in relative prices does not result automatically in a change in the pattern of production: much depends on the rate of investment. That is, economies with high rates of physical and human capital formation are highly flexible and can respond quickly to income earning opportunities. They can react to changes in relative prices by channelling investment into newly profitable industries and in effect alter the composition of output through changes in the direction of growth, not through a static reallocation of a given volume of capital, human and natural resources. Thus, once again, policies which ensure high rates of physical capital formation and high levels of expenditure on human development are central to success.

THE INFORMAL SECTOR

Large numbers of people in developing countries are self-employed either as small peasant farmers or as owners of small family-based enterprises or as providers of personal services. Many others are employees in small enterprises, possibly working on a part-time basis. This heterogeneous group of activities often is described as the informal sector in contradistinction to the formal sector where employment typically is organized in large firms using relatively capital intensive techniques of production.

One can encounter a variety of views about the informal sector and a range of policy postures extending from tight control through benign neglect to moderately supportive. There are those who view the informal sector as economically backward and tradition bound, as a remnant of pre-capitalist modes of production and as a residual sector which is destined to disappear as development proceeds. Those who view the informal sector as economically unimportant, i.e., a residual, and as a sector which is likely to shrink in size, are inclined to advocate a policy of benign neglect, i.e., to ignore it.

More common, however, is the view that the informal sector acts as a sponge which absorbs those who cannot obtain employment in the formal sector. Informal sector activities are an alternative to unemployment, they are a product of survival strategies by the poor, and they include (in addition to ordinary workers) the lumpenproletariat, the criminals and the misfits. Moreover, because of rapid population growth, rural-to-urban migration and the limited absorptive capacity of the formal sector, the urban informal sector is likely to grow for the indefinite future. This growth is a threat to public order (because of crime), to health (e.g., because of food sold from street stands under unsanitary conditions), to safety (e.g., because of dangerous, unregulated vehicles being used to transport goods and passengers) and even to political stability (because the unorganized masses can be manipulated by demagogues). The policy response of those who hold this view of the informal sector is to suppress it where possible, to move it out of sight and to adopt firm measures to contain it. Regulations are tight, housing codes and zoning restrictions are rigidly imposed, health and safety measures are stringent and periodic crackdowns by the police often are brutal.

A radically different view, however, is gradually winning adherents. According to this view, the informal sector is neither a collection of residual activities that soon will disappear nor a sponge that expands and absorbs the destitute and the undesirables who threaten the rest of society but rather a potential source of economic dynamism, creativity and initiative, entrepreneurship and growth.[19] The appropriate policy response, it is argued, is to support informal sector activities by bestowing secure property rights on the land, squatter housing and other productive assets assembled by the poor; by removing administrative obstacles and controls which prevent the growth of microenterprises and small scale businesses and inhibit entrepreneurship; and by reallocating credit so that the poor have access to finance capital, as in the example of the Grameen Bank. The poor, and the majority of ordinary working people who obtain a livelihood in the informal sector, are thus seen not as a problem, but as part of the solution, a collection of valuable human resources who in the right conditions can transform the economy and improve the well-being of all.

GUARANTEED EMPLOYMENT

Even under the best of circumstances, however, there is likely to be considerable slack in the labour force in both rural and urban areas. This can take the form of year-round or seasonal unemployment or part-time employment with lengthy periods of joblessness. Young people and women are especially vulnerable to unemployment and are likely to welcome opportunities for wage employment. A number of countries have experimented with labour intensive public works programmes[20] and their experience suggests that a guaranteed employment scheme could be a viable and valuable policy initiative in many other developing countries.[21]

In China, prior to the dissolution of the commune system, the mobilization of surplus labour was a key mechanism for rural capital construction. In the state of Maharashtra, India, a successful employment guarantee scheme has been in operation since 1975. In Bangladesh there has been a large food-for-work programme for about three decades. Labour intensive schemes to construct basic infrastructure facilities also have been created under Indonesia's Kapupaten programmes, South Korea's Saemul Undong movement, Bolivia's emergency stabilization programme and in many African countries. Much can be learned from these experiences.

The point of departure of an employment guarantee scheme should be recognition of the right of everyone to work, i.e., to guaranteed employment for performing low skilled manual labour. A programme of guaranteed employment would thus act as a residual source of employment, at a wage no higher than the going market wage for landless agricultural labourers. It would thereby become a safety net for those capable of productive work.

The guaranteed employment programme should concentrate on the construction of productive assets that can be expected in future to raise output and incomes. It should not be regarded as a short-term measure to provide relief in an emergency or as a transfer or welfare programme. Rather, it should be seen as a mechanism for mobilizing otherwise unused resources for physical capital formation and growth. That is, the main purpose of the scheme is to generate employment and reduce poverty and inequality by accelerating labour intensive investment and thereby promoting faster growth.

Care must be taken, however, to ensure that the programme, contrary to its intentions, does not actually increase inequality in the distribution of income and wealth. A successful guaranteed employment scheme will create a number of valuable productive assets. These assets will raise both rural and urban land values and hence the incomes of those who own the land. Since landowners are likely to be better off than the low skilled and otherwise unemployed male and female labourers who work at subsistence wages to create the assets, the effect of the employment programme, paradoxically, could be to increase inequalities.

The workers who participate would receive two types of benefits from an employment scheme. First, they would receive subsistence wages during the period when the work is undertaken. In Maharashtra, for instance, more than three-quarters of the beneficiaries are landless workers or small farm households; about 40 per cent of those employed are women. The subsistence wages in some cases account for between one-third and two-thirds of total household incomes. Thus the direct benefits accrue largely to the poor and are not negligible when seen from their perspective.

Second, to the extent that the assets created under the scheme generate a permanently higher demand for labour, the workers should enjoy in future higher market wages or more days of employment, or both. Most of the benefits, however, are likely to accrue to landowners in the form of lower costs (e.g., if road construction reduces the cost of transport), higher output (e.g., from irrigation projects), higher land rents and hence higher land prices. Moreover, the benefits to landowners are likely to rise more than proportionately with the size of holding. This would occur, for instance, if a project lowers transport costs and the marketable surplus increases with farm size.

One way to overcome this problem would be to transfer ownership of the assets created by unemployed workers to the workers themselves. This could readily be done by forming a multi-purpose cooperative or worker-managed enterprise, the shares in which would be proportional to the number of days worked on the construction project. In effect, state assets would be privatized. The cooperative would be responsible for maintaining the assets, managing them and distributing profits among the shareholder-cooperators. Unemployed workers would thereby gradually be converted into asset-holders, although they should be free to cash in their shares with the cooperative if they wished.

Not all assets created by a guaranteed employment programme could be managed in this way, but considerable scope exists for simultaneously transforming idle labour into physical capital and workers into shareholders in cooperative enterprises. For instance, a cooperative could be organized around an irrigation project and water sold to farmers; a timber, firewood or fruit cooperative could be organized around a tree planting project; a toll-charging company could be organized around a bridge-building project; a fishing or duck cooperative could be based on an artificial pond, and so on. These individual cooperatives could then be grouped into multi-purpose cooperatives that would have overall responsibility for managing the collectively constructed assets. Such an approach could combine job creation and poverty alleviation with an improvement in the distribution of wealth.

ECONOMIC SECURITY IN POOR COUNTRIES

Globalization and the economic forces associated with it – restructuring, commercialization and market penetration – were expected to result in higher average incomes and the higher incomes, in turn, should make it possible for governments in developing countries to increase social provisioning and social protection. Instead, globalization often has led to reduced social provisioning and social protection and – in both developed and developing countries – to a move away from the universal approach to economic security that was a basic principle of the welfare state. Instead of universal provisioning of social services, policy makers increasingly limit their objectives to providing residual protection to vulnerable groups, targeting benefits on those classified as poor and creating a social safety net to prevent people from falling into severe distress.[22] The result of these minimalist policies is that human development and human capital formation are under threat in a great many countries, particularly in sub-Saharan Africa, parts of West Asia and Latin America and in the former socialist countries in transition from a centrally planned to a market guided economy.

Perhaps for the time being one must abandon hope for universal social protection, but this does not imply that provision of a modicum of economic security for poor people in poor countries is beyond the means of government policy or that economic security for the poor is of low priority.[23] The poor do not have easy access to capital markets (and hence cannot borrow when income temporarily falls below subsistence expenditure), and neither do they have access to insurance markets (and hence cannot protect themselves against, say, incapacitating illness or crop failure). The poor, in other words, face a case of 'market failure' and consequently there are grounds for the government in effect to act as lender and insurer of last resort. The non-poor also face market failures, but their means are greater and consequently their ability to cope and provide for themselves is greater. Hence public measures to provide economic security, if they cannot be universal, should focus on the poor.

In terms of cost, the most important component of a set of policies to provide economic security is pensions for the elderly. Yet it should be possible, perhaps in stages, for all developing countries to finance and implement a pension scheme in which all working people participate, not just urban residents employed in the formal sector, as is often the case. The age at which women and men become eligible for a pension and the monthly payment obviously will have to reflect the demographic, economic and fiscal circumstances of the country but, in principle, it should be possible to provide a measure of economic security to the elderly even in the least developed countries. If this is too ambitious in the first instance, then one can begin by providing a pension to those most in need, namely, to the lowest income groups, rather than to the upper-income groups, as is almost always the case now.

Public expenditure on a pension scheme can be justified in part on economic grounds, and this strengthens the case for universality of provision. It is now widely recognized that one of the motives for having children is provision of economic security in old age. Children, once they become adult workers, are a form of insurance for their parents: not just insurance against the infirmities of old age, but insurance against many of the catastrophes that can occur without warning. Children, thus, are a substitute for economic security measures that protect the livelihood of people and, in particular, they are a substitute for old-age pensions. It follows from this that state-funded pension schemes in developing countries are likely to result in a reduction in the demand for children, a decline in the fertility rate and a slower rate of growth of the population. This in turn is likely to lead to a faster rate of growth of per capita income.

Lastly, there is the empirical observation that in fact a number of developing countries have given priority to expenditures on economic security. Among the socialist developing countries, there are China and Cuba, and among the more market-oriented countries, there are the cases of Sri Lanka, Costa Rica and, in India, the states of Kerala and Tamil Nadu. In each of these six cases public expenditure has contributed to impressive gains in human development and in none, with the possible exception of Cuba in recent years, has expenditure on human development – and specifically on economic security – resulted in unacceptably slow rates of growth. If there is a conflict between growth and economic security, it must be a very mild one. Probably no such conflict exists. Indeed it is likely that a well designed programme to increase economic security – by lowering risk, encouraging investment and reducing the desired number of children per household – actually would increase incomes and growth.

THE DISTRIBUTION OF PRODUCTIVE ASSETS

Most developing countries are characterized by an abundance of labour relative to natural, human and physical capital. As a result the wages received by low skilled labour (and the incomes of many of the self-employed) tend to be low whereas profit rates, the returns to education, and land rental rates tend to be high. This in turn implies that the share of wages in national income will tend to be low in developing countries, compared to the wage share in countries where labour is relatively scarce. Unless natural, human and physical capital are evenly distributed, a low share of wages in total income will be translated into an unequal distribution of income among persons. The combination of high income inequality and low wage rates means that poverty will be widespread.

That is, even if everyone is fully employed, the problem of poverty among labouring households will remain as long as labour is abundant and the distribution of productive assets is unequal. It is not enough to create employment; in many countries the result would be to enlarge the class of the working poor. If the objective of policy is to reduce poverty substantially within a reasonable period of time – say, one generation – some redistribution of productive assets is likely to be necessary. One obvious possibility, important historically, is a redistribution of land.

Indeed in the highly successful East Asian economies, asset redistribution, and notably a land reform, occurred before the commencement of accelerated growth. Land reform was a central feature of the development policies of Japan, China, South Korea and Taiwan and helped to reduce poverty and inequality. In many other developing countries a redistribution of property rights in land and water, accompanied as necessary by technical assistance, credit to small farmers and improved marketing, is very likely to improve allocative efficiency[24] as well as create employment, reduce poverty and improve the distribution of income. Moreover, there is no evidence that land reform reduces the long run rate of growth and in some circumstances it could well promote it.

In some countries water reform is almost as important as land reform. State-owned tube wells could be privatized by turning them over to groups of landless people who would have the right to pump and sell irrigation water and the responsibility to maintain the wells and pumps. The beneficiaries could be organized into cooperatives similar to those suggested for the management of assets created under guaranteed employment schemes. One local NGO in Bangladesh has experimented with such an arrangement and its experience has demonstrated that the idea is viable.

A redistribution of productive assets in rural areas evidently will reduce poverty and inequality in the countryside, but the benefits of land and water reforms are not confined to the rural areas. The benefits spread to the urban areas as well. One reason for this is that asset redistribution raises the average income of the rural poor. This increases the opportunity cost of rural migrants, raises their 'reservation wage' (i.e., the wage that would just induce them to emigrate) and hence exerts upward pressure on urban wages, particularly on the wages of low skilled labour. This linkage between land reform and a higher wage rate in the urban industrial sector is one important reason why Taiwan, for instance, enjoys a high degree of equality in the overall distribution of income, and not just low inequality in the rural areas.[25]

These arguments can be generalized. First, in countries where the distribution of assets is highly unequal, the structure of incentives is warped and resources tend to be allocated inefficiently. In the rural areas, inequalities in the distribution of productive assets lie behind the commonly observed inverse relationship between farm size and yields and they contribute as well to the monopsonistic power of landowners in local labour markets.[26] Inequality in asset ownership also tends to be associated with sub-optimal investment in human capital and the neglect of productivity increasing expenditures on human development.[27] In the developed countries, the erosion of the welfare state may actually have harmed economic performance. Samuel Bowles and Herbert Gintis have made the point this way:

> Equally suggestive of a positive relationship between egalitarian institutions and policies on the one hand and economic performance on the other is the fact that the advanced capitalist countries, taken as a whole, have grown faster under the aegis of the post World War II welfare state than in any other period for which the relevant data exist. In historical retrospect, the epoch of the welfare state and of social democracy was also the golden age of capitalism.[28]

Second, a political point with economic implications, societies with a highly unequal distribution of wealth are likely to be characterized by pronounced class conflict, unstable political regimes and periodic episodes of civil violence. Such conflicted societies will find cooperation between workers and asset owners to be difficult, be the asset owners large landowners or urban capitalists. Each will be suspicious of the other; each will resist changes proposed by the other. The result will be greater risk, lower levels of investment, slower rates of technological and institutional change and a slower long term rate of growth. The contrast between East Asia and Central America illustrates the point. Everyone ultimately would be better off in Guatemala, Honduras, El Salvador and Nicaragua if the distribution of assets in those four countries approximated the distribution of assets in Taiwan and South Korea.

Following on from this, third, is the point that inequality can be costly to maintain. Social conflict, if it is not resolved through a redistribution of income, assets and power, will have to be contained and permanent containment requires resources, namely, a large police force, a well equipped army, an active internal intelligence service, a vigorous judicial system and a full complement of local jails, national prisons, rehabilitation centres and the like. The opportunity cost of these resources in terms of investment and growth can be high, as the history of Latin America and the Middle East attests. Moreover, the apparatus of containment usually seems to require an authoritarian and undemocratic state, as one can see in Haiti. Thus a highly unequal distribution of productive assets can entail high costs, political and economic, whereas a redistribution of assets can contribute significantly to improved economic performance and, perhaps, to a greater chance of social peace.

SUMMARY AND CONCLUSIONS

Globalization has weakened the economic power of the state but it has not made the state impotent. Government policy in developing countries has a major role to play in creating more and better employment and income earning opportunities, reducing poverty and improving the distribution of income and wealth. What is needed is not a smaller state but a different state which places greater emphasis on human development and creating appropriate institutions and an efficient set of incentives. Sustained economic growth is not sufficient but it is a *sine qua non* if the objective is to improve the well-being of ordinary working people.

Rapid growth requires high levels of physical capital formation and an incentive structure that ensures that investment is allocated efficiently. There is considerable scope for improving the allocation of investment in both the public and private sectors, and thereby raising the productivity of capital on the margin and hence the average rate of growth. In particular, an improvement in the allocation of finance capital could contribute much to improved economic performance and greater equity.

Human capital formation is no less important than physical investment. Indeed it can help to accelerate growth and reduce poverty while simultaneously tempering inequalities in the distribution of wealth and income. Most of the discussion surrounding a human development strategy has overlooked the potential contribution of human capital formation to improving the distribution of income earning assets.

While structural issues are almost always more fundamental than relative prices, serious price distortions can have very harmful effects. It once was thought that the formal sector labour market was seriously distorted and that this had adverse consequences for employment, the alleviation of poverty and income distribution. It is more common today, however, for problems to arise in the capital market (in the form of low real rates of interest in the formal sector) and in the market for foreign exchange (in the form of an overvalued exchange rate). These price distortions harm employment prospects and inhibit the development of small scale, informal sector enterprises.

Even if prices are 'right', i.e., even if the set of incentives accurately reflects social costs and benefits, the ability of an economy to reallocate resources in response to changed incentives depends on the rate of capital formation, both physical and human. The composition of output is changed by altering the pattern of investment, not by shuffling around a given endowment of resources. Thus, once again, human and physical investment are the keys to success. Moreover they are complementary: investment in one increases the productivity of investment in the other.

Thus policies concerned with employment, income inequality and poverty must be viewed in a broad context. Partial implementation of an investment, growth and price liberalization strategy can lead to disappointing employment and distributional outcomes, and policies which address labour market distortions while ignoring malfunctionings in the capital markets may actually worsen the condition of many working women and men. This is especially true during the transition from one economic regime to another – most dramatically in countries switching from central planning to a market guided system – and special care will have to be taken to reduce the adverse distributional effects of liberalization and privatization.[29] It is here, in fact, that the encouragement of the informal sector and the implementation of a guaranteed employment scheme can be of enormous importance.

The informal sector should be seen as a potential source of dynamism, entrepreneurship and growth. Policies concerned to increase employment, create additional income earning opportunities, to secure more stable livelihoods and to reduce poverty and inequality should ensure that barriers to the expansion of small scale, informal activities are removed. Moreover, the poor who obtain a living in the informal sector are as entitled to secure property rights (in land, housing and productive assets) as those in the formal sector and they are also entitled to access on equal terms to finance capital. The enforcement of such 'entitlements' could go some way towards improving the distribution of wealth and increasing economic efficiency.

The informal and formal sectors should also be seen as linked to one another. That is, the character of the informal sector depends in part on the characteristics of the formal sector and hence the reform of the formal sector may be necessary to permit dynamism and growth to take place in the informal sector. The two sectors, in other words, are not dualistic and separate but rather closely interconnected.

The poor should also be guaranteed a livelihood through employment at a subsistence wage. Guaranteed employment schemes can contribute to faster growth by concentrating on the construction of productive assets. The ownership of the assets created by unemployed workers should then be transferred to the workers themselves, organized into cooperatives with shares being distributed in proportion to the number of days worked. In this way a programme to create employment and reduce poverty can be combined with institutional innovation which leads to a permanent improvement in the distribution of wealth.

Public works schemes can be designed to ensure security of employment and livelihoods for able-bodied women and men and hence the insecurity of the poor that arises from the volatility of income earning opportunities can be attenuated. Insecurities which arise, for example, from sudden illness or crop failure can in principle be handled by the capital market (e.g., borrowing during periods of distress) or by the insurance market (e.g., crop insurance). The poor, however, do not have access to capital and insurance markets and hence there is a case for government to act as lender and insurer of last resort. Perhaps the greatest insecurity faced by the poor comes with old age and hence state pensions for the elderly, particularly the elderly poor, should have high priority. A well designed state pension scheme not only will increase economic security, it also is likely to result in a lower fertility rate and a faster rate of growth of per capita income.

Finally, if the objective of policy is to reduce poverty substantially within a reasonable period of time, some redistribution of productive wealth, including land and water rights, is likely to be necessary. Asset redistribution, moreover, if well designed, can help to create employment, raise allocative efficiency and improve the overall distribution of income. In some circumstances, asset redistribution can help to accelerate the aggregate rate of growth, e.g., by creating an economic and political environment conducive to investment in human capital, by reducing social conflict, lowering risk and stimulating physical investment, technological change and productivity enhancing institutional innovation and, lastly, by allowing unproductive expenditure on the apparatus of conflict containment to be reduced and reallocated to more constructive purposes. The political, social and economic benefits of an equitable distribution of wealth often are underestimated.

Notes

I am grateful to Azizur Rahman Khan, Eddy Lee, Samir Radwan and Hamid Tabatabai for comments on an earlier draft.

1. See Keith Griffin and Azizur Rahman Khan, *Globalization and the Developing World* (Geneva: UNRISD, 1992).
2. Keith Griffin and Terry McKinley, 'A New Framework for Development Cooperation', paper presented at the UNDP Roundtable on 'Change: Social Conflict or Harmony?', Stockholm, 22–4 July 1994.
3. Quoted in *The Economist*, 9 July 1994, p. 55.
4. This point is emphasized by John Langmore, 'One Inseparable Humanity: A Global Employment Strategy', paper presented at the UNDP Roundtable on 'Change: Social Conflict or Harmony?', Stockholm, 22–4 July 1994.
5. Ibid.
6. Alfred Maizels, 'Commodity Markets, Institutional Support Measures and Challenges for Developing Countries', paper presented at the colloquium in honour of Gerald K. Helleiner, North-South Institute, Ottawa, 22–4 June 1994.
7. Comparing the two periods 1970–80 and 1980–92, the growth of GDP in the high income countries declined from 3.2 per cent per annum to 2.9 per cent, and the growth of world GDP declined from 3.4 to 3.0 per cent per annum. (See World Bank, *World Development Report 1994*, New York: Oxford University Press, 1994.)
8. See, for instance, Lawrence Mishel and Jared Bernstein, 'Is the Technology Black Box Empty?: An Empirical Examination of the Impact of Technology on Wage Inequality and the Employment Structure', Economic Policy Institute, mimeo, April 1994.
9. For an analysis of President Clinton's economic policies see David Gordon, 'Clintonomics: A Glass Half Empty', *Contention*, Vol. 3, No. 1 (Fall 1993); also see in the same issue Keith Griffin, 'David Gordon on Clintonomics: A Comment'.
10. *The Economist*, 9 July 1994.
11. See Chapter 2.
12. China is the most important example of a country which enjoyed accelerated growth and a substantial reduction in poverty. There was also an increase in inequality in the distribution of income, although compared to other developing countries, inequality is relatively moderate. See Keith Griffin and Zhao Renwei (eds), *The Distribution of Income in China* (London: Macmillan, 1993).
13. This argument is developed at greater length in Keith Griffin (ed.), *Poverty and the Transition to a Market Economy in Mongolia* (London: Macmillan, 1995), Ch. 1.
14. See UNDP, *Human Development Report* (New York: Oxford University Press), published annually since 1990; Keith Griffin and John Knight (eds), *Human Development and the International Development Strategy for the 1990s* (London: Macmillan, 1990); Keith Griffin and Terry McKinley, *Implementing a Human Development Strategy* (London: Macmillan, 1994).
15. The capability approach to development policy has been pioneered by

Amartya Sen. See, e.g., his *Inequality Reexamined* (Cambridge, MA: Harvard University Press, 1992).

16. See, for instance, World Bank, *The East Asian Miracle* (New York: Oxford University Press, 1993) and Keith Griffin, *Alternative Strategies for Economic Development* (London: Macmillan, 1989), Ch. 7.

17. The notion of wage rigidity in urban areas in strongly challenged in Vali Jamal and John Weeks, *Africa Misunderstood, or Whatever Happened to the Rural-Urban Gap?* (London: Macmillan, 1993).

18. Because of the nature of capital markets, credit can never be allocated entirely by price – some rationing is inevitable – but this does not imply that the level of the real rate of interest is therefore irrelevant. See, for instance, J.E. Stiglitz and A. Weiss, 'Credit Rationing in Markets with Imperfect Information', *American Economic Review*, Vol. 71, No. 3 (June 1981).

19. The leading advocate of this view is Hernando de Soto, *The Other Path: The Invisible Revolution in the Third World* (New York: Harper & Row, 1989), originally published in Spanish under the title *El Otro Sendero: La Revolución Informal* (Lima: Instituto Libertad y Democracia, 1987).

20. Jacques Gaude and Steve Miller, 'Rural Development and Local Resource Intensity: A Case Study Approach', in Griffin and Knight (eds), *Human Development*.

21. See Griffin and McKinley, *Implementing a Human Development Strategy*, pp. 71–9, from which most of this section is taken.

22. See Jessica Vivian, 'Social Safety Nets and Adjustment in Developing Countries', paper presented at the UNDP Roundtable on 'Change: Social Conflict or Harmony?', Stockholm, 22–4 July 1994.

23. For a full discussion see Ehtisham Ahmad, Jean Drèze and Amartya Sen (eds), *Social Security in Developing Countries* (Oxford: Clarendon Press, 1991). Also see Griffin and McKinley, *Implementing a Human Development Strategy* pp. 90–5 on which the discussion below is based.

24. See, e.g., Keith Griffin, *The Political Economy of Agrarian Change* (London: Macmillan, 1974).

25. John C.H. Fei, Gustav Ranis and Shirley W.Y. Kuo, *Growth and Equity: The Taiwan Case* (New York: Oxford University Press, 1979).

26. Griffin, *The Political Economy of Agrarian Change.*

27. See Griffin and McKinley, *Implementing a Human Development Strategy.*

28. Samuel Bowles and Herbert Gintis, 'Efficient Redistribution in a Globally Competitive Economy', paper presented for a Colloquium on Social Justice and Economic Constraints, Université Catholique de Louvain, 3 June 1994, p. 9.

29. See Griffin (ed.), *Poverty and the Transition to a Market Economy in Mongolia*, Ch. 1, for a detailed discussion of policy alternatives during a change of economic regime.

7 The Transition to Market Guided Economies: Lessons for Russia and Eastern Europe from the Chinese Experience*

with Azizur Rahman Khan

The process of economic reform in China began in 1978 and continues to this day. The process is far from over – there is much that remains to be done – but a great deal has been achieved in the last fifteen years and much can be learned from the Chinese experience. Our purpose, however, is not to attempt a comprehensive evaluation of the economic reforms in China but to consider what lessons from the Chinese experience might be applicable to Russia and Eastern Europe as they attempt a transition from centralized quantitative planning to an economy guided by market forces. China would seem to be an obvious point of comparison for socialist countries in transition since China was and remains a socialist country which none the less aspires to harness market forces to serve national purposes. It would perhaps be an exaggeration to claim that China has led the way in the transition from socialism as practised in the communist ruled countries, since there were numerous experiments with economic reform in Russia and Eastern Europe going as far back as the 1950s, but the Chinese reforms have lasted longer, penetrated more deeply and apparently been more successful than any of the reforms introduced in other socialist countries.

The traverse from a quantitatively planned to a market guided economy is a journey into unknown territory. There are no models to follow, no leaders to emulate, not even well founded theories that can be used as a guide. Much is known about how market economies function, al-

* First published in Bernd Magnus and Stephen Cullenberg (eds), *Whither Marxism? Global Crises in International Perspective* (New York and London: Routledge, 1995).

though periodic malfunctioning demonstrates how much remains to be learned. Less is known about the efficient management of a planned socialist system, although our ignorance is not as great as has sometimes been claimed and neither are the accomplishments of socialism as meagre. Still less is known about how to move from one system to another and we find ourselves groping in the dark, searching for a match and candle to light our way.

One potential source of enlightenment is the experience of Western Europe in the years after the Second World War. The wartime economies of Europe were essentially planned economies and the methods used to allocate resources were not so different from those used in socialist countries. The reconversion of the Western European economies to market guided economies was a slow and painful process, assisted after 1947 by generous quantities of foreign aid. There were several false starts, controls were removed gradually and sometimes hesitatingly, and progress was punctuated periodically by crises of various sorts. Food rationing did not end in Britain until 1951, six years after hostilities ceased. Yet the reconversion of Western Europe to a market guided economy arguably was less difficult than the transition being attempted today by Russia and Eastern Europe. Western Europe, after all, possessed the institutions needed by a capitalist economy: secure property rights, legal codes and a court system to enforce laws of contract, a well developed capital market with specialized financial enterprises, and a dense network of markets capable of transmitting information quickly and cheaply. In the case of Western Europe, the preconditions for success already existed. In the case of Russia and Eastern Europe, however, the foundations are missing and this inevitably makes the transition more difficult.

A second possible source of enlightenment is the experience of some developing countries. Particularly during the 1980s a number of developing countries had to cope with problems which at least on the surface appear to be similar to those faced by Russia and Eastern Europe today: severe balance of payments difficulties, heavy foreign indebtedness, rapid inflation occasionally accelerating into hyper-inflation, slow and even negative rates of growth, rising unemployment and poverty and in some sectors, a collapse of production. No doubt there are lessons to be learned from Bolivia and Ghana, from Mexico and South Korea about stabilization, adjustment and restructuring, and it would be foolish to turn one's back on whatever wisdom can be gleaned from history, but the fact remains that the circumstances in the developing countries in the 1980s were very different from the circumstances in

Russia and Eastern Europe in the 1990s. Above all, stabilization and restructuring in developing countries occurred within an established economic system. However prominent in economic affairs the state might have been, the economies of the developing countries were mixed capitalist economies in which resources for the most part were allocated via the market mechanism and not through quantitative controls. Stabilization and restructuring, in other words, were not accompanied by systemic change.

The problem confronting the developing countries in the 1980s, difficult but ultimately not intractable, was how to improve their existing market guided economies in order to absorb external shocks and overcome internally generated disequilibria. The problem confronting Russia and Eastern Europe in the 1990s is how to effect a transition to a market guided economy while simultaneously absorbing massive shocks such as the reconfiguration of national boundaries, severe disruption of long established trading relationships, loss of export markets and curtailment of vital supplies of imported raw materials and energy. The combination of systemic change, multiple shocks and serious macroeconomic disequilibria in a large number of countries at the same time is unprecedented and one should be cautious about drawing analogies with developing countries a decade ago.

Of course one should also be careful about drawing analogies from China, particularly since China officially remains committed to some form of socialism whereas Russia and Eastern Europe do not. Our argument, however, is not that China is the sole or even the best source of relevant experience but that China is one source of relevant experience, and moreover a source that has been neglected in the discussions of economic reform in Russia and Eastern Europe. In what follows we shall concentrate on four topics where China may be able to shed some light. We begin with a discussion of macroeconomic financial stability during the reform process. This is followed by an analysis of the pace of growth and the level of investment during the period since the reforms. We then turn our attention to property relations and the reform of state economic enterprises. Lastly, we discuss changes in the distribution of income that have accompanied the reforms.

China has its own way of doing things, its own style, and this is reflected in several features which are characteristic of the reform process. Perhaps paradoxically for a centrally planned economy,[1] the economic reforms in China were not planned at the centre and imposed from the top down in conformity with a predetermined grand scheme. On the contrary, the reform process has been highly pragmatic, experimental and sequential. Reform has proceeded by trial and error on a step by step basis. Policies have been flexible, amendments have been frequent, enforcement has been far from uniform and reverses have occurred. An outside observer of this process might be bemused and regard the Chinese as marching to an uncertain drummer, but we believe the methods used by the Chinese reformmongers[2] account for much of their success. Indeed one of the lessons from China is the advantage of proceeding in a flexible and incrementalist way.

The economic reforms began in agriculture and only when their success had been demonstrated were they extended to the industrial sector. Within agriculture, numerous experiments with alternative arrangements to the commune system were conducted.[3] These experiments initially were confined to a single county and then spread to an entire province, or to several counties within a province, and hence during this experimental period several different approaches to agricultural reform were being tested simultaneously. The eventual national model – the household responsibility system – was not adopted until the various local experiments had been evaluated at the centre, but once a national model was selected, it was introduced throughout the country very swiftly, albeit with considerable local variation.

The process of reform in agriculture set the pattern for reforms in other sectors. The process was characterized by (i) an experimental approach to policy making, (ii) a tolerance for diversity, (iii) a willingness of policy makers at the centre to learn from the experience at the grass roots and (iv) a tendency of reformmongers to concentrate their efforts where rapid and substantial gains from reform could be anticipated.

The pattern was repeated when the industrial reforms began. Rather than confront the difficult problem of the state economic enterprises head on, the reforms were launched initially in the countryside by transforming the township and village enterprises into cooperatives, private and individual enterprises. Space was created for the private sector to expand – at first only in the rural areas but later also in the cities – without altering property relations in the large, economically dominant, state owned urban industrial sector. Privatization of state enterprises, in other words, was avoided but the weight of the state sector in industrial output was rapidly reduced by allowing small scale private enterprise to emerge.

The pattern was repeated yet again with the reform of foreign trade policy. China did not open up all at once by reducing tariffs, eliminating quotas, welcoming foreign capital, dismantling exchange controls and declaring the currency convertible. Indeed by these criteria China still is far from being an open economy. Instead it moved cautiously, gradually liberalizing trade, encouraging a few joint ventures in selected industries and slowly adjusting the exchange rate. Radical experiments with a semi-free trade regime were conducted in four Special Economic Zones located in two eastern coastal provinces, of which the most famous is Shenzhen adjacent to Hong Kong. When these experiments proved to be successful, fourteen important coastal cities were allowed to engage directly in foreign trade and investment without the necessity to go through the centre. Foreign economic policy thus became rather patchy, with considerable regional variation. The lack of uniformity, abhorrent to a Western trained economist, had positive advantages during a period of transition: it enabled policy makers to avoid the political confrontations that would have been created by an attempt to impose a uniform national policy from the beginning, it provided valuable experience and information which could be used to fine tune policies, and it gave policy makers time to build political support on the basis of demonstrated achievements. Russia and Eastern Europe could do worse than emulate the methods of the Chinese reformmongers.

MACROECONOMIC FINANCIAL STABILITY

The transition from an economy where resources are allocated by quantitative controls to one where resources are allocated by price is likely in the best of circumstances to be disruptive. Prices, by design, will become much more important and relative prices are likely to change dramatically. This will harm some consumers and producers and benefit others. The losers almost certainly will oppose reforms while the gainers are likely to support them. Society will thus be divided, and if the reforms are introduced in a brusque manner intense social conflict may emerge. This suggests that the transition is likely to proceed more smoothly, both politically and economically, if reforms are introduced gradually and if producers and consumers are given time to adjust.

Macroeconomic financial stability in particular will provide a favourable environment for reform. Above all, high rates of inflation should be avoided. Rapid increases in the average level of prices will magnify perceptions of gains and losses and accentuate social conflict. Moreover, rapid and especially accelerating inflation almost always is accompanied by sharp and unpredictable changes in relative prices –

Table 7.1   The annual rate of inflation in China, 1981–91
(percentage change in the GDP deflator)

Year	Rate	Year	Rate
1981	2.6	1987	8.8
1982	2.0	1988	20.7
1983	1.9	1989	16.3
1984	2.8	1990	2.2
1985	11.9	1991	3.0
1986	7.0		

Source: United Nations, *World Economic Survey 1992*, Annex Table A.14 (New York, 1992), p. 197.

complete indexation is neither possible nor desirable – and this will lead to changes in the distribution of income that could undermine public support for the reform process as a whole. Inflation often is accompanied by erratic changes in relative prices and this harms consumers while making it difficult for producers to make sensible production and investment plans. As a result, rapid inflation could well lead to a fall in the level of output and a decline in the rate of growth. If average living standards fall precipitously, the transition to a market guided economy could be aborted. The stakes thus are high.

China, unlike Russia and most of Eastern Europe, has been quite successful in maintaining macroeconomic financial stability. Prior to the economic reforms, during the era of comprehensive central planning and quantitative controls, inflation was repressed, prices on average were highly stable and the prices of individual commodities often remained fixed for many years. During the period from 1965 to 1980, for instance, the annual rate of inflation in China was minus 0.3 per cent per annum. During the next 11 years, 1981–91, the average rate of inflation was much higher, namely 7.2 per cent a year, but in six of the 11 years the rate was 3.0 per cent or less. (See Table 7.1.) In only three years did inflation achieve double digits and in only one brief period, 1988–89, did inflation threaten to get out of control.

In 1988 the economy became overheated as a result of an investment boom. The authorities reacted quickly and in late 1988 a stabilization programme was introduced. Government current expenditure was cut, state financed investment was reduced sharply and the supply of bank credit was restricted. Tight monetary and fiscal policies were maintained until 1991, by which time the rate of inflation had been brought under control again and financial stability restored. It would appear, at least on the surface, that even during a lengthy transition period the authorities have been able to maintain a firm grip on the aggregate level of spending.

Beneath the surface, however, there are signs that the grip is less firm than at first appears. All the banks are owned by the state and banks are by far the most important source of credit. The financial system in China is poorly developed: the bond market is small and stock markets are embryonic. Hence in principle the government should have little difficulty maintaining an orderly financial environment. In practice, however, the control of the central government over the volume of bank credit and its allocation is weak. In times of impending crisis the government can impose austerity, but in other, more normal times its ability to control the volume of credit is rather tenuous. Actual bank lending usually exceeds authorized lending as local bank managers are more responsive to the demands of local and provincial officials than to control figures issued by the centre. Financial stability in China thus tends to be rather fragile and the danger of overheating from excessive investment demand is ever present.

The money supply increased 25.4 per cent a year between 1980 and 1990. In a fully monetized market economy this would have resulted in persistent rapid inflation. China, however, is not a fully monetized economy and a significant proportion of the increase in the money supply was held as money balances rather than spent on goods and services. This is reflected in changes in the ratio of the stock of money to national income, which rose from 33.6 per cent in 1980 to 74.7 per cent in 1990. The money–income ratio now falls within the range characteristic of fully monetized economies and it is therefore likely that if the money supply continues to grow by 25 per cent a year, China will encounter severe inflationary pressures.

The authorities seem to have recognized the danger and emphasis within the monetary system has shifted away from money creation to greater reliance on the flotation of government bonds and foreign borrowing. At present the bond market is not a major source of finance for long term investment although it can be expected to grow rapidly in future. Foreign borrowing increased from almost nothing at the beginning of the reform process to a small but significant source of finance today. Between 1980 and 1990, for instance, external debt increased from 1.5 per cent of GNP to 14.4 per cent and the debt service ratio rose from 4.4 per cent of total exports to 10.3 per cent. China, evidently, has been prudent about foreign borrowing; it now needs to become more prudent about domestic money creation.

Table 7.2   Rates of inflation in Eastern Europe and the Soviet Union, 1981–91 (per cent per annum)

Year	Bulgaria*	Czechoslovakia†	Hungary	Poland‡	Romania*	Soviet Union*
1981	0.4	0.9	4.6	24.4	1.9	1.4
1982	0.3	4.7	6.9	101.5	16.9	3.4
1983	1.4	1.1	7.3	23.0	5.3	0.7
1984	0.7	0.9	8.3	15.8	1.1	−1.3
1985	1.7	1.3	7.0	14.4	0.4	0.8
1986	2.7	0.4	5.3	17.3	0.3	1.9
1987	2.7	0.1	8.6	25.5	0.4	1.9
1988	2.4	0.2	15.5	59.0	1.7	2.3
1989	6.2	1.5	18.8	259.5	0.9	1.9
1990	19.3	9.9	28.9	584.7	5.7	5.3
1991	249.8	57.9	35.2	70.3	305.5	196.0

* Retail prices in the state sector.
† Cost of living index for workers and employees.
‡ Cost of living index for workers and employees in the socialist sector.

Source: United Nations, *World Economic Survey 1992*, Annex Table A-11 (New York, 1992), p. 194.

China's financial stability may be a little fragile, but it compares very favourably with the instability in Russia and much of Eastern Europe. Of course the extent of repressed inflation in pre-reform Russia and Eastern Europe was higher than in China, but the fact remains that the Chinese managed their financial affairs rather well and the Russians and Eastern Europeans did not. The collapse of communism beginning in 1989 was followed almost everywhere by an explosive increase in inflation. (See Table 7.2.) In Poland the rate of inflation increased from 59 per cent a year in 1988 to 259.5 per cent in 1989; in Czechoslovakia (since divided into two countries), inflation rose from 9.9 per cent in 1990 to 57.9 per cent in 1991; in Bulgaria, from 19.3 per cent to 249.8 per cent; in Romania, from 5.7 to 305.5 per cent. Among the Eastern European countries in the table, only in Hungary was an explosion avoided and even there inflation accelerated steadily, reaching an annual rate of 35.2 per cent in 1991, far higher than even the worst year in China.

In the then Soviet Union the price explosion occurred in 1991, when the rate of inflation reached 196 per cent a year. Prices were liberalized in Russia at the beginning of the following year and matters went from bad to worse. By the final quarter of 1992 the average rate of inflation in Russia was 25 per cent a month. The target for inflation in 1993, announced on 20 January, was a rate no more than 5 per cent a month by the end of the year.[4] It will not be easy to achieve the target because price indexation is spreading rapidly – to the working capital of enterprises, to minimum pensions and to wages. Unless the government is able to establish macroeconomic financial stability quickly, rapid inflation may become institutionalized in the Russian economy.

If this happens the transition to a market guided economy will become much more difficult. Rigidities will be built into the economy, allocative inefficiency will increase and, if hyperinflation should occur, barter transactions will replace market transactions. Output, employment and incomes might then begin a downward spiral. Support for economic reform probably would collapse, with unforeseeable consequences.

The Chinese experience suggests that financial stability can contribute to the reform process by creating an environment in which changes in relative prices are undisturbed by rapid movements in the general level of prices. In such an environment price signals are strong and clear, their effects on incentives are powerful and consequently both producers and consumers are likely to respond quickly. This, in turn, implies that the economy will be more flexible, more responsive to profit opportunities and hence more likely to sustain high levels of output and investment. If investment can be sustained, production and incomes will rise, possibly at an accelerating rate if the economic reforms result in a greater efficiency of investment, i.e., in a rise in the incremental output-capital ratio. Sustained and possibly accelerating growth will result in increased support for the reform process, thereby creating a virtuous circle of reforms leading to growth and growth leading to more reforms.

The connections between financial stability, systemic reform and economic growth are thus crucial to the transition to a market guided economy. The Chinese reformmongers seem to have understood the importance of these connections and their experience is highly relevant to Russian and Eastern European policy makers as they struggle to transform their own economies.

GROWTH AND INVESTMENT

Despite all the inefficiencies of the central planning system, Russia and Eastern Europe continued to achieve a moderate rate of growth of GDP throughout the pre-reform period. Thus in the former Soviet Union the average annual rate of growth was 3.5 per cent during the seven year period ending in 1988. In Eastern Europe during the same period the average growth rate was close to 3 per cent. Negative rates of growth did not arise until these countries attempted to convert to a market guided economy.

As can be seen in Table 7.3, the introduction of reforms was accompanied by a sharp deterioration in economic performance. Indeed in all six countries included in the table, growth rates became highly negative almost immediately. Hungary suffered the least (output declined by 8 per cent in 1991), while Bulgaria suffered the most (output declined by 23 per cent in the same year). Only in Poland are there signs of recovery, with a positive growth of output of 3 per cent in 1992. Moreover, the decline in investment often was even more severe than the decline in output. In the worst year, investment fell 30 per cent in the then Czechoslovakia (1991), 38.3 per cent in Romania (1990) and 50 per cent in Bulgaria (1991). The former Soviet Union, so far, has escaped rather lightly, but the worst is yet to come. The so-called 'big bang' or 'shock therapy' seems to have destroyed inefficient but functioning economies with little sign so far that they have effected a traverse to a more productive system.

The Chinese experience has been very different. Economic reforms in China, far from lowering the growth of output and investment, led to a slow but unmistakable acceleration. This is a remarkable achievement, particularly given the good performance in the period prior to the reforms. In fact China's growth rate during the pre-reform period already was very high by international standards, namely, 5.8 per cent a year during the decade ending in 1978 and 6.8 per cent a year during the period 1965–80. As can be seen in Table 7.4, the rate of growth of GDP accelerated to an average of more than 9 per cent a year in the ten years after the introduction of the reforms. Moreover, in no year did output actually fall: the least good performance was in 1989, the year of stabilization, when GDP increased only 3.2 per cent.

There was a strong tendency in China during the transition for investment to grow more rapidly than output and consequently the ratio of investment to GDP tended to rise, reaching a peak of more than 39 per cent in 1986 and 1987. The transition to a market guided economy in China stimulated an investment boom and policy makers often were concerned with the problem of 'overinvestment'; the collapse of output commonly associated with the implementation of 'shock therapy' elsewhere never arose in China. Domestic savings increased as rapidly as investment and hence, except for 1985 and 1986, China relied very

Table 7.3 The growth of output and investment in Russia and Eastern Europe (per cent per annum)

	Gross Domestic Product					Investment			
	1988	1989	1990	1991	1992	1988	1989	1990	1991
Former USSR	5.3	3.3	-2.1	-17.0	-15.0	6.2	4.7	0.6	-7.0
Bulgaria	2.6	-1.4	-11.8	-23.0	-9.7	4.5	-10.1	-12.0	-50.0
Former Czech.	2.6	1.3	-4.7	-16.0	-5.3	4.1	1.6	7.7	-30.0
Hungary	2.7	3.8	-4.0	-8.0	n.a.	-9.1	5.6	-8.7	-11.0
Poland	4.4	0.2	-12.0	-9.3	3.0	5.4	-2.4	-10.1	-8.0
Romania	-0.5	-5.8	-8.2	-13.0	-9.6	-2.2	-1.5	-38.3	-16.8

Source: United Nations, *World Economic Survey 1992* (New York, 1993).

Table 7.4   Growth, investment and saving in China

Year	Growth rate of GDP (%)	Gross investment as percentage of GDP	Gross domestic saving as percentage of GDP
1975	8.3	30.3	30.6
1976	–5.4	28.4	29.0
1977	7.9	29.0	29.5
1978	12.5	33.4	33.2
1979	7.0	34.9	34.6
1980	6.4	32.2	32.2
1981	4.9	29.2	30.0
1982	8.3	29.7	31.6
1983	9.8	30.4	31.5
1984	13.3	32.4	32.8
1985	12.5	38.7	34.5
1986	7.9	39.3	36.1
1987	10.1	39.2	39.1
1988	9.9	38.9	38.0
1989	3.2	36.4	35.7
1990	5.2	39.0	42.5
1991	7.0	n.a.	n.a.

Sources: 1975–89: World Bank, *World Tables 1991* (Washington, DC, 1992); 1990–91: United Nations, *World Economic Survey 1992* (New York, 1993).

little on external capital to finance investment. That is, domestic rather than foreign savings financed capital formation, and high rates of investment – possibly accompanied by increases in the efficiency of investment – led to accelerated growth.

The difference in performance as regards growth and investment between China on the one hand and Russia and Eastern Europe on the other tells us much about the approach to reform and the transition to a market guided economy in the two cases. In China emphasis was placed on growing out of systemic inefficiencies and on using a high rate of investment to reallocate resources and increase microeconomic efficiency. In Russia and Eastern Europe, in contrast, policy makers seem to have been unduly preoccupied with systemic reform and static allocative efficiency at the cost of stifled growth.

It is misleading to characterize the Chinese approach to reform as 'gradualism' and the Russian and Eastern European approach as the 'big bang'. The boldness of reform and the rapidity of change in China have far exceeded what has been attempted in other economies seeking to move from a centrally planned to a market guided system. The Chinese reform of the rural economy is an outstanding example of boldness of conception and speed of implementation. The transformation of the commune system into a system of private peasant farming was completed in a remarkably short period of three or four years. Rural institutions were totally restructured and every aspect of the rural economy and society was affected. Yet this transformation was accomplished without disrupting production. In fact the level of agricultural output rose and the rate of growth actually accelerated in the early years.

In order to appreciate the magnitude and significance of what was achieved, one must remember that the Chinese commune was much more than a collective farm. The communes owned and operated rural industries; they were responsible for tasks normally undertaken by local government, including the provision of basic social services; they were even responsible for the local militia. All the functions of the commune were transformed and new institutions created, and this was done at a breathtaking pace. Agriculture was reorganized on the basis of household farming. Commune industries were reorganized as collectively managed corporations, and these reorganized enterprises spearheaded industrial growth during the period of transition. Local government institutions were created to take over services previously supplied by communes. The only comparable experience in history of such a rural upheaval is the process of collectivization in China itself a quarter of a century earlier, between 1955 and 1958.

The transformation of the commune system was not a unique achievement. China also is remarkable for the speed with which a highly dynamic, small scale, private sector emerged after the restraints on private entrepreneurship were removed. No less noteworthy has been the speed with which export-oriented industrial zones were created and the success China has had in penetrating foreign markets. China today exports a higher fraction of its total output than do, say, India and Brazil. Even in the area of macroeconomic stabilization China has been more decisive than Russia and the Eastern European countries. Of course, as we have seen, China never quite lost control of its macroeconomy, but when stabilization did become necessary in the late 1980s, it did not hesitate: orthodox measures were applied quickly and vigorously.

Compared to Eastern Europe, China may be said to have followed a gradualist path in two areas, namely, price reforms (including reform of the system of exchange controls) and the privatization of state enterprises. It is clear with hindsight that the Chinese policy of gradualism in these two areas was pragmatic and far more sensible than the alternative of rushing simultaneously to free all prices and privatize most public enterprises. Had the reformmongers freed all prices at once, there would have been massive and largely unpredictable effects on the distribution of income and that, in turn, would have required very large compensatory income readjustments and protective measures. Compensation on a massive scale would have been very difficult; it probably would have introduced many distortions and inefficiencies, and almost certainly would have resulted in huge government deficits and loss of macroeconomic control. Similarly, a wholesale privatization of the state enterprises would have disrupted the entire industrial sector and caused an immediate reduction in output. The consequence would have been a shortage of consumer and producer goods, as has occurred in Russia and Eastern Europe.

Had China not sustained macroeconomic stability and normalcy of supply of goods and services, it would have been impossible for entrepreneurship to emerge and flourish on the scale that it did outside the state sector, namely, in township and village enterprises, in the private sector and in cooperatives. Had China tolerated rapid inflation and a regime of shortage, private sector initiatives would have been distorted and entrepreneurial talent diverted to speculative activities and rent seeking to a far greater extent than in fact occurred. Productive investment would have fallen and growth would have come to a halt.

There is a clear lesson to be learned from the Chinese experience. There is a conflict during the transition between maintaining control over macroeconomic variables and reducing inefficiency within the existing economic structure. The faster one attempts to remove inefficiency, the more difficult it will be to maintain macroeconomic equilibrium. The course of wisdom is to accept a slower rate of improvement in allocative efficiency in order to avoid losing control over the macroeconomy and adversely affecting investment and growth. A gradual reform of existing enterprises, avoiding whenever possible a fall in output, creates an opportunity for the economy to grow. Policy should concentrate on the incremental increase in output – on the marginal additions to capacity – and create incentives and institutions which channel incremental effort and resources into socially profitable activities. If growth is rapid, incremental output will be large, and if these large increments are allocated efficiently, the effect on the economy as a whole soon will be quantitatively important. The Chinese experience strongly suggests that a high rate of investment may bring about a more rapid improvement in efficiency than a direct attempt to restructure state enterprises within a context of slow or negative growth.

PROPERTY RELATIONS AND INDUSTRIAL REFORMS

There are over 86 000 state industrial enterprises in China. At the beginning of the reform process state enterprises accounted for nearly 79 per cent of industrial output whereas today they probably account for about half. The rapid expansion of the collective, cooperative, private and individual enterprise sectors and the relative decline of the state sector occurred not as a result of a transfer of ownership from the state to the private sector but as a consequence of the explosive growth of output within the non-state sectors themselves. Privatization of state enterprise, in other words, has played almost no role in China's transition to a market guided economy. The state sector has continued to expand at a rapid rate throughout the transition, but the non-state sector has expanded even faster and as a result a mixed economy has been created in which the weight of the non-state sector has steadily increased.

This is in marked contrast with Russia and Eastern Europe where great emphasis has been placed on transforming property relations by privatizing state industrial enterprises. A large number of schemes have been devised including the sale of state enterprises by auction, the transformation of state enterprises into joint stock companies, the distribution to the entire adult population of vouchers or 'rights' to acquire shares in a portfolio of state enterprises, the distribution of some shares to those who work in state enterprises, etc. The implicit assumption seems to be that privatization is a precondition for a successful transition to a market guided economy. The Chinese experience contradicts this assumption and suggests that the opposite may be closer to the truth: namely, that an attempt in the early stages to privatize state enterprises may slow down the transition rather than accelerate it. Why might this be so?

The state enterprise in China approximates to what sociologists call a 'total institution'. It is of course an institution that produces industrial goods. In addition, it is an instrument used by the state to implement physical output targets, a vehicle for state investment and a major source of government revenue from the taxation of profits. The state enterprises also are providers of social services. They provide pensions for their retired workers, housing for their employees, guaranteed employment for the urban work force in the absence of unemployment insurance and even child care and holiday facilities. Some state enterprises also are responsible for the operation of health and educational facilities. Services that in other countries are provided by the state, in China are provided by state enterprises. Hence privatization of state enterprises would entail not only a change in property relations but a complete overhaul of employment policy and the introduction of state financed unemployment compensation, a reform of the system for allocating housing and the creation of a housing market, and the design and implementation of a state funded pension scheme for the elderly. The health and education services also would have to be reorganized.

Many of the state enterprises are regional or national monopolies. Hence privatization would have to be accompanied by a well conceived and implemented competition policy, including a liberal import policy, in order to prevent the newly privatized firms from exercising market power and engaging in uncompetitive behaviour. In the absence of anti-monopoly measures, privatization could actually result in greater inefficiency in the allocation of resources.

Moreover, it is not obvious how the government could efficiently transfer state enterprises to the private sector when relative prices are subject to very large change. Yet this will almost always be the case during a period of transition to a market guided economy. There are two problems here, a revenue problem and a valuation problem. First, privatization would lead to a fall in government revenues from state enterprises precisely at a time when, as we have seen, it is important to maintain macroeconomic stability and contain inflationary pressures. Prior to the reforms, taxes on the profits of state enterprises accounted for about 60 per cent of government revenue.[5] The proportion is much lower today, partly because the top marginal tax rate has been reduced from 100 per cent to 55 per cent and partly because the changes in relative prices that have already occurred have increased the number of state enterprises in deficit. Given this situation it would appear to be unwise to aggravate the government's fiscal problems by transferring sources of revenue to the private sector, even if those sources are of diminishing significance. In time, of course, tax reforms can be designed and implemented which raise offsetting revenues from the private sector, but until such reforms are in place, privatization would lead to a fall in government revenue.

Privatization, furthermore, as we have seen, would generate a need for higher government expenditure. If industrial enterprises are relieved of the responsibility for providing pensions, housing, child care facilities, guaranteed employment and other social services, the state will have to step in and provide these services itself. This, inevitably, will be costly. Prudence suggests that privatization should be postponed until reforms of the social services and taxation have been completed.

Second, let us turn to the problem of valuing state enterprises prior to privatization. If state industrial enterprises are given away or sold at bargain basement prices, the government will relinquish an opportunity to obtain revenue from the sale of assets (as well as the revenue from profits taxes) and, depending on how the privatized assets are distributed among the entire population, probably will create inequalities in the distribution of wealth and income. Assuming the government wants to avoid these consequences, state enterprises should be sold at their full market value. The question then becomes how to estimate full market value. Given the distorted prices that are present during the transition period, it is virtually impossible to know which state enterprises are likely to be socially profitable at the end of the transition and which are likely to operate at a loss, and hence should be allowed to become bankrupt. In theory it might be possible to calculate shadow prices and estimate social profitability using those prices, but in practice this is likely to prove to be impracticable, given that China has over 86 000 state enterprises. The only realistic way to determine which enterprises are socially profitable is to remove all or at least the most important price distortions. This indeed is one of the main objectives of the reform process. But as long as actual prices are highly distorted and do not reflect social costs and benefits, it will be impossible to estimate accurately the true value of state enterprises. This suggests, again, that privatization should be postponed until the price reforms have been completed.

For all these reasons the Chinese have neither privatized state enterprises nor allowed loss making state enterprises to go bankrupt. The arguments for delaying privatization are even stronger in countries which have adopted a strategy of 'shock therapy' and experienced a sharp fall in output and incomes. An attempt to dispose of state assets through sale in such countries is almost certain to lead to disappointment. If buyers are restricted to citizens of the country, the sales price is likely to be depressed because of lack of purchasing power; if foreigners are allowed to bid for the assets, valuations are likely to be higher, but the most profitable state enterprises are likely to end up in foreign hands. Neither outcome is attractive unless for ideological or other reasons privatization is desired at almost any price.

The Chinese reformmongers took the view that changing property relations was less important during the transition than (i) increasing the efficiency of state enterprises by lowering costs of production, increasing the quality of output and improving the marketing and servicing of products and (ii) gradually subjecting state enterprises to market forces and heightened competition, both domestic and foreign. In 1984 a number of reforms were introduced, the effect of which was to give state enterprises greater autonomy over their production, marketing and financial affairs.[6] Managers were given freedom to produce more than the planned quota, to market above-quota output as they wished and to sell above-quota output at negotiated or free market prices. This last provision created a dual pricing system in industry to which we will return. Managers also were given more freedom to reorganize their enterprise, to acquire inputs from outside the state marketing system, to introduce bonus schemes and modify the wage structure and, after paying a profits tax which ranged from 7 to 55 per cent on the largest enterprises, to retain profits and use them as they wished.

Decision making was devolved to the managers of state enterprises, but property relations were not altered. The state enterprises continued to be responsible for providing a wide range of social services while the reformmongers began to explore ways to divest firms of these responsibilities and devise alternative ways to provide housing, social services and unemployment compensation to the urban population. Because of the incremental and gradual nature of the reform process, the reforms were inconsistent and incomplete, and numerous anomalies arose. We shall mention some of the most important ones.

First, enterprise reform, and particularly reform of the payments system, proceeded more rapidly than price reform. Managers of profitable state industrial enterprises distributed some of the profits to the workers by introducing generous bonus schemes. The profits, however, often reflected not superior technical performance or greater than average effort by the labour force but rather an arbitrarily high quota price for the firm's output. Firms with losses or low profits could not afford to offer generous bonuses to their workers even when the losses were due to irrationally low quota prices rather than the failures of management or workers. The distribution of workers' incomes across state enterprises, while remaining relatively equal, became somewhat arbitrary and served no incentive or allocative function. The solution to the problem is not to terminate the wage reforms and bonus schemes but to complete the price reform.

Second, under the reforms state enterprises were allowed to retain all their profits after payment of taxes, but those firms which operated at a loss were not allowed to go bankrupt. The state thus found itself in something approaching a no-win situation. It was fully responsible for the losses of state enterprises but was entitled to only a portion (usually about half) of the profits of state enterprises. A primary justification for this policy was a desire to avoid creating massive unemployment among those who worked in unprofitable state enterprises. Given that there was no centrally funded scheme to compensate the unemployed for the loss of employment, bankruptcies of state enterprises would have caused considerable hardship in the urban areas. Moreover, since workers in China did not freely choose their jobs but had been assigned to them by the state, it could be argued that there was an implicit contract under which the state had a continuing obligation to provide employment. Another justification for the policy was recognition that during a time of transition bankruptcy did not necessarily imply that a firm was socially unprofitable. This is especially true when the costs of providing health, education and other social services are charged to the profits of state enterprises rather than financed out of taxation. As long as prices failed to measure social costs and benefits, reported profits and losses could not be relied upon in allocating resources. Again, this is an argument for completing the price reform as expeditiously as possible, not for supporting loss-making state enterprises indefinitely.

Third, the asymmetric treatment of the profits and losses of state enterprises has created serious financial problems for the state which threaten to undermine macroeconomic stability. Decentralized management of enterprises combined with partial price liberalization has changed relative prices and greatly increased the number of state enterprises operating at a loss. Indeed at present about a third of all state industrial enterprises fail to make a profit. As a result, an increasing proportion of government expenditure has had to be used to cover the deficits of state enterprises and this has occurred at a time when the reduction in profits taxation has greatly reduced the ratio of tax revenues to national income. The losses of state enterprises have been covered in part by direct subsidies from central government and in part by government-ordered low interest loans from the banking system. Whatever the technique used – subsidies or loans – the deficits of state enterprises, partly a consequence of the reforms, have created financial difficulties for the government and hamper the continuation of the reform process.

Let us consider, finally, the dual pricing system. Dual prices were an integral part of the agricultural reforms of the late 1970s when quota prices were supplemented by free or negotiated prices for above-quota output sold on free markets or to the state, respectively. The low quota prices formed the basis for the urban food rationing system under which grain, cooking oil, and a few other products were supplied in fixed quantities at subsidized prices. During the 1980s agricultural procurement prices were raised repeatedly while the prices paid by urban households were held steady. The cost of the food rationing system thus increased continuously and this contributed to a growing government deficit. Important steps towards the resolution of the problem were taken in 1991 and 1992 when urban food prices were sharply increased to bring them closer to procurement and free market prices. At the same time the effect of higher food prices on urban living standards was tempered by a rise in money wage rates.

Dual pricing in industry began in 1984 when the government allowed the state enterprises to sell above-quota output at above-plan prices. This provided strong incentives on the margin to increase total output and to alter the composition of output in favour of goods which enjoyed strong market demand. Moreover, market prices for industrial goods could be used by planners to guide the direction of adjustment of fixed, planned prices, thereby gradually unifying the price system. There were thus good reasons to favour a dual price system during the transition to a market guided economy. On the other hand, dual prices for industrial products have resulted in a series of problems which are likely to persist until the price reform is completed.

First, the dual price system has encouraged managers to engage in arbitrage, i.e., to obtain industrial inputs from the state at planned prices and resell them in the parallel market at above-plan prices. This, in turn, has undermined the state supply and marketing systems and made it more difficult to create orderly markets. Major industries have been affected – coal, steel, petroleum – and because profits from arbitrage have not been recorded, government revenue from profits taxation has been harmed. Second, dual pricing and the associated official and parallel markets have created numerous opportunities for corruption and this, in turn, has in some cases undermined public support for continuation of the reform process and for greater reliance on the market mechanism. Finally, the dual pricing system has been highly profitable for the managers of some state enterprises and this, in turn, has encouraged widespread rent seeking activity within the state enterprise sector as a whole. The presence of a dual price system has created vested interests among managers in favour of its continuation and this, too, has weakened support for continuation of the reform process.

All of this suggests that price reform is the key to creating a market guided economy. The Chinese reformmongers were right to leave property relations unchanged and to treat privatization as a secondary issue. Space was created for the private sector and entrepreneurs took advantage of this to establish new enterprises. Most of the new enterprises are very small, but there are many of them and they have grown rapidly. As a result the private sector now rivals the state sector in industrial output. Meanwhile, the state industrial enterprises are being subjected to market disciplines. Competitive pressures have increased from three sources, the domestic private sector, joint ventures between Chinese and foreign enterprises, and liberalized imports from abroad. Relative prices have changed but a dual price structure remains in many industries and this has created anomalies. Continued movement towards a unified price structure is therefore important. About a third of the state enterprises fail to make a profit, but none the less firms are not allowed to go bankrupt. There are three reasons for this: (i) until prices come to reflect social costs one cannot be certain that a loss making enterprise is socially unprofitable; (ii) until a scheme for unemployment compensation is in place, the government, rightly, is unwilling to make large numbers of workers jobless; and (iii) until a state-funded pension scheme is created and the system for allocating housing is reformed, bankruptcies in the state enterprise sector would create massive social problems in the urban areas. The solution, again, is to push ahead with price reforms and reorganize the social services.

Only when this is done would it make sense to consider altering property relations and privatizing the large state industrial enterprises. The time to consider this is thus some years away. Moreover, it is likely that when the price reforms and reforms of the social services are completed, it will be discovered that many of the state enterprises are economically viable. China could then choose, if it wishes, to have a mixed economy with a large and efficient state enterprise sector.

INCOME DISTRIBUTION AND THE SOCIAL SAFETY NET

China under the old economic regime, in common with the other centrally planned economies, enjoyed a relatively egalitarian distribution of income and possessed a social safety net that protected the great majority of the population. Compared to other developing countries with a comparable level of income per head, the degree of equality in pre-reform China was high and the incidence of poverty was low. However the policies and institutions which were responsible for creating a relatively egalitarian society also contributed to inefficiency in the allocation of resources, to defective production incentives and to a lower rate of growth than would otherwise have been possible. The sorts of policies and institutions that had these conflicting effects include (i) guaranteed employment of peasants on communes and workers in state enterprises and severe restrictions on firing workers, (ii) lack of profit incentives in state enterprises and the so-called soft budget constraint,[7] and (iii) a payments system in state enterprises and in the collective sector which failed to reward differences in skills, effort and performance.

Some policies, moreover, not only created inefficiencies, they also accentuated inequality. In China and many other socialist countries the terms of trade were deliberately turned against agriculture, thereby discouraging agricultural production and greatly widening inequalities between rural and urban areas. Within the urban areas, the system of subsidies probably included several elements of benefit disproportionately to the well-to-do. In general, however, it appears that on balance the arbitrary controls and policies that one associates with central planning resulted in distributional equality at the expense of economic efficiency.

The process of economic reform, on the one hand, has led to a gradual correction of policies that create inefficiencies and, on the other, to the removal of policies and institutions that ensured a high degree of equality and an effective social safety net. The result has been a tendency for inequality to increase. To offset this, it will be necessary within the reform process to create alternative institutions and to devise new policies to replace those which created the inefficient egalitarianism characteristic of centrally planned regimes. If this task is neglected it is unlikely that a worsening of the distribution of income and an increase in the number of those in poverty can be avoided.

Four points are relevant here. First, the rate of growth of the economy during the transition to a market guided system is critical. If the rate of growth is high, it is far less likely that an increase in inequality will be accompanied by an increase in the proportion of the population living in poverty. In addition, rapid growth generates extra resources, some of which can be used to extend the social safety net and assist those who fail to benefit during the transition to a market guided economy. Both a reallocation of resources and a compensatory redistribution of income are greatly facilitated by rapid growth in overall output and incomes.

Second, it is important to pay attention to the distribution of assets during the transition and to equitable access to productive resources. In the Chinese case the distribution of land, the allocation of credit and the composition of expenditure on human capital have been central issues. There is always a danger that during the reform process the ownership of assets will become heavily concentrated and the market guided economy that emerges at the end of the transition will be characterized by a polarization of wealth. This can be avoided by ensuring (i) that equality of access to land is preserved if and when collective agriculture is replaced by private farming, (ii) private sector enterprises (including especially the small firms) are treated the same as state enterprises when it comes to the allocation of credit and material inputs and (iii) that price and distribution reforms are introduced in such a way that rent seeking activities are minimized and such rents as are created during the transition are not systematically appropriated by those who have power and influence.

Third, high priority should be given to reforming policies and institutions which contribute both to inefficiency and to inequality in the distribution of income. The number of such cases may be relatively small, but they are obvious candidates for attention during the early stages of reform. Examples of what we have in mind are improvements in the terms of trade for agriculture, the abolition of payments in kind to senior officials and the elimination of subsidies that benefit higher income groups.

Fourth, if an increase in poverty during the transition is to be prevented, a new social safety net will have to be created and carefully targeted on those who are most vulnerable. Under the old system many social services such as health and education were provided in large part by the collective sector, i.e., by the collective farms or communes in the rural areas and by the state enterprises in urban areas. During the transition to a market guided economy many of these services are likely to disappear, particularly if the reform process includes changes in the structure of ownership and an increase in the degree of autonomy enjoyed by managers of state enterprises. Moreover, as the composition of output changes in response to a new set of incentives, there may be a large (even if temporary) increase in the level of unemployment. Hence it will be necessary to reorganize the social services and the social safety net and change the basis of their financing, while placing responsibility on state and local government institutions for the efficient delivery of services.

The question that arises is how well did China perform under each of these headings during the early years of its transition? The country clearly deserves high marks for accelerating its rate of growth. The average annual rate of growth of per capita income has been approximately 8 per cent since the beginning of the reform process. This exceptionally rapid growth has made it possible for China to absorb an increase in inequality in the distribution of income without experiencing an increase in the incidence of poverty. There is indeed no evidence that the proportion of the population falling below the poverty line has risen except possibly in small localities or for short periods of time. The contrast with Russia and Eastern Europe is vivid. In both these regions there have been sharp reductions in the level of per capita income – growth rates actually have been negative – and it has consequently been impossible to avoid an increase in the incidence of poverty. This would have occurred even if the distribution of income had remained unchanged, whereas in fact inequality seems to have increased quite markedly.

China also appears to have done well as regards the distribution of assets and access to productive resources. After the dismantling of the commune system there was an orderly transition to an egalitarian peasant farming system. Landlessness is virtually unknown and all households within a locality have approximately equal access to land. Inequalities in the distribution of land in the country as a whole are due in large part to differences across regions (and in types of terrain) in per capita land endowments.[8]

Less is known about access to productive resources outside the agricultural sector although there are indications that credit and material inputs have been made widely available to township and village enterprises and to small entrepreneurs in both rural and urban areas. This reflects in part the policy of increasing the share of non-state enterprises by creating opportunities for entry into a range of activities rather than by privatizing existing state enterprises. Since the new private enterprises tend to be small and labour intensive while the existing state enterprises almost always are large, the policy has resulted in a relatively equal distribution of assets.

The comparison of the Chinese experience with Russia and Eastern Europe is instructive. The ex-Soviet bloc countries are committed in principle to abolishing collective ownership, but they have yet to find a way to transform their systems of collective agriculture into an egalitarian peasant farming system. Moreover in Poland, where private farming predominates, the distribution of landownership is relatively unequal. In the non-agricultural sectors, Russia and Eastern Europe have concentrated their efforts on privatizing existing state enterprises and, although success so far has been meagre, there is a danger that this policy will result in a concentration of ownership of private assets. Polarization is likely to be further accentuated because of the acute market disequilibria and greater scarcity of goods and services in Russia and Eastern Europe compared to China and consequently the higher scarcity premia or rents that can be appropriated by private entrepreneurs who acquire state-owned assets. Even without privatization, the existence of very large rents would enable those who appropriate them to create their own private enterprises and this, in turn, would lead to a concentration of wealth and income.

China has had only limited success in removing distortions which simultaneously produce inefficiency and inequality. Here an opportunity has been missed. Two major sources of income inequality in post-reform China are, first, the large gap between rural and urban incomes and, second, the high level of subsidies in the urban areas. Let us consider each of these in turn.

The per capita income of urban households in China is 2.42 times the per capita income of rural households. This income differential is much larger than one typically finds in other developing countries in Asia. Moreover, research has shown that an increase in any component of rural income, be it an agricultural or non-agricultural source of income, would reduce overall income inequality in China as measured by the Gini coefficient.[9] The only exception is rural wage income, but wages account for only 9 per cent of total income in rural areas.

The distribution of urban subsidies has a moderately disequalizing effect on the distribution of income in urban areas, but it has a hugely disequalizing effect on the distribution of income in China as a whole. Urban subsidies constitute 39 per cent of urban household incomes on average and these subsidies account for 41 per cent of the inequality observed in urban areas. In China as a whole, urban subsidies represent less than 17 per cent of total household income but they account for more than 32 per cent of overall inequality in the distribution of income.[10] A reduction in urban subsidies thus would improve the distribution of income both in China as a whole and within the urban areas. At the same time, a reduction in urban subsidies would make it possible to increase the efficiency of the labour market by making resources available to raise the average level of wages and increase wage differentials.[11]

Given the large gap between the cities and the countryside, any reasonable scheme for the reduction of inequality between the urban and rural areas will reduce overall inequality in the distribution of income for China as a whole. One of the most effective ways to reduce the rural–urban gap would be to improve agriculture's terms of trade. This indeed is what was done during the initial phase of the reform process. In 1979 there was a sharp increase in agricultural procurement prices and this resulted in a 15 per cent rise in the terms of trade of the agricultural sector.[12] The initial improvement, however, was not maintained and agriculture's terms of trade apparently began to erode in the early 1980s. We say apparently because the system of reporting prices changed in 1984 and consequently after that date it is no longer possible to measure the terms of trade on a comparable basis. While quantification of changes in agriculture's terms of trade during recent years is much more difficult, available reports suggest that purchases of agricultural products by the state have been on increasingly unfavourable terms. In some cases payments to farmers by the state have been delayed for a considerable time and this, inevitably, has damaged incentives.

There is a direct link between the two policies on which we have focused, urban subsidies and agriculture's terms of trade. Indeed they represent competing claims for public expenditure. A principal reason why state purchase prices for agricultural products were not raised in line with increases in prices of goods purchased by farmers is that higher agricultural prices would have increased the government's budget deficit. Had it been possible to reduce urban subsidies, however, the budgetary constraint would have eased and more resources would have been available to raise farm prices.

Let us turn now to the last of the four issues we have raised, namely, the provision of a social safety net. In rural China the social safety net and much of the pre-existing structure of public services disappeared when the communes were dismantled. Responsibility for the social services and for providing a safety net was transferred to the newly created organs of local government. This transfer often occurred relatively smoothly, but there is some evidence that the new network of services is less extensive and less effective than that which existed under the old communes. This is particularly true of basic health services: the number of barefoot doctors, medical workers and midwives declined sharply after the economic reforms were introduced. (See Table 7.5.) In addition, the number of hospitals, hospital beds and medical personnel in the townships declined 14 per cent, 4 per cent and 6 per cent, respectively, between 1978 and 1985.[13] Although comparable information for Russia and Eastern Europe is impossible to obtain, reports

Table 7.5 Medical workers in rural areas (million persons)

Year	Barefoot doctors	Medical workers	Midwives
1977	1.76	n.a.	n.a.
1979	1.58	n.a.	n.a.
1980	1.46	2.36	0.64
1981	1.40	2.01	0.59
1982	1.35	1.65	0.55
1983	1.28	1.39	0.54
1984	1.25	1.16	0.52

Source: Athar Hussain and Nicholas Stern, 'On the Recent Increase in Death Rates in China', Suntory-Toyota Centre for Economics and Related Disciplines, London School of Economics, Research Programme on the Chinese Economy, CP8, September 1990.

Table 7.6 Gini coefficients, death rates and infant mortality rates in China

Year	Rural Gini coefficient	Urban Gini coefficient	Crude death rate (0/00)	Infant mortality rate (per 1000 live births)
1976	—	—	7.8	44.9
1977	—	—	7.7	41.0
1978	0.32	—	7.5	37.2
1979	0.28	—	7.6	39.4
1980	0.26	0.16	7.7	41.6
1981	0.23	—	7.7	43.7
1982	0.22	—	7.9	45.9
1983	0.25	—	8.0	48.0
1984	0.27	—	8.0	50.1
1985	0.30	—	—	—
1986	0.31	—	—	—
1988	0.34	0.23	—	—

Note: — means data not available.
Sources: Gini coefficients: Azizur Rahman Khan, Keith Griffin, Carl Riskin and Zhao Renwei, 'Household Income and its Distribution in China', *China Quarterly*, December 1992. Death rates and infant mortality rates: J. Banister, *China's Changing Population* (Stanford, CA: Stanford University Press, 1987).

by well informed observers suggest that the deterioration of services there has been far greater than in China.

Further evidence of China's performance during the transition to a market guided economy is presented in Table 7.6. This table contains

Gini coefficients for the distribution of income in both rural and urban areas, the figures for crude death rates and the infant mortality rate. The period covered, with many gaps in the data, is 1976 to 1988.

In the rural areas the distribution of income actually improved during the early years of the reforms: the Gini coefficient declined from approximately 0.32 in 1978 to about 0.22 in 1982. One reason for this is that the reforms began in the relatively poorer regions and proved to be highly successful. As a result, average incomes in the economically more backward rural areas increased substantially, thereby reducing intra-rural income inequality. The reduction in inequality among regions offset a tendency for inequality to increase within each region and hence overall inequality diminished.[14] This effect ceased to operate, however, when the rural reforms were extended to the already more prosperous regions. Once that occurred, policies intended to counter what has been called 'arbitrary egalitarianism' at the local level tended to increase inequalities both at the local level and in the rural areas as a whole. As a result, the Gini coefficient began to rise steadily after 1982 and by 1988 rural inequality in China, as measured by the Gini coefficient, was comparable to that in India.

It is less easy to be certain about trends in the distribution of income in urban areas because there are only two observations. Between 1980 and 1988, however, there was a significant increase in the Gini coefficient in urban areas, suggesting that inequality in the distribution of income must have increased. None the less, the low value of the Gini coefficient in 1988 (0.23) suggests that the degree of inequality in the distribution of income in urban China still is remarkably low. Indeed urban inequality in China appears to be much lower than in all other developing countries for which evidence is available.

In China as a whole the Gini coefficient for 1988 was 0.38. This is higher than the coefficient in either the urban or rural areas. Unfortunately there are no comparable estimates for earlier years of the overall degree of inequality and hence one cannot be certain about trends during the transition period. There is, however, evidence that differences in income between rural and urban areas have widened, at least since 1985.[15] It is therefore likely that in China as a whole the Gini coefficient has increased rather rapidly, again, at least since 1985.

The data in the last two columns of Table 7.6 show that by some measures the well-being of certain groups declined even though there was no increase in poverty. Because of the deterioration of health services the infant mortality rate increased dramatically between 1978 and 1984. This is but one symptom of a general rise in age specific mortality rates. Indeed the crude death rate rose from 7.5 per thousand in 1978 to 8.0 per thousand in 1983 and 1984, and this cannot be fully explained by changes in the age distribution of the population. The rise appears to have been greater in the countryside than in the cities. Thus the available evidence suggests that China has been only moderately successful during the transition period in providing a social safety net and preventing an unacceptable increase in inequality.

The egalitarianism of the pre-reform era rested in large part on policies and institutions, the abolition of which was a precondition for increased economic efficiency. It was almost inevitable therefore that the reform process would unleash economic forces which would result in greater inequality. Attempts were made by policy makers to counteract the tendencies accentuating inequality by ensuring equality of access to productive resources (especially in agriculture) and by constructing a new safety net. Some of the distortions that combined inefficiency and inequality, however, have yet to be eliminated. More important, the social safety net that existed prior to the reforms has not been replaced by a new safety net that is equally effective. As a result, there has been some increase in inequality and some deterioration in the social services targeted on specific vulnerable groups, such as infants and young children.

The economic reforms were very successful, however, in promoting a high rate of growth and this provided a cushion of rising incomes which prevented poverty from increasing. There is no reliable time series evidence on the incidence of poverty in China although it has been suggested by some analysts that poverty did increase during certain, relatively short, time periods.[16] It is unlikely, however, that the number of persons living in poverty in the nation as a whole, or the proportion of the population below the poverty line, has increased during the 15 years since the transition to a market guided economy began. Indeed it is unlikely that poverty increased during any significant subperiod of that 15 year period. In this respect the Chinese experience differs sharply from the experience of Russia and Eastern Europe.

What, then, can Russia and Eastern Europe learn from China about managing inequality and poverty during the transition? First, it must be recognized that in shifting from a centrally planned to a market guided economy, it is highly likely that the distribution of income will become more unequal. The reason for this is that under a centrally planned regime the same policies and institutions that provide economic security and a relatively high degree of equality also are responsible for a high level of inefficiency in the allocation of resources. Hence reforms intended to encourage greater efficiency are likely at the same time to reduce economic security and the degree of equality. In order to avoid a polarization of incomes, economic reforms should be supplemented by measures designed to protect the poor and the vulnerable from a deterioration in their standard of living.

Second, it is important that during the transition the rate of growth of output and of average income per head should be high. A stagnant economy is a difficult environment in which to introduce reforms of the economic and social structure. Rapid growth acts as a cushion and prevents an increase in inequality from being translated into an increase in poverty. Rapid growth also provides additional resources which can be used to finance policies which compensate the losers during the reform process. The faster is the rate of growth, the more resources are generated which in principle can be used for compensation. And of course, to complete the circle, the faster is the rate of growth, the less is likely to be the need for compensation.

Third, the package of policies intended to compensate loses must be designed with care. The Chinese experience in this area contains both positive and negative lessons. The policy package should concentrate initially on removing policy induced distortions that result simultaneously in inefficiency and inequality. Examples include untargeted subsidies that are appropriated largely by the non-poor and price controls that reduce the earnings of the poor. The Chinese reformmongers have missed several opportunities in this general area.

When replacing old institutions with new ones that are more compatible with a market guided economy, there should be a strong emphasis on equality of access to productive resources and a wide distribution of human capital. To ensure that this occurs, reforms of the system of ownership should concentrate on creating new, small scale, competitive enterprises rather than privatizing large state enterprises. In agriculture the Chinese were particularly successful in creating a system of egalitarian peasant farming to replace collective farming under the commune system. This experience may be difficult to replicate in Russia and Eastern Europe where agriculture is far more mechanized and where there is greater scope for economies of scale, but even there it might be useful to experiment with greatly enlarged private plots on the collective and state farms. Elsewhere, e.g., in the newly independent Central Asian republics, the Chinese experience may be more directly applicable. Certainly the general approach of the Chinese to property rights and the structure of ownership deserves careful consideration.

The Chinese experience also is instructive about the difficulties of creating a new social safety net. Indeed the Chinese are just beginning to address this issue in the urban areas, and in the countryside, where the reforms began, they have not yet succeeded fully in replacing the collective institutions that in the past provided a high level of economic and social security. If the Chinese have achieved only modest success despite firm political control and exceptionally rapid growth, the likelihood of quick success in Russia and Eastern Europe must be very low. The Chinese experience suggests that if the collective economy is abolished, society is likely to lose much of its control over the economic surplus and this will severely limit the ability of the state to organize and deliver basic services and protect those who are vulnerable. In Russia and Eastern Europe, where growth rates have been negative, it is hardly surprising that it has been extremely difficult to put in place an effective social safety net.

CONCLUSIONS

The transition to a market guided economy in Russia and Eastern Europe roughly coincided with the reform of the political system: 'openness' (*glasnost*) and 'restructuring' (*perestroika*) were initiated more or less simultaneously. Political reform, however, led to a loss of political control and that, in turn, had an adverse effect on economic reform. In China economic reforms were introduced first and political reforms followed with a long lag. Indeed one might say that serious political reforms have yet to get under way. Throughout the process of economic reform the Chinese authorities have maintained firm control over political change, at the cost of denying political democracy.

Does the sequence matter? Looking back, it appears that it does. The 'Russian model' has so far been a huge failure. Countries following this model have in general achieved neither political stability nor economic success. In Russia itself there is continuous political turmoil (even a threat of national disintegration) and a rapidly deteriorating real economy (combined with a threat of hyper-inflation). The situation in Eastern Europe is less bad, but nowhere in Eastern Europe is it good. China, in contrast, has enjoyed a prospering economy albeit within a political framework that remains highly authoritarian.[17] The 'Chinese model' has some similarities with the approach adopted in an earlier stage of development in South Korea, Taiwan and Singapore. One must be careful not to push historical parallels too far, but the

Chinese experience does suggest that maintaining firm political control during a period of systemic change in the economy has enormous advantages. This is especially true if the 'style' of reform is experimental, flexible and incremental – as it was in China – so that the reformmongers receive a steady flow of information that enables them to monitor progress during the transition.

Another lesson from the Chinese experience is the importance of maintaining macroeconomic stability during the shift from central planning to reliance on the market mechanism. Rapid inflation should be avoided: it weakens the incentive effects of changes in relative prices, it leads to unpredictable and arbitrary changes in the distribution of income and, because of the resulting high uncertainty, it makes it difficult for enterprises to plan production and investment efficiently. The Chinese seem to have understood the close connections that exist between financial stability, economic growth and systemic reform.

Indeed sustained growth is central to a successful transition. Policy makers in Russia and Eastern Europe have behaved as if they believed that a successful transition would result in sustained growth. The Chinese have reversed the direction of causality: sustained growth permits a successful transition while falling output and incomes greatly hamper it. This is yet another important lesson from the Chinese experience. In fact the economic reforms in China have led to an investment boom and an acceleration in the rate of growth of output. Incomes have risen rapidly and this has made it easier to continue the reform process.

The Chinese, in effect, decided to grow out of systemic inefficiencies, whereas the Russians and Eastern Europeans have tried to reduce inefficiency by reallocating a given volume of resources within the existing production structure. The Russians, in other words, have tried to convert swords into ploughshares whereas the Chinese have used the increments from growth to channel new investment not only into ploughshares but into a wide range of consumer goods industries. The Russian approach has been unsuccessful; the Chinese approach has been very successful. The Russians today have fewer swords and ploughshares than they had five years ago, while the Chinese have more of both, particularly the latter, and much else besides.

One can also learn much from the Chinese experience about privatization and the reform of property relations. The Chinese concentrated their efforts on creating space for the private sector to expand. No overt attempt was made to reduce the absolute size of the state sector by privatizing state industrial enterprises. (The transformation of communes into a small peasant farming system is another story.) In Russia and Eastern Europe, in contrast, enormous efforts have been made to transform state enterprises into private ones, so far with little beneficial effect.

The key to creating a market guided economy is price reform. Privatization is a secondary matter and, in fact, premature privatization may slow down the transition rather than accelerate it. In the Chinese context, and probably elsewhere too, privatization would weaken macroeconomic stability by simultaneously reducing government revenues (from profits of state enterprises) and creating pressures for increased government expenditure (on social services and unemployment compensation). This would make it more difficult to sustain high levels of investment and almost certainly would cause the rate of growth to fall. In addition, privatization, if hastily implemented, almost certainly would result in greater inequality in the distribution of wealth and income.

Privatization is thus a low priority reform. It should follow price reform, tax reform, housing reform and reform of the social services. Meanwhile, Chinese experience indicates that if obstacles to private enterprise are removed, the private sector will expand spontaneously and very rapidly and the relative importance of the state sector will decline steadily. It is not necessary to destroy the state enterprise sector to create a dynamic and strong private sector.

Finally, one can learn a lot from the Chinese experience about poverty and inequality during the transition to a market guided economy. Once again, growth is critical. This is because the reforms are likely to result in an increase in inequality in the distribution of income. If growth is rapid, however, greater inequality need not be accompanied by an increase in the number of people living in poverty. Moreover, if poverty does increase, growth ensures that resources will be available to create a new social safety net or extend the existing one.

Much depends on the distribution of productive assets and on whether there is equality of access to credit. The Chinese reforms began in the countryside and care was taken when the communes were dismantled to ensure that land and other agricultural assets were widely distributed among the rural population. The transition thus began with an egalitarian distribution of private wealth in the sector where the majority of the people lived and worked. In addition, when the restraints on the growth of the private sector were removed, care was taken to ensure that private entrepreneurs had ready access to bank credit to finance investment. This enabled large numbers of very small, labour intensive enterprises to be created quickly and helped to prevent private non-farm capital from becoming heavily concentrated. Hence, although accelerated growth in China was accompanied by greater inequality, the increase in inequality was only moderate and the distribution of income in China still is relatively equal compared to other developing countries.

The Chinese also understood the need to set up a new network of social services in place of the one that began to crumble, particularly in the rural areas after the abolition of the commune system. None the less, some people did fall through the safety net. Real incomes rose and there was no significant increase in poverty, but the well-being of some declined because of a deterioration in the provision of social services. This is most evident in the case of health services: both infant mortality rates and crude death rates rose. Thus, despite an equitable distribution of assets and rapid growth of incomes, human development suffered a setback, at least in some dimensions. The Chinese experience thus underlines the necessity to create an effective social safety net to protect those who are harmed during the transition to a market guided economy.

Notes

1. The degree of centralization in China often is exaggerated. See Carl Riskin, *China's Political Economy: The Quest for Development Since 1949* (Oxford: Oxford University Press, 1987).
2. The word was first used by Albert O. Hirschman, *Journeys Toward Progress: Studies of Economic Policy-Making in Latin America* (New York: Twentieth Century Fund, 1963).
3. Some of the experiments are described in Keith Griffin (ed.), *Institutional Reform and Economic Development in the Chinese Countryside* (London: Macmillan, 1984).
4. 'Russia's Road to Ruin', *The Economist*, 6 February 1993, p. 51.
5. See Athar Hussain and Nicholas Stern, 'Economic Reforms and Public Finance in China', Suntory-Toyota International Centre for Economics and Related Disciplines, London School of Economics, Research Programme on the Chinese Economy, CP23, June 1992.
6. The early phase of the industrial reforms is analysed in Keith Griffin, *World Hunger and the World Economy* (London: Macmillan, 1987), Ch. 5.
7. The soft budget constraint in effect ensured that state enterprises could never become bankrupt and would always have a claim on resources regardless of how inefficient they might be. See János Kornai, *Economics of Shortage* (New York: North-Holland, 1980).

8. Terry McKinley and Keith Griffin, 'The Distribution of Land in Rural China', *Journal of Peasant Studies*, Vol. 21, No. 3 (October 1993).

9. The data on income distribution in China in this paragraph and those that follow refer to 1988. For details see Azizur Rahman Khan, Keith Griffin, Carl Riskin and Zhao Renwei, 'Household Income and its Distribution in China', *China Quarterly*, December 1992.

10. The contribution of a component of income to overall income inequality (as measured by the Gini coefficient) is equal to the product of the share of the component in total income and its 'concentration ratio'. The concentration ratio, in turn, is estimated from the 'concentration curve' in exactly the same way as the Gini coefficient is estimated from the Lorenz curve. The concentration curve represents the proportion of income from the given source received by the lowest x proportion of *income* recipients (not the lowest x proportion of the recipients of *income from the given source*).

11. The concentration ratio of urban wages (0.18) is so much lower than the concentration ratio of urban subsidies (0.31 for housing, 0.13 for ration coupons and 0.21 for other subsidies) that a reallocation of public expenditure from subsidies to wages would make it possible to increase wage differentials substantially without increasing inequality in the urban areas.

12. The terms of trade for agriculture that we use is the ratio of the index of farm product purchase prices to the index of rural retail prices of producer and consumer goods.

13. State Statistical Bureau, *Yearbook of Rural Social and Economic Statistics of China 1986* (Beijing, 1987).

14. This is the explanation given by the World Bank in *China: Long-term Issues and Options* (Baltimore, MD: Johns Hopkins University Press, 1985), pp. 29–30.

15. The Household Surveys carried out by the State Statistical Bureau (SSB) show that the ratio of per capita urban household income to per capita rural household income increased steadily from 1.88 in 1985 to 2.31 in 1989. See SSB, *China Statistical Yearbook 1990* (Beijing, 1991). Note that these SSB ratios of urban/rural inequality are not comparable with the 1988 estimate (2.42) cited above which is based on a different and more comprehensive system of accounting. See Khan *et al.*, 'Household Income', for evidence that the SSB estimates understate the urban/rural income differential.

16. The World Bank, for example, claims in *The World Development Report 1990* that the incidence of rural poverty increased from 10 per cent of the rural population in 1985 to 14 per cent in 1988.

17. Whether political control can be combined with democratization is an issue worth investigating. If they cannot be combined there is a possible trade-off between political democracy and successful economic reform. We merely note this possible conflict here without expressing our own preferences about the trade-off.

Appendix: Simultaneous versus Sequential Reforms during Periods of Systemic Change*

(with Azizur Rahman Khan)

We are pleased that our paper on 'The Chinese Transition to a Market-Guided Economy: The Contrast with Russia and Eastern Europe' was sufficiently interesting to stimulate a polemical comment from Laszló Csaba and we welcome the opportunity to continue the dialogue in the pages of this journal. We have seen only a very rough translation into English of Laszló Csaba's comment and it is quite possible that we have not fully understood some of the points he was trying to make. We shall therefore ignore the minutiae of his contribution – even when they are highly critical and appear to misrepresent our position – and concentrate instead on a few of the central issues where our views evidently differ from his.

It might be useful to our Hungarian readers, however, to say a word about the origin of our paper and our intellectual background. Laszló Csaba refers to the 'flood of papers in the Western literature lecturing stumbling East Europeans with Chinese examples' and claims our paper is 'a characteristic piece of this intellectual trend'. In fact the paper was not originally addressed to East Europeans, and neither was it our purpose to lecture anyone, whether stumbling or not. The paper was originally presented at a conference in San Francisco attended primarily by economists based in North America and was first published in English in *Contention*, a US journal devoted to debate on controversial issues. Our purpose in writing the paper was to challenge the view, then dominant in the United States, that the transition from central planning to a market-based economic system could best be accomplished by applying 'shock therapy' or undergoing a 'big bang', to use the popular phrases of the day. We believed then, and still believe, that there is a superior alternative and that China came closer than most countries to adopting that alternative. We were swimming against the 'flood' of professional and political opinion that favoured views similar to those of Laszló Csaba, and which regarded our views as seriously mistaken. It is a little odd therefore to be accused by him of contributing to a flood of Western literature advocating that Eastern Europe and Russia adopt the Chinese path. Ours is the Western minority opinion.

Laszló Csaba describes us as 'American analysts' and 'American authors'. That is incorrect: although we teach at an American university, one of us is British (Griffin) and the other is from Bangladesh (Khan). Both of us are development economists with experience in many parts of Asia, Africa and Latin America. Neither of us is a specialist on China, although we have conducted research there for many years, and we look at the experience of China through the lenses of a development economist. In the eyes of Laszló Csaba,

---

* First published (in Hungarian) in *Közgazdasági Szemle*, Vol. XLII (July–August 1995). This was written in response to a comment published in the same journal by the Hungarian economist, Laszló Csaba. The comment, in turn, was provoked by a shorter, Hungarian version of the essay reproduced in Chapter 7.

this seems to disqualify us from analysing the problems of transition in Russia and Eastern Europe since he regards it as highly inappropriate – indeed 'unique in the history of science' – to offer 'a less developed country. . . as an example for more developed ones'.

We do not share Csaba's Eurocentric view. On the contrary, we believe that much can be learned by studying other economies that is relevant to problems of transition in Russia and Eastern Europe. There is, for instance, an enormous literature on 'structural adjustment' in Latin America and Africa that could be of interest to those concerned with the economics of transition. There is also a literature on the effects of privatization in developing countries which could be of interest. Similarly, we suggest that the experience not only of China but also of countries such as Vietnam is relevant to problems of transition in the more developed countries undergoing systemic change. Of course historical circumstances, initial conditions, institutions and cultural characteristics differ from one country to another and should be taken into account when conducting an analysis, but it is foolish to disregard information available from other countries or to regard the countries conventionally classified as developed as special cases which have nothing to learn from countries classified under different labels.

Let us turn now to matters of greater substance.

Simultaneous versus Sequential Reform

The core of the disagreement is over the question of simultaneous versus sequential economic reforms in countries engaged in a transition from a centrally planned to a market economy. László Csaba and the theorists of 'shock therapy' and 'big bang' in the West – of whom Jeffrey Sachs is perhaps the best known – believe that reforms should be introduced instantaneously, all at once (in a 'big bang') and that this will concentrate the inevitable economic dislocations and personal hardships that accompany a process of systemic change into a short period of time ('shock therapy'). That is, it is believed that simultaneous reform of the entire economy will speed up the transition and minimize hardship, thereby raising the well-being of the population as a whole above what would be possible under any other alternative strategy. This is a reasonable position to take, but we believe that it is profoundly wrong.

Our view is that the advocates of simultaneous reform confuse the speed and scope of policy intervention with the speed of constructive economic change. An attempt to reform all aspects of the economy simultaneously is likely, we argue, (i) to produce great financial and price instability, (ii) to create severe declines in real output and incomes in the short run, (iii) to increase inequality, accentuate poverty and possibly create substantial unemployment, all of which will lower the well-being of the population during the transition period and beyond and (iv) increase the length of the period required to complete the systemic change. This last point is fundamental: rapid, simultaneous reform will result in a slow transition and in arbitrary, unpredictable and probably large changes in the distribution of income. Because of this, the transition is almost certain to be very painful, with the consequence that support for the reform process in general could be seriously eroded.

László Csaba and others of his persuasion appear to misunderstand this point. They pose the issue as a choice between rapid reform and gradualism. This is incorrect: we favour completing the transition process as quickly as possible and believe that the way to do this is by introducing reforms sequentially – concentrating on a few key issues and a few key sectors – rather than by trying to do everything at once. Simultaneous reforms will lead to a slow transition; sequential reforms will lead to a rapid transition.

Csaba may not agree with this proposition, but let us at least agree on the correct formulation of the question. The question is not whether reforms should be introduced slowly or rapidly but whether they should be introduced sequentially or simultaneously. Those of us who favour sequential reform have a professional responsibility to indicate how a disequilibrium system might be managed and what are the top priorities, i.e., what things should be done first. This we tried to do in our article, focusing on economic stabilization, reform of key prices, creating opportunities for the growth of new private sector enterprises and rebuilding a social safety net. There is no need to repeat the analysis here; instead we will reiterate one or two points where our views differ sharply from those of Laszló Csaba.

Growth and Efficiency

The switch from central planning to a market guided economy is a difficult undertaking. It requires overcoming macroeconomic imbalances, changing relative prices dramatically, altering the composition of output to reflect actual and potential comparative advantages, reallocating labour from one sector to another, restructuring enterprises and changing the composition of the stock of physical capital. None of this is easy, but we believe these tasks can be accomplished more readily if they are attempted within a context of growth rather than within a context of economic contraction. If one accepts this view, then growth as such merits high priority within a transition strategy.

Unfortunately, however, the highest priorities in most countries undertaking systemic change have been (i) privatization and (ii) simultaneous and wholesale price liberalization. Both of these may be desirable – we are not uncritical advocates of state ownership and price controls as Csaba seems to suppose – but neither can be expected to make a significant contribution in the short run to accelerating the rate of growth. Privatization is concerned with the transfer to the private sector of the ownership of the existing stock of state-owned capital. It is not concerned directly with increasing the total stock of capital or raising the rate of growth. Privatization may increase efficiency in the use of resources and raise the productivity of investment, and hence contribute indirectly to faster growth, but there can be no guarantee that it will do so. Privatization of public enterprises in Western Europe – beginning with the United Kingdom – has had a mixed record so far, and it has sometimes resulted in the creation of private monopolies which then require state regulation to prevent efficiency losses. Industrial restructuring, mergers and acquisitions in the United States similarly have had a mixed record and certainly provide no evidence that transfers of ownership – in this case within the private sector – produce rapid payoffs. And privatization in the ex-socialist countries – often a sham if not outright theft by officials and factory managers – has yet to demonstrate that it leads to faster growth.

Price liberalization, too, is not directly concerned with accelerating growth. The primary purpose of price liberalization is to improve the static allocation of resources, not to accelerate the pace of expansion. We do not wish to denigrate efficiency, and neither do we deny the crucial importance of liberalizing key prices (interest rates, the price of foreign exchange, the price of energy), but we do not believe that it is enough to change property relations and 'get prices right' to ensure that the transition will be completed successfully. Growth is essential, in part to increase efficiency.

Mindless accumulation which ignores allocative efficiency will of course lead to a waste of resources. Presumably this is what Csaba has in mind when he claims there is an inverse correlation between high investment and allocative efficiency in Russia and Eastern Europe.[1] This does not imply, however, that price liberalization in the absence of investment will result in greater efficiency. It could just as easily result in a contraction of output in the unprofitable enterprises and sectors, a rise in unemployment and a fall in living standards. That is, it could result in macroeconomic inefficiency. Changes in relative prices are signals to change the composition of output. One can change the composition of output by reducing production in unprofitable sectors or by increasing production in the profitable sectors: the former is likely to result in a recession whereas the latter requires investment, which in turn will lead to growth and higher incomes.

Csaba asks whether a society actually can choose its desired rate of growth. The answer is no, but it can choose and adopt policies which encourage growth. One such policy, which we believe is far more important than privatization of existing state enterprises, is to create opportunities for new private enterprises to emerge and expand. This entails removing prohibitions on private initiative; reducing red tape, unnecessary regulations, licences and the like; eliminating police harassment; easing barriers to entry, breaking the monopoly of state enterprises in certain sectors and encouraging competition; ensuring that private sector entrepreneurs have access on equal terms to finance capital; opening export and import markets and providing access for private sector businesses to raw materials; establishing a judicial system that can enforce contracts and provide a reliable system of commercial law. There is much that can be done and should be done that has nothing to do with privatization, whether sham or genuine, which will promote growth and simultaneously increase efficiency.

Note that all of these proposed measures are neutral as regards the branch of economic activity. Csaba seems to think that we believe countries in transition should begin their reforms in the agricultural sector. This is a misunderstanding. True, China reformed agriculture first, but we do not recommend that other countries should mechanically reproduce the Chinese sequence. Rather we suggest that one should begin where reforms are likely to make the biggest impact on raising output and employment and reducing poverty. Depending on the country concerned, it could be agriculture, but one might regard the opportunities as more promising in small service activities, or tourism, or rural industry, or small and medium size urban manufacturing, or in exporting. There is nothing special about agriculture. The objective is to pick a set of activities where rapid gains are possible and then concentrate effort on those activities, be it through institutional change, legal reforms, changes in property relations, or allocation of credit and other resources. One cannot leave the choice of sector to the market, since during the process of transition markets by definition are incomplete and do not function properly and the overall economy is in structural disequilibrium.

The Economics and Politics of Systemic Change

A rapid transition from one economic system to another therefore requires the government to play an active role. This is an inescapable fact of life. Systemic change will not occur spontaneously, and certainly not speedily in the absence of carefully constructed government policies. Our belief in a 'strong role for the government' has nothing to do, as Csaba seems to think, with our personal experiences or our education or psychological predispositions; it reflects the logic of our argument and our understanding (admittedly highly imperfect) of how one can most rapidly and humanely effect the transition to a market guided economy. Both in the title of his comment and at various points in the text, Csaba suggests that we regard democracy as incompatible with reform, that we favour authoritarian regimes and that we condone (or at least find charming) the killing of demonstrators by the state, as occurred in China in 1989. At some point a polemical argument can become scurrilous, but since we are unable to read the original Hungarian text, we must leave it to the reader to judge whether Mr Csaba has crossed that threshold.

In raising in passing the role of political stability and democracy during the transition process, we were not hiding in a footnote our political preferences or expressing a 'value judgement' but touching upon an issue that cannot be ignored by serious scholars of the development process. The issue can be posed as a question. Given that one has an authoritarian political regime and a centrally planned economy, what should one liberalize first, the economy or the polity? Alternatively, given that one has a multi-party, democratic political system, do particular problems arise in effecting a transition from a centrally planned to a market guided economy?

These are not easy questions, and our conclusions are put forward tentatively, but it does not help to advance understanding by trivializing and misrepresenting our views, as Laszló Csaba does. It is perhaps instructive to note that in all the successful advanced market economies of Western Europe, North America and Japan the sequence was first economic transformation and then political democracy. Voting rights, a *sine qua non* of democracy, were initially restricted to men of property, then extended to working men and only much later – in the twentieth century – was the female half of the population allowed to vote. The construction of capitalism in the United States, for instance, was accompanied by a sequence that included the extermination of the indigenous population, the introduction of slavery, massive importation of immigrant labour without voting privileges and the installation of formal, legal discrimination against African-Americans which denied them their civil rights until the 1960s. Historically, economic liberalization clearly preceded political liberalization whether one considers the first industrial revolution in England or the much later transformation of Japan from feudalism to capitalism.

Similarly, in the case of the four 'baby tigers' of East Asia – namely, Taiwan, South Korea, Singapore and Hong Kong – and in the other newly industrializing countries as well, the political regime typically was authoritarian, being either a single-party state or a dictatorship or, as in Hong Kong, a colonial regime. Indeed in Hong Kong there was not even the pretence of democracy for a century or more: the first small steps were not taken until a few years ago, just before the territory is scheduled to be returned to China.

The patterns of history are merely suggestive and certainly do not illustrate iron laws of political and economic transformation, but the patterns have occurred with sufficient frequency to make a disinterested observer pause before dismissing or condemning the sequence of economic and political change adopted by China. It should also be noted that since 1978, when the economic reforms began, the level of state violence in China – killings, imprisonment for political crimes and political repression – has declined as compared to the earlier period of communist rule. Moreover, China's record during the reform period does not compare unfavourably with that of the former Soviet Union and Eastern and Central Europe where, depending on the country, there has been a rise in anti-semitism, ethnic conflict, civil strife and international wars between countries that until recently were republics within the same state. Many more people have died in the former Soviet Union in the last five years than have died in China in the last sixteen. The situation in the former Yugoslavia is even more harrowing. This does not imply that suppression of opposition movements in China is 'charming', but it does put the transition process in that country in its proper perspective. Why is it that systemic change tends to be accompanied by political turbulence and political turbulence, in turn, makes systemic change difficult? This is a complex question and we do not pretend to know the answer. However, a part of the explanation, perhaps a small part, may have to do, once again, with the timing of events and the distribution of benefits and costs.

The costs of systemic change occur largely in the short term, as is obvious to everyone who is witnessing the painful transition to a market economy in the centrally planned economies. The benefits from systemic change, in contrast, occur only after a lag, sometimes after quite a long lag, but can then persist into the indefinite future. Hence the net benefit of systemic change, i.e., the difference between benefits and costs, can be negative in the early years of the transition, and if the implicit social discount rate is relatively high, cumulative negative net benefits can exist for many years. In other words, one needs a long time horizon to appreciate fully the advantages of systemic change.

A competitive political process, such as one finds in a liberal democracy, is characterized by a short time horizon. Elections occur at regular, relatively short intervals and politicians competing for the support of the electorate are under constant pressure to seek short term benefits for their constituents. Politicians ideally would like to avoid short term costs altogether, but when this is impossible, they usually try to shift the costs to those ineligible to vote or to the supporters of parties other than their own. Long term costs can be ignored by politicians, since they tend to arise after the next election and are thus beyond the relevant time horizon. A liberal political system, in other words, tends to select policies in which benefits are concentrated in the near future and costs are concentrated in the distant future. Systemic change, however, seems to require policies which concentrate the costs in the near future and distribute the benefits in the more distant future. There is thus a dissonance between economic liberalization and political liberalization, a dissonance which has been overcome in some countries by concentrating first on economic reform and only later moving towards political democracy. Those like László Csaba who favour moving simultaneously on both the economic and political fronts run the risk of encountering not only a political 'backlash', with which he begins his comment on our paper, but also an economic impasse.

Note

1. We have not made a careful analysis of the relationship between the rate of investment and the degree of allocative efficiency. It seems to us, however, that Csaba's claim of an inverse relationship between the two reflects distortions arising from systemic characteristics of a centrally planned economy. An inverse relationship in the past might have been due to the fact that the system of central planning simultaneously promoted high investment and low efficiency of resource use. Once the comparison is limited to market economies, a positive relationship appears more likely. This is suggested by the observation that without exception the countries of the most rapidly growing regions of the world economy – East and Southeast Asia – have been characterized by rates of investment as high as, or higher than, the rates of investment in the former centrally planned economies.

8 The State, Human Development and the Economics of Cocaine: The Case of Bolivia*

The state in Bolivia is weak in the sense that it has not been able to organize economic development on a sustained basis or to ensure that the benefits of development reach those most in need. The economy of Bolivia is the poorest in South America. In 1988 its per capita GNP as officially measured was $570. The average income of the next poorest country on the South American mainland, Ecuador, was 96 per cent higher than Bolivia's. In a world context Bolivia is classified as a middle income developing country but its average life expectancy at birth of 53 years would place it among the very poorest countries in the world.[1] Human development evidently has not kept pace even with the modest progress the country has experienced in expanding material production, and in recent years there has been economic and social retrogression. Indeed the country has been in a severe economic crisis for a decade and GNP per capita is lower today than it was in 1965, a quarter of a century ago.

Poverty is very widespread. The population of the country is about 6.9 million and of these about one million live in such extreme poverty that they suffer from inadequate nutrition and another 3 to 4 million people are unable to satisfy their basic needs for food, shelter, clothing, potable water, etc. Population growth, estimated to be between 2.2 and 2.7 per cent a year, has in recent years added more to poverty than to the human resources of the country.[2]

The infant mortality rate is about 108 per thousand in the nation as a whole and in the rural areas it rises to 120. It is estimated that 46.5 per cent of the children under 5 years of age suffer from undernutri-

---

* A shortened version was published in a Festschrift in honour of Rehman Sobhan: Abu Abdullah and Azizur Rahman Khan (eds), *State, Market and Development* (Dhaka: The University Press, 1996).

tion and the figure rises to 50.8 per cent in rural areas and to 62.2 per cent in the rural altiplano. Illiteracy among those older than 15 is 18.9 per cent and increases to 31.1 per cent in the rural areas; among rural women it is 43 per cent. Rural housing conditions are very poor: only 30.5 per cent of rural houses have piped water (as compared to 83.3 per cent in urban areas), only 2.9 per cent have a proper sewage disposal system (43.2 per cent in urban areas) and only 26.5 per cent are served by electricity (91.7 per cent in urban areas). Nearly 73 per cent of rural households use wood as their cooking fuel while nearly 84 per cent of urban households use gas. Primarily because of the primitive conditions in rural areas, per capita consumption of commercial energy in Bolivia, at 258 kg of oil equivalent, is well below the average of 297 kg in the 'low income countries', once again illustrating the acute poverty in which most Bolivians live.

Development in Bolivia has historically been uneven and inequitable. The urban areas have been favoured by the state while the rural areas have been ignored. Some regions, e.g., Santa Cruz today, have received much attention while others (Pando, Beni, Potosí) have been neglected. Efforts have been concentrated on the development of some sectors (mining, petroleum and gas, commercial agriculture for export) while other sectors (transport, peasant agriculture, education and health) have been starved of resources. Women have been discriminated against in favour of men. Lastly, the distribution of income has been highly concentrated, reflecting a general disregard for the well-being of the poor. Data for 1975, for instance, indicate that the richest 15 per cent of households accounted for 68 per cent of total income whereas the poorest 40 per cent of households received only 13 per cent of total income. The figures for today are unlikely to be any better and in some respects may be worse.

Present conditions in Bolivia, and the record over recent decades, make it evident that a transformation of economic policy will be required if the well-being of the great majority of people is to be improved significantly within a reasonable period of time. This in turn almost certainly will require a transformation of the state. The depth and magnitude of Bolivia's problems are such that nothing less than a fundamental reorientation of the country's development strategy will suffice.

A new strategy is needed in which the state makes broadly based human development its primary focus. That is, public policy in future should be reoriented in favour of raising the capabilities of all members of society: poor and rich, women and men, those who dwell in rural as well as in urban areas. There is a pressing need to reassess all policies in terms of their impact on human resources, i.e., in terms of their ability to create employment, increase the productivity of labour, raise levels of education, training and skill, and encourage inventive and innovative activity, capital investment and entrepreneurial initiative in all sections of the community. Only in this way is it likely that Bolivia will be able to escape the deep malaise that affects it.

The malaise would be greater than it is – indeed, as we shall see, much greater – were it not for the international boom in cocaine. The explosion of world demand for cocaine happened to coincide with the emergence of a prolonged crisis in the rest of the Bolivian economy and the incomes generated in the coca economy undoubtedly prevented economic and social conditions from being worse than they are. Coca production, processing and shipping dramatically affected the macroeconomy of Bolivia and any development strategy that pretends to reverse Bolivia's economic decline must pay careful attention to the drugs economy. Indeed the attitude of the state towards the coca economy will tell us much about the relationship between government and the poorest people in Bolivian society.

MAINTAINING MACROECONOMIC EQUILIBRIUM

The 'new economic policy' introduced in late 1985 often is blamed for the development crisis in which Bolivia finds itself. This is a mistake: the rather orthodox stabilization programme was a response to deteriorating economic conditions, not a cause of them. Indeed by 1985 the economy of the country was retrogressing at an accelerating rate. For example, during 1979–81 the growth of GDP per capita was minus 1.8 per cent per annum and during 1982–85 the deterioration accelerated further to minus 5.6 per cent per annum. Similarly, the rate of inflation in 1979 was 19.7 per cent, rising to an annual rate of 24 000 per cent by September 1985. Income per head in 1985 was down by about 25 per cent from its previous peak and, even worse, real wages fell approximately 50 per cent between 1980 and 1985.

By then the government had lost control of the economy. It was no longer able to collect taxes, because in a period of hyper-inflation even a modest postponement in paying taxes results in a sharp fall in real tax receipts. In fact taxes were only 2.3 per cent of GNP in 1984 and general government revenues were sufficient to cover only 20 per cent of consolidated government expenditure, including the huge deficits of public sector enterprises. Before the stabilization programme was introduced the public sector deficit was equivalent to a quarter of GDP as officially measured.

Incomes have continued to fall since the introduction of the 'new economic policy' and economic distress is painfully evident. Many people lost their jobs at the beginning of the stabilization programme, especially miners in state enterprises and other public sector employees; unemployment rose, depending on the estimate, to somewhere between 11.5 and 25 per cent of the labour force; self-employment in the informal sector expanded rapidly and indeed the informal economy, including the drugs sector, came to dominate employment and output in the economy as a whole. Symptomatic of disarray in the formal economy is that even as late as 1987 general government expenditure was only 14 per cent of GDP, gross investment was only 9 per cent, and gross domestic savings a derisory 2 per cent. In that same year a currency reform was implemented under which the new boliviano was introduced in exchange for 1 000 000 of the old pesos.

ALTERNATIVE DEVELOPMENT PRIORITIES

The government of a state with a strong commitment to improving the well-being of its poorest citizens would have different priorities from the actual ones. Although fundamental changes in Bolivia's development strategy are urgent, one cannot of course do everything at once: choices must be made and priorities agreed. Meanwhile it would be sensible to do nothing to disrupt the coca economy. Incomes from coca and cocaine are sustaining the rest of the Bolivian economy and preventing a catastrophic fall in the standard of living of the majority of the population. The coca economy is in effect providing the government with a little room for manoeuvre which it could use to seek ways to reverse a deeply entrenched process of material retrogression. The best way forward is no doubt subject to debate, but many informed observers would agree that the initial priorities should ideally reflect four criteria. First, they should help to initiate a resumption of long term growth. This is particularly important because of the sharp fall in average incomes experienced in recent years. Second, they should contribute directly to human development and expanding the capabilities of the entire population. Third, they should begin to address the country's most serious problems of poverty and inequality. Fourth, they should be mutually reinforcing and thus constitute a coherent programme rather than an *ad hoc* collection of isolated and unconnected projects.

Three areas of concentration meet these tests. They are (i) education and training, (ii) internal transport and (iii) employment creation. I will comment briefly in turn on each. In the next section I will turn to the vital question of policies towards the illegal economy.

Education

The educational system in Bolivia is widely recognized to be inadequate and in need of major restructuring from top to bottom. That of course is a long term task, but a start could be made by reallocating public expenditure on education so that it contributes more directly to solving the country's problems. Carefully planned and implemented expenditure on education can be expected to produce a rate of return that is at least as high as the rate of return on physical plant and equipment.[3]

The most urgent tasks are (i) to reallocate resources away from education in urban areas and in favour of rural areas, so that the great inequalities in rural education can be reduced; (ii) to shift resources from expensive university education, which favours the relatively better off, to improving the quality of primary and secondary education, which is both less expensive and favours the less well off; (iii) to concentrate improvements at the primary and secondary levels on the education of women, in order to reduce the pronounced gender bias in the educational system and (iv) to provide instruction in the rural areas, at least at the primary level, in the native tongue (Quechua and Aymara) of the pupils.

These four reforms, modest as they are, will contribute directly to human development, will help to reduce poverty and inequality and can be expected to have a high rate of return in terms of economic growth. That is, even within the present meagre spending levels, the composition of expenditure on education and training is such that a reallocation of resources within the sector could lead to higher productivity of labour as well as to a more equitable distribution income.

Internal Transport

The transportation system in Bolivia is woefully inadequate because the sector has been starved of resources for decades. As a result the country is spatially fragmented, much of the rural population is physically isolated and the development of an integrated domestic market has been inhibited. Broadly based, well integrated national development will not be possible until the internal transport system is substantially enlarged and improved.

Bolivia is a vast country of 1.1 million square km, yet it has only 37 600 km of roads. Approximately 10 000 km consists of the principal highway connecting Santa Cruz, Cochabamba and La Paz with international routes. Of this, only 1500 km are paved. Another 4000 km are passable year round; 1490 km are passable in the dry season and the rest are usually impassable. The state of the remaining 26 600 km of roads defies description.

The immediate priority is to improve the impassable roads and greatly increase the number of secondary rural roads. The intention should be to reduce the isolation of rural communities, make it easier for farmers to get their marketable surpluses to market and reduce the cost of transport to cultivators so that prices at the farm gate can rise. This implies a shift in government expenditure from air transport (which benefits the rich) to rural road building and a major effort to develop a capability to implement a widely dispersed, labour intensive construction and road maintenance programme (which would benefit the poor). How much easier it is to buy a few aircraft and hire international contractors (with foreign aid) to build an airport!

Employment Creation

Employment creation should be an integral part of any strategy that emphasizes human development. Employment creation serves three functions: it contributes to increased output, it provides an income to the otherwise unemployed and it gives dignity to those who work and a sense of useful participation in the community. In addition, employment creation in Bolivia for the foreseeable future could be a vehicle to accelerate capital formation and hence economic growth. The strategy should emphasize small scale, labour intensive projects which are locally organized and implemented while being evenly spread throughout the country. In the rural areas the strategy implies a need to strengthen locally based organizations of the poor. This, in turn, implies a state which views a well organized peasantry as an asset rather than a threat.

Projects should focus on agriculture as well as industry, and within industry the policy should be to search for opportunities to invest in rural, small scale industries such as mills, food processing facilities, brick-making and other construction materials, workshops and storage facilities. The intention should be to reduce the concentration of investment in the cities of La Paz, Santa Cruz and Cochabamba and bring the benefits of employment creation and industrialization to the countryside. The possibilities for doing so in Bolivia would appear to be quite considerable. Two examples illustrate what could be done.

First, there is great potential for mobilizing seasonally available labour in the Altiplano and valley regions for investment in small scale irrigation. The Altiplano and Valles contain 38 and 42 per cent of the country's population, respectively, and a disproportionate number of the rural poor. Small holding, *campesino* agriculture has been totally neglected; farming is based on rain-fed systems and yields are low and droughts common. Yet much could be done to repair and extend older irrigation facilities and to construct new ones. This would help to stabilize output, increase yields and in some cases permit double cropping.

Results from United Nations pilot projects in the field show that such projects are technically feasible and can be managed by a committee of local beneficiaries. Experience in Bolivia indicates clearly that labour will be forthcoming for such investment projects at zero money cost to the project. The total costs are extraordinarily low, namely, on average US $181 per hectare (excluding the value of labour supplied gratis by the beneficiary community) as compared to US $4000 per hectare on large projects. The additional income generated varied between US $500 and US $3300 per hectare, indicating very high rates of return on investment.

The return would be even higher if investment in small scale irrigation were complemented by investment in rural roads, small scale rural industry and rural education (as discussed above), and if extension services and credit were made available to small holder farmers.

The second example is the employment created by the Emergency Social Fund (*Fondo Social de Emergencia* or FSE). The background to the FSE is the collapse of real wages in the 1980s, the slow growth of urban employment (only 0.8 per cent per annum during the period 1976–86), the sharp rise in urban unemployment (especially among the miners) and the swelling of the informal sector, including the illegal drug sector, which acted in part as a sponge and absorbed many of those who were driven out of the shrinking formal sector.

Created towards the end of 1986, roughly a year after the beginning of the stabilization programme, the FSE was intended to provide short term employment during a three to four year period until such time as 'restructuring' was completed, growth resumed and new employment opportunities were generated. The FSE was thus seen as a palliative, a temporary measure providing employment on labour intensive infrastructure projects as well as, in some cases, providing free or subsidized public services (health, nutrition).

What is significant about the FSE from a long run development perspective is not that it solved the country's urban employment problems or significantly reduced poverty – it was indeed only a palliative in those respects – but that it pointed the way to government sponsored employment creation linked to investment in infrastructure and other projects. Experience with the FSE showed that employment could be created at modest cost, working largely through private contractors and NGOs, and that the projects financed by the Fund could in principle be given a strong development orientation as opposed to being merely a welfare payment.

The government could build on this experience and create a guaranteed employment scheme for those who cannot earn a livelihood at a minimum subsistence wage in other parts of the economy. The purposes of the scheme would be, first, to protect the standard of living of the very poor, to provide greater security and reduced uncertainty, while, second, promoting economic development through labour intensive capital construction programmes. Public works schemes of this type have a great advantage in that they can be designed to discriminate strongly in favour of the poor, since at the meagre wage envisaged only the poor would be interested in taking up an offer of employment. Thus public works schemes can provide good coverage of the needy but able-bodied while not extending benefits to the non-needy.

COCAINE AND THE INFORMAL SECTOR

The informal sector in Bolivia is huge and accounts for more than half of the country's output, much of it illegal. The alternate development strategy outlined above, emphasizing human development, is designed to benefit disproportionately those who obtain a livelihood in small scale agriculture or are self-employed in the legal part of the informal urban sector. As far as urban poverty and unemployment are concerned, the informal sector is the key to progress.

According to the 1976 census, 47 per cent of the urban working population is engaged in the informal economy. This includes the self-employed (who account for two-thirds of total informal employment) and family enterprises with fewer than five employees, but excludes the large numbers of domestic servants (who account for 9 per cent of the labour force). The proportion today, because of the contraction of the public formal sector (including the large mines), undoubtedly is higher and it is safe to assume that well over half of the urban population is dependent upon informal sector activities. If domestic servants also were included, the proportion probably would be over 60 per cent.

In the principal cities, over a quarter of informal sector workers in 1983 (again excluding domestic servants) were ambulatory or used mobile stands, 16.4 per cent worked from fixed stands and 58 per cent worked in establishments that hired five employees or less.[4] We thus are concerned with occupations that require little fixed capital, are highly labour intensive, provide mostly services, and are characterized by a low productivity of labour and low incomes.

The informal economy always has had strong links to illegal activities, notably smuggling, but these links have become much stronger in recent years as a result of the boom in the demand for cocaine in the United States and Europe and the consequent expansion of supply in the Andean countries of South America. Where once it may have been possible to ignore the illegal sector when formulating economic policy, this is no longer the case. The production and export of cocaine have become such an important part of Bolivia's economy that it is impossible to overlook this.

Cultivation of coca leaf for domestic consumption is of course legal in Bolivia and local use of coca as a mild narcotic goes back many centuries. What is new is the cultivation of coca as a commercial crop, and its processing into cocaine for export to the United States and Europe where demand is high and possibly still growing. This is technically illegal although until recently the authorities refrained from adopting vigorous methods to eliminate the drug trade. Today, however, it is illegal to grow coca outside certain designated 'traditional' areas and steps have been taken to eradicate coca outside the designated areas and to 'interdict' trade in coca paste and cocaine as well as trade in the raw materials used in drug processing.

Very large numbers of people are dependent on coca leaf production and processing. These include the coca leaf cultivators and their hired labour, transporters and retailers of coca leaf, truck owners and drivers, wholesalers, owners of clandestine laboratories and those who work in the labs (the so-called *pisadores*), armed guards, the owners of small aircraft and their pilots, and the businessmen engaged in shipping both the raw materials to process coca and the finished products. It is impossible to know how many people are engaged in the various activities, but a cautious estimate might be 121 000 people engaged in cultivating coca ultimately destined for illegal export[5] and between 300 000 and 390 000 persons in the coca economy as a whole,[6] including everyone from cultivators to shippers.

The production of coca leaf increased from about 9000 metric tonnes a year in 1972–74 to about 152 000 tonnes in 1987. The value of coca leaf output varies of course with international prices, but rough estimates indicate a value in 1985 of $300–$400 million a year, falling to about $238 million in 1987. This, however, is merely the tip of the iceberg.

The Size of the Illegal Coca Economy

About 16 per cent of coca leaf production is destined for traditional consumption within Bolivia while the remaining 84 per cent is processed into coca paste or increasingly into cocaine and is destined for export. This 84 per cent is illegal and it is this illegal coca economy that is the object of analysis.

The coca economy has of course expanded very rapidly since the 1960s and for much of the last 25 years has been almost the only sector that has enjoyed sustained rapid growth. The area under cultivation, output per hectare and production have all increased substantially, even dramatically. The broad contours of the coca leaf sub-sector of the illegal coca economy in 1987 were as follows:

Area planted (ha)	60 956
Yield (metric tonne, mt/ha)	2.5
Output of coca leaf (mt)	151 992
Price per mt	US$1567
Value of output	US$238.17 million
Value of output per ha	US$3907.26
Number of producers (families)	61 641
Coca ha per family	0.99
Persons employed in cultivation	120 827
Employment days per ha	216

Nearly 62 000 families were engaged in growing coca for ultimate processing and export. Most families had only one hectare of coca on average and yet that hectare produced nearly $4000 of income, almost all of which was value added (i.e., returns to land and labour). This income was much higher than the amount that could be earned from any alternative crop. The next best traditional crop probably was oranges, yet in 1987 a hectare of oranges yielded an income only 20 per cent as high as a hectare of coca. Some non-traditional crops (such as ginger and macadamia nuts) might have approximated the return to coca, but markets for non-traditional crops are poorly developed and rather thin, and the estimated comparability of returns is more hypothetical than real.

The price of coca leaf fell sharply between 1987 and 1990 and one might have expected cultivators to change their crop mix and reduce the area devoted to coca. This did happen, but only to a very modest extent, even in those areas where *campesinos* were paid $2000 for each hectare of coca voluntarily eradicated. Evidently most cultivators decided to wait and see if prices recovered rather than destroy their coca plants. Indeed, far from reducing their involvement in coca, after 1987 many *campesinos* in Beni and the Chapare responded to the fall in the price of coca leaf and the disruption of marketing channels in Colombia by up-grading their activities and processing their coca leaves into coca paste and even cocaine. The rise in the price of paste by 24 per cent between 1987 and 1989 more than offset the decline in the price of coca leaf.

Just as marijuana is the most valuable cash crop in the United States, so too the cultivation of coca leaf is today the most valuable crop in Bolivia. In 1980 coca accounted for about 1.94 per cent of the total cultivated area and 10.2 per cent of the value added in agriculture. By 1988 coca occupied 4.68 per cent of the land and (in 1987) accounted for about 28.5 per cent of agricultural output. It was by far the most important crop.

Value added in the entire coca economy, including processing of coca leaf, was US$ 1422 million in 1987. This was equivalent to 24 per cent of the country's GDP. This was much below the 44–7 per cent estimate for 1985, possibly the peak year, but still represents a very large percentage of the total income generated in Bolivia. The entire industrial sector of Bolivia, for instance, accounted for only 12.2 per cent of GDP and agriculture minus coca for 15 per cent of GDP. The coca economy, in other words, was by far the largest sector of the economy.

The gross value of exports of coca paste and cocaine in 1987 is estimated to have been US$1470 million. Exports other than coca paste and cocaine were only US$570 million. That is, exports from the coca economy were 2.58 times as large as all other exports combined, including of course exports of the major legal commodities, hydrocarbons and minerals. When, however, one decomposes exports of coca paste and cocaine into value retained by the Bolivian economy and export receipts held abroad in safe havens, the resource cost to the Bolivian economy of declaring such exports to be illegal becomes apparent.

Only US$490 million of export earnings from cocaine, coca paste and coca leaf was retained by the economy as foreign exchange available to finance imports and alleviate the foreign exchange constraint on development. The remaining US$980 million left the country and was transferred abroad where it contributed to the development of the highly industrialized, wealthy, cocaine consuming countries. That is, Bolivia was able to enjoy only one-third of the benefits of exports from the coca economy; two-thirds of the benefits were enjoyed by the countries which received the financial deposits of the drug traders.

It can be argued that the loss each year of US$980 million of foreign exchange earnings arises directly from the fact that in response to external pressure Bolivia has declared exports from the coca economy to be illegal. If such exports were legal, most if not all of the foreign exchange earnings would be available to promote the economic development of the country. This large transfer of resources from a very poor country to some of the richest financial centres in the world does not arise from market forces but from political decisions imposed on Bolivia by foreign powers.

Having said this, however, it must also be recognized that the government of Bolivia has allowed itself to become vulnerable to foreign pressure by becoming heavily dependent on foreign aid. A large portion of total investment, and virtually all public sector projects, are financed by external grants and loans. If forced to choose between foreign exchange earnings from exports of the coca economy and foreign aid, the behaviour of the government suggests that it would prefer the latter. This may reflect the fact that foreign aid accrues directly to the government and can be used to favour those who support the regime, whereas earnings in the coca economy are largely outside government control and accrue in large part to the rural poor, who often are indifferent if not hostile to whatever group happens to hold power in La Paz. Thus what to the poor may be regarded as an externally imposed burden may be regarded quite differently by those who control the state.

POLICY ALTERNATIVES

Be that as it may, Bolivia has come under increasing pressure to adopt vigorous measures to reduce and preferably eliminate the production, processing and trade in coca and cocaine. The pressure on Bolivia is not inspired by a concern for the well-being of the Bolivian people but by the self-interest of some industrialized countries, led by the United States, as perceived by their governments. That is, Bolivia is being urged to take measures to solve a problem arising in rich countries rather than to solve its own pressing problems.

If in fact Bolivia were to reduce the size of the coca economy significantly, this would lower average incomes in the country by a non-negligible amount. Given that per capita income in Bolivia has fallen dramatically, it is not obvious that Bolivia should add to her misery through self-inflicted injury. Moreover, if the coca economy were to disappear, the fall in average incomes would not be distributed uniformly. The brunt of the decline would fall on the poor. Poverty, inequality and social discontent would increase, with unpredictable political consequences. The poorest and most deprived people in South America would find their economic position deteriorating further.

A number of specific policy alternatives can be identified and I will comment on each briefly. These are (i) *laissez faire*, (ii) foreign financed replacement of the coca economy in its entirety, (iii) eradication of coca plants, (iv) interdiction, (v) crop substitution, (vi) rural development in the highlands, (vii) a combined strategy and (viii) decriminalization.

Laissez Faire

The policy pursued for many years was a version of *laissez faire*. That is, while coca processing and shipping were technically illegal, criminal prosecutions were rare and the government in effect turned a blind eye on the coca economy. In the early days this did not matter very much, but now that the coca economy accounts for 25–50 per cent of Bolivia's total income, circumstances are rather different. The coca economy is largely outside the control of government; it is a huge parallel economy to the legal economy. The question is whether it is in Bolivia's interest that it should remain so.

The gravest danger is that the parallel, illegal economy could gradually develop its own political institutions (police, armed forces, judiciary) and territorial base (no-go areas) and in effect become an anti-state within the state, possibly threatening the integrity of the formal state itself, as has happened in Colombia and Peru. Bolivia is happily far from that situation at present, and it could be argued that *laissez faire* has served the country reasonably well, but the situation could change very quickly in response to internal or external pressures.

One consequence of *laissez faire*, of economic policy makers ignoring the illegal economy, is that the government has no way of influencing the largest and most dynamic sector in the country. The national accounts are a totally misleading statement of what is produced and how much income is generated. The balance of payments accounts do not record accurately either exports or smuggled imports used to 'launder' earnings from cocaine, and neither do they present a correct picture of capital flows into and out of the country. Policy makers literally cannot know what is going on.

Turning a blind eye probably no longer is feasible. It is not possible to ignore a sector that at times is nearly as large as the legal economy; the activity is too extensive and the amounts of money involved are too large to pretend they don't exist. In geometry, parallel lines do not meet, but in a small country like Bolivia a large, illegal parallel economy is bound to touch and ultimately infect and corrupt the legal economy.

Replacing the Coca Economy

We saw earlier that value added in the illegal part of the coca economy was estimated to be $1422 million in 1987. An alternative to turning a blind eye to the coca economy would be to replace the income derived from coca leaf, coca paste and cocaine by other activities which in aggregate yield a comparable level of income.

Replacing the coca economy in its entirety would of course require massive investment. Just how much investment would be needed is uncertain, but it is reasonable to assume that the incremental capital–output ratio in Bolivia is 3.7, i.e., that it takes $370 of investment to produce an annual income of $100.[7] Given this assumption, replacement of the coca economy would require an investment programme of about $5262 million. Funds of this order of magnitude could only come from abroad, and to make it economically worthwhile for Bolivia to destroy its coca economy, the funds would have to be provided in the form of grants (not loans) and they would have to be additional to the foreign aid the country currently receives.

This sum, large as it is by Bolivian standards, is the minimum amount the country should seek from foreign aid donors. It is the minimum sum because the theoretically correct base of reference is not 1987 value added in the coca economy but the value added that would be generated if the coca economy were free to respond to unhindered market forces. This hypothetical level of income is difficult to calculate with precision, but it is obvious that if the coca economy were decriminalized and if all legal inhibitions to the cultivation, processing and sale of coca were removed by the government, output, employment, exports and income would be significantly larger than they are today. As things stand, value added in the coca economy in 1991 is almost certainly significantly larger than it was in 1987, primarily because the disruption of the Colombian market has led Bolivia to process more of its coca itself and it appears that about 40 per cent of coca leaf is now processed into cocaine before exporting. The proportion no doubt would be higher still if the trade were decriminalized.

By the standards of the United States, $5262 million is not a large sum. Spread over eight years to enable Bolivia to absorb the investment, it comes to only $658 million a year. This is much less than the retail or street price of cocaine in the consuming countries and represents a low estimate of full compensation to Bolivia for bearing part of the burden of solving the drug problems of rich countries. Having said this, however, it must be recognized that donor countries are unlikely to increase their grants by $658 million a year but will prefer instead to pursue less costly alternatives. One such alternative is eradication of illegal coca plants.

Eradication of Coca Plants

As mentioned, a law has recently been passed which makes it illegal to cultivate coca outside certain traditional coca growing regions. Bolivia is now being urged forcibly to eradicate this 'illegal' coca. This policy almost certainly will not work. Given the high international prices for coca paste and cocaine, a policy of forced eradication of farmers' coca crops will simply result in *campesinos* moving to other, more remote and inaccessible areas to grow coca. The area where coca is grown will increase, not diminish, and the problems of control will become more difficult, not less so. A policy of forced eradication will encourage coca to spread to other geographical regions, it will deepen the penetration of coca into the Bolivian economy and it will increase the hostility of a large section of the rural population to the central authorities. It is hard to imagine a more foolish policy.

The United States has attempted to implement a policy of forcible eradication of marijuana within its own borders. After years of effort the policy has yet to yield positive results. Marijuana remains a major commercial crop in California, where cultivation first began, and has now spread to other states hundreds of miles away, such as Kentucky, Tennessee, Missouri and Hawaii. With a farm-gate value of more than $13 billion a year, marijuana has become the largest commercial crop in the country. If the United States with its advanced technology, its large number of well trained officials and its vast financial resources is unable to eradicate marijuana successfully, it is totally unrealistic to imagine that Bolivia can forcibly eradicate coca. Yet the United States admits that the recent 'crackdown [on marijuana eradication] is intended primarily for foreign consumption'.[8] The cynicism is transparent.

Interdiction

Another policy being urged upon Bolivia is 'interdiction', by which is meant harassment of processors and destruction of processing facilities, cutting off the supply of inputs used in processing and interception of trade in coca leaf, coca paste and cocaine. Not only the police (the Rural Police Unit trained by American Special Forces and advised by agents of the US Drug Enforcement Administration) but also the armed forces (including the navy) have become involved. In fact the police, air force and army are allowed to keep the spoils of war – captured aircraft, boats and apparently even coca paste – and thus they have a vested interest in perpetuating a policy of interdiction indefinitely.

The weaknesses of this policy are obvious. First, there is a great danger that it will lead to the militarization of the rural economy. The use of the armed forces and the police inevitably will provoke violence and loss of life. Second, the policy will result in corruption within the lower ranks of the armed forces and police (and possibly the higher ranks as well) and undermine their effectiveness. Collaboration with drug traffickers will increase; the commercial activities of the traffickers will not decrease.

In any case, third, even under the best of circumstances a strategy of interdiction will fail because most of the coca paste laboratories are in remote regions of the country and can readily be moved to other sites or, if destroyed, rebuilt. The capital cost of the facilities is very low. Similarly, the numerous airstrips (over 700 are known to exist) and their location in remote regions make it difficult to intercept traffic in coca paste and cocaine.

Fourth, many of the transporters and processors of coca leaf are poor people. The claim that 'interdiction' can be targeted on the large operators is not credible. Most of the victims of interdiction will be *campesinos*, i.e., small growers, small transporters, workers in paste making facilities and small processors. Finally, even if interdiction could be limited to the larger operators, *campesinos* are not fools: the poor would recognize that their market is being destroyed by the government and that their livelihood is being undermined. There is a danger that many *campesinos* will come to identify their interests with those of the large operators. In that direction lie Peru and Colombia.

Substitution of Alternative Crops for the Cultivation of Coca

A more positive policy would be to create incentives to cultivators of coca leaf to switch to alternative crops. Indeed many attempts have been made to introduce new crops in the coca producing areas of the Chapare and other sub-tropical regions in an attempt to induce small cultivators to abandon coca and adopt alternative cropping patterns. In an effort to find an economically viable alternative to coca, over a hundred crops have been tried, including citrus, pineapple, papaya, watermelon, ginger, black pepper, rubber trees, coconut palms, macadamia nuts and flowers. All such attempts have failed so far and future attempts, too, almost certainly are doomed to failure so long as demand for cocaine in the consuming countries and international prices remain high. Given the present international price structure for coca and competing crops, there is little economic incentive for *campesinos* to alter the composition of their farm output. This does not imply that continued research is of no value, for surely some day the world price of cocaine will fall, and when that time comes it will be important to know what is the next best alternative.[9] But for the moment it is not realistic to assume that crop substitution represents a viable policy for reducing the supply of coca.

Moreover, even if the supply of coca leaf were to be reduced, total farm income from the cultivation of coca almost certainly would rise. Since the farm price of coca leaf is only a small fraction of the retail street price of cocaine in the consuming countries, the successful introduction of alternative crops in the coca producing regions would be offset by an offer of higher farm prices by coca wholesalers, processors and traffickers. That is, the demand for coca leaf over the relevant range probably is inelastic and hence any reduction in the quantity supplied would lead to a more than proportionate increase in price. This in turn implies that a policy of crop substitution, if successful in physical terms, would actually increase total revenue from the cultivation of coca. Up to a point, the less coca leaf is produced in Bolivia, the more income Bolivia earns from the coca sector.

Finally, there is evidence that unless aid projects are handled carefully, programmes intended to encourage *campesinos* to reduce the cultivation of coca will actually stimulate it. If eligibility to partici-

pate in crop substitution and other alternative development programmes
in the coca zones depends upon *campesinos* being able to demonstrate
that they grow coca, then *campesinos* not at present cultivating coca
will have an incentive to begin doing so. If only coca cultivators are
eligible for aid, then everyone will become a coca cultivator. Foreign
aid will have precisely the opposite effect to that which is intended.

Rural Development in the Highlands

A far more sensible policy would be to channel substantially greater
efforts towards rural development in the altiplano. The largest concentration of poverty is of course in the highlands; it is from the highlands that the migrant coca farmers come; and the fundamental source
of the supply side problem of coca is in the highlands. In fact 62 per
cent of the coca farmers in the Chapare were landless or near-landless
peasants in the altiplano before they migrated to the coca producing
zones.[10] If one wants to get at the root of coca production in Bolivia,
one will have to concentrate on improving living standards in the altiplano. This will not be easy, it cannot be done quickly, and it will not
be cheap.

Coca production will continue to increase rapidly as long as there is
an attractive and reasonably stable market and as long as there are no
attractive alternative income earning opportunities, be they in agriculture or in non-agricultural activities. What is required is general development targeted on the poor: the provision of rural roads, electricity,
water supplies and sanitation; the improvement of animal husbandry
and crop varieties; the creation of employment opportunities; the provision of rural health clinics and of improved primary and secondary
education. A properly conceived strategy of human development should
be an integral part of an anti-drugs programme. There is a happy coincidence between what is needed in the long run to solve the coca
production problem and what should be the general development priorities of the country. A government concerned with the well-being of
the impoverished majority should build on this in formulating its strategy for the coca sector and not allow itself to become distracted by
external pressures seeking quick and facile solutions.

The Illusion of a Balanced Strategy

It is tempting to argue that a balanced coca policy should include both
disincentives and incentives, both sticks and carrots, both eradication

and interdiction, on the one hand, and crop substitution plus rural development, on the other. The temptation should be resisted.

Coercion and persuasion cannot be combined effectively. Coca cultivators typically have mixed farms in which only part of the land is
devoted to coca and the rest to other crops. If a *campesino*'s coca
plants are destroyed by the state, he is unlikely to believe claims that
the state is genuinely interested in promoting his non-coca activities.
Moreover, what is true of an individual *campesino* and his family is
equally true of *campesinos* as a class. If the state uses force against
the rural population, it cannot expect to enjoy their cooperation in a
development effort. The harvest of forced eradication and interdiction
will be hostility. If the police and armed forces threaten the security of
campesinos, the conditions necessary for long term investment and growth
will be destroyed. If suppression is chosen, a government's development strategy will be stillborn and the hopes of the poor for a better
life will lie in ruins.

Decriminalization

The final policy alternative is to decriminalize the cocaine sector, to
treat it in exactly the same way that other countries, including the
United States and other developed countries, treat the production and
export of tobacco products and alcoholic beverages, or lethal weapons
for that matter. Coca farmers could be registered and production controls gradually introduced; output and sales could be systematically
recorded; land area or production or exports could be taxed in order to
support the general development of the economy, even if initially taxation
would have to be at low rates so as not to drive the activity underground again. Such an approach would have the advantage of bringing
the largest sector back into the formal economy where the authorities
could begin to measure, control and tax it. Profits generated in the
drugs sector could then be used to finance the development of Bolivia
rather than the expansion of other countries. The producers of coca
leaf (mostly small and impoverished farmers) and the processors and
shippers (some of whom are wealthy businessmen) would cease to be
criminals in their own country, and a threat to society at large, and the
burden of responding to the drug problem would fall on the importing
countries (where the demand originates) and within those countries,
on those who choose to consume narcotic substances. This, surely, is
where the burden should fall.

It could be asked whether the state could in fact control the coca economy effectively if coca production, processing and trade were decriminalized. Would 'government failure' rather than economic expansion be the outcome of decriminalization? While the former is possible, it seems too pessimistic a view. It is indeed existing policies which are best described in the phrase 'government and administrative failure'. At the micro level, agents of the government prey upon those working in the coca economy, extorting bribes and payoffs and weakening the moral authority of the state through the corruption that always accompanies illegal activities. Government agents as often as not act as much in their self-interest as in the general interest. Moreover, at the macroeconomic level there has been massive 'government failure': policies have neither succeeded in suppressing the coca economy nor in harnessing the value added generated in the sector for capital accumulation and growth. What is needed is less interference by government in the coca economy plus a change in policy instruments used to regulate it. The former would occur automatically after decriminalization; the latter implies a shift from reliance on the military, the police and the judiciary to the use of tax policy, credit allocations and public sector investment policies. Such changes could bring considerable benefits to the people of Bolivia.

None the less, it is prudent to consider the reaction of the rest of the world to a policy of decriminalization in Bolivia. The fear, of course, is that aid donors and trading partners would retaliate and in consequence the costs to Bolivia of foreign retaliation would exceed the benefits of decriminalization. This seems an improbable outcome, however. First, the argument assumes that most foreign governments would not only be unsympathetic to Bolivia's policy dilemma but be actively hostile to the country and would react to decriminalization by seeking to isolate Bolivia. Should such tendencies materialize, Bolivia obviously should make a major diplomatic effort to counter them by presenting its case internationally in the United Nations and elsewhere and by attempting to increase understanding abroad of its development problems and policy alternatives. Such an effort might not be fully successful, but neither is it likely to be a complete failure.

Second, assuming all donor countries immediately terminate their foreign aid programmes, Bolivia still would be a net gainer in economic terms: per capita income would rise, not fall; the availability of foreign exchange would increase, not diminish; and the incidence of rural poverty would decline. The fall in aid would be more than offset by a rise in output and incomes in the coca economy, an increase in retained value from coca exports and, almost certainly, by an improvement in investment allocation and the productivity of capital. Growth would almost certainly accelerate.

Third, if foreign governments retaliated by imposing a trade boycott, the economic blockade would surely fail. After all, exports from the coca economy already are illegal, yet they account for about three-quarters of the country's total exports. Decriminalization, even if accompanied by a foreign trade boycott, would lead to a rise in the value of total exports and an increase in foreign exchange retentions. The boycott would be equally ineffective as regards imports. Bolivia's borders with Peru, Brazil, Paraguay, Argentina and Chile are highly porous and impossible to police, as the already highly developed smuggling networks attest.

We are left then, finally, with the possibility of a military invasion, a Panama-type operation but on a much larger scale with extraordinarily severe logistical problems. Quite apart from the fact that the adventure in Panama failed to achieve its objective of reducing the flow of drugs from that country to the United States, and setting aside too the likely repetition of failure were a similar attempt made in Bolivia, it is most improbable that Bolivia's Latin American neighbours would tolerate armed intervention by the United States, let alone actively cooperate by allowing invading troops to cross their frontiers. The consequence of an attempted military invasion would not be the strangulation of the coca economy in Bolivia but the eruption of a major international crisis throughout the western hemisphere. Retaliation against decriminalization, if it were more than a gesture, would be an act of supreme folly.

Were it not for the fact that the production and export of cocaine are illegal, the cultivation of coca would be an ideal vehicle for raising living standards of some of Bolivia's poorest people. Coca farming is labour intensive and thus generates considerable employment; it requires only simple tools; the plant grows well on poor soils, is not subject to pests or disease and yields four or five harvests a year, and thus ensures a steady flow of income; the plant continues to produce for about 18 years and thus the investment is long lasting; and finally, the product enjoys a high value-to-weight ratio and thus is able to overcome the high cost of transport in remote areas ill served by the country's road system.[11] Income per hectare from growing coca is estimated to be between $1500 and $4000, which of course is a multiple of the income that can be obtained from alternative crops. Moreover, the processing of coca also is suitable for poor peasants because the technology is simple and readily learned, the required equipment is cheap and the method used to produce coca paste is labour intensive. Thus decriminalization has its attractions.

Moreover, experience shows all too clearly that attempts to suppress and destroy a flourishing drugs economy are bound to fail and, more important, the attempt to eliminate the drugs economy will provoke a violent reaction from those whose interests are damaged and this reaction, in turn, can inflict a heavy cost on the rest of society. This is no idle speculation in the case of Bolivia. The coca growers already have formed two associations to defend their interests, the peasantry in general is vociferous and well organized and there is a tradition of rural insurrection and revolution.

Even if the cost to society were light, however, an attempt to suppress the drugs economy would bring the government into conflict with a large section of the peasantry, many rural school teachers involved in the trade, parts of the rural elite and even some members of the armed forces and police. There is of course no presumption that conflict should be avoided at all costs, but it would be an unfortunate paradox if the government of Bolivia which came to power in 1989, committed as it was to improving the well-being of the poor, were to find itself in conflict with the peasantry, historically the most deprived, exploited and impoverished section of the community. Confrontation between the central authority and the *campesinos* undoubtedly would raise tension in the rural areas, reignite class conflict and precipitate social unrest in a country already suffering from a weak economy. If the confrontation were seen to be supported by foreign governments, above all by the United States, strong nationalist feelings could easily be aroused, adding fuel to a domestic political backlash.

Depending on international prices of legal exports (minerals and hydrocarbons) and cocaine, the drugs sector probably accounts for somewhere between 25 and 50 per cent of the total income and output produced in the country. It is not realistic to imagine that a sector of this size can be suppressed. A vigorous attempt by the state to do so would require the militarization of the society, would be costly in both political and economic terms and in any case would surely fail, as experience elsewhere in Latin America and Asia has shown. The consequences of successful suppression would be equally horrific since it would imply a sharp increase in poverty among a large group of people who already are very poor. Suppression would also contribute further to the alienation of the peasantry from the state. A far better approach would be to decriminalize the cocaine sector and then gradually to measure, regulate and tax it, thereby transforming it into an engine of

development. A simultaneous emphasis on human development in Bolivia would in the long run go further to restrain the growth of the
drugs sector than any other alternative. The pairing of decriminalization with human development, seemingly odd bedfellows, would enable the country to combine sustained growth with equity and security.

Notes

1. Bolivia is ranked fortieth out of 130 countries, and classified as a country
   of 'médium human development' by the UNDP. This relatively high ranking,
   however, largely arises from (i) using a PPP estimate of income and giving it a one-third weight in compiling a 'human development index' (HDI).
   Life expectancy and literacy also are given one-third weights in the HDI.
   See UNDP, *Human Development Report 1990* (New York: Oxford University Press, 1990).
2. Unless otherwise noted, data in this essay are based on government statistics (both official and unofficial) made available to me at the Ministry
   of Planning and Coordination.
3. For evidence in support of this proposition, and for a more general discussion of policies in support of a strategy of human development, see
   Keith Griffin and John Knight (eds), *Human Development and the International Development Strategy for the 1990s* (London: Macmillan, 1990).
4. José Blanes Jiménez, 'Cocaine, Informality, and the Urban Economy in
   La Paz, Bolivia', in A. Portes, A. Costells and L.A. Benton (eds), *The
   Informal Economy: Studies in Advanced and Less Developed Countries*,
   (Baltimore, MD: John Hopkins University Press, 1988), Table 7.5, p. 142.
5. Government of Bolivia, *Estrategia Nacional del Desarrollo Alternativo
   1990*, Presidencia de la Republica, La Paz, Bolivia, 1990.
6. See CEDIB, 'Todo Sobre la Coca Cocaina-1', *Realidad Nacional Bolivia
   1989*, No. 16 (April 1989) and Carlos F. Toranzo Roca, 'La Otra Cara de
   la Estabilización', Revista *Cuarto Intermedio*, July 1989.
7. This is the assumption used in Government of Bolivia, *Estrategia*.
8. See the *Los Angeles Times* report of 16 May 1990.
9. The fall in the price of coca leaf reportedly has led one State Department
   official to describe the coca economy as a 'dying industry' and some observers to claim that 'in just a few years, Bolivia's part in the cocaine
   business could be reduced to a minor role'. (See the *New York Times*, 20
   May 1990.) These reports of the death of the coca economy clearly are
   premature.
10. See Kevin Healy, 'The Expanding Drug Economy and Rural Underdevel-
    opment and Unrest in Bolivia: The Boom Within the Crisis', paper pre-
    sented at Cornell University for the conference on 'Coca and its Derivatives:
    Biology, Society and Policy', 1985.
11. Healy, 'The Expanding Drug Economy'.

9 Observations on Economic Policy in Post-Revolution Nicaragua*

What is new for our revolution at the present time is the need for a 'reformist', cautious and roundabout approach to the solution of the fundamental problems of economic development.

The greatest, perhaps the only danger to the genuine revolutionary is that of exaggerated revolutionism, ignoring the limits and conditions in which revolutionary methods are appropriate and can be successfully employed.

> (V.I. Lenin, *Collected Works*, Moscow: Progress Publishers, Vol. 33, pp. 109–11, cited in Roy Medvedev, *The October Revolution*, London: Constable, 1979, p. 186)

The Sandinista revolution of 1979 transformed the polity and economy of Nicaragua. Dictatorship was replaced by a more democratic and participatory political system and the 'repressive agro-export model' of development of the previous three decades (Barraclough, 1982) was replaced by a model based on socialist principles. No one concerned with justice, equality or the alleviation of poverty should weep over the passing of the Somoza regime. The Nicaraguan version of an agro-export model of development resulted in peasants being forced off the land and an increasing proportion of the cultivated area being held by large estates. The process of polarization went so far that by 1970 it is estimated that the poorest 50 per cent of the population consumed less than 1800 calories per capita per day. Growth did indeed occur, at least between 1950 and the early 1970s, and rates of investment were in general quite high, but the growth that occurred was accompanied by impoverishment and increased inequality.

The crisis of the repressive agro-export model was precipitated not

---

* First published in the *Review of Radical Political Economics*, Vol. 20, Nos 2 and 3 (Summer and Autumn 1988).

by the impoverishment of the peasantry and an intolerable increase in inequality but by a decline of the economy into a depression in the early 1970s and a sharp fall in average incomes.[1] This produced conflicts within the propertied class and made it possible to form an alliance among disaffected groups of the property owning class, intellectuals and other members of the urban elite and a majority of the urban and rural poor. This alliance eventually was able to destroy the Somoza regime and to do so with relatively little difficulty as compared to the long and violent struggles that took place, e.g., in Algeria, Vietnam, Angola and Mozambique.

The Sandinista government that followed the revolution expropriated the properties of the Somoza group and its allies and as a result by 1980 the state owned the entire banking system, half the agroprocessing facilities, one-third of manufacturing capacity, one-fifth of the cultivated land and all of the construction, mass transport, fishing and forestry industries. In addition, foreign assets in mining and bananas were nationalized and compensation agreed with the previous owners. These changes in ownership meant that the state acquired direct responsibility for enterprises accounting for about 40 per cent of GDP (FitzGerald, 1988:19). That is, the state clearly owned and controlled the commanding heights of the economy and was well poised to launch a socialist strategy of development.

Centralized planning was introduced; multiple exchange rates were adopted; the nationalized banking system was used to guide credit to projects and sectors of high priority; foreign exchange resources were allocated centrally. Other controls were used to regulate the private sector. Thus if socialism is equated with planning and public ownership of the most important means of production, Nicaragua became a socialist country. The government, however, always said that its intention was to create a mixed economy.

Looking back on the early years of post-revolution Nicaragua, it is evident that the Sandinista government intended to use state power to achieve two major objectives. The first was to reallocate resources towards the poor, largely in the form of state provided services. There was a considerable expansion of health, education, nutrition and literacy programmes. Attempts were made to foster popular organizations (although they functioned poorly) and some effort was made to liberate women and, later, meet the specific demands of the minority Indian populations. The 'basic needs' component of economic policy certainly led to an initial improvement in the living conditions of the poor although, as we shall see, the improvement would not be sustained.

The second objective was to establish the state as the engine of growth by assuming responsibility for capital formation, and presumably for maintaining it at the relatively high levels characteristic of the earlier agro-export model of development. This objective also was achieved but only in the limited sense that state investment rose sharply while private investment collapsed. Indeed, in 1984–86 private sector investment amounted only to 3.4 per cent of GDP, clearly not enough to maintain the existing stock of private sector capital in good working order. State investment, moreover, was channelled towards projects with long gestation periods and was characterized by low efficiency (Irvin and Croes, 1988). The large textile combine at Esteli, the huge 'Victoria de Julio' sugar refinery and the deep water port on the Atlantic are examples of large, slow maturing, inefficient investment projects with negligible (and even negative) rates of return. As a result of projects such as these the contribution of state investment to growth was lower than it might have been.

Some may be tempted to argue that a collapse of private investment is, if not inevitable, certainly to be expected when a left-wing government takes power. The argument is suspect in principle since private investment – including investment by small peasant landowners, small businessmen, traders and merchants in the informal sector – depends largely on profit expectations and there is no reason to assume that left-wing governments inevitably are hostile to all forms of private property or inevitably damage profit expectations. On the contrary, an improved distribution of income and other measures introduced by a left-wing government might in some circumstances raise the rate of return in, say, that part of the private sector producing wage goods and hence might actually stimulate private savings and investment. More important in the present context, the argument was never made by the post-revolution government in Nicaragua, which always claimed that its policies were designed to build a mixed economy with a significant private sector.

The 40 per cent of GDP represented essentially by Somoza property proved to be more than the state could handle efficiently and it was foolish of the government to take on the additional responsibility for all investment in the country. Much would have been gained by being more conciliatory towards non-Somoza property owners. At the very least, state-acquired agricultural land should have been redistributed to the peasantry rather than organized into state farms, and incentives to save and invest in agriculture should not have been destroyed.

While in the event the state did assume responsibility for maintaining a high level of investment, it appeared to take no responsibility for generating the high level of savings necessary to finance that investment. This was a fatal error. Gross domestic savings fell from 18 per cent of GDP in 1965, during the expansion phase of the agro-export model, to minus 2 per cent in 1986. This is to say, in 1986 Nicaragua was dependent on foreign aid and loans to finance 100 per cent of its investment programme (equivalent to 19 per cent of its GDP) plus a portion of expenditure on private consumption and government services as well (which together accounted for 2 per cent of GDP).

It is no excuse to blame the decline of savings on unanticipated and unavoidable happenings, such as the emigration of sections of the capitalist class, capital flight, and the like. Such problems could in fact have been anticipated and at least partially avoided by the leadership: they should, for instance, have learned from the fatal errors of Allende's Chile as well as from the experience of Cuba (which at least succeeded in 'forcing' households to save and in 'suppressing' inflation, although at considerable cost in terms of a misallocation of resources). Financial mismanagement in Nicaragua was so serious that by 1984 the government deficit was about a quarter of total output. Not surprisingly, by 1985 inflation was running at 300 per cent a year, rising to 600 per cent in 1986.

The two objectives of government – increasing the volume of state supplied services and gaining control over investment – were achieved at very high cost. The terms of trade were deliberately turned against the peasantry. As a result, food supplies in the towns declined and overall food and total agricultural production per head also declined. Credit, input allocation and capital investment policies discriminated against small scale producers, be they peasant farmers or small urban establishments engaged in petty commodity production. Conversely, there was a pronounced bias in favour of large scale production, be it in the state or even in the private sector. There was also a bias against private commerce, the government preferring instead to create a state monopoly of trading in rural areas combined with state supermarkets, food rationing and factory commissaries in urban areas.

The net effect of these policies was adverse to the poor. The bureaucratic style of economic management also resulted in enormous inefficiency. Exports were penalized while imports (for use by the government) were subsidized. As a result, exports fell from 29 per cent of GDP in 1965 to less than half that share, namely 14 per cent, in 1986. Indeed, the volume of exports declined in absolute terms. Prices became so seriously distorted that at one time 'the street-price of unobtainable tractor tires was higher than the official price of a tractor' (Irvin and Croes, 1988:38).

To be fair, economic policies were modified in late 1983, largely because the war against the Contras forced a change in approach. The war of course increased the pressure of demand on resources and put the economy under even greater strain. Spending on defence and security rose from about 6 per cent of GDP in 1980 to 21 per cent in 1987 (FitzGerald, 1988:22). Had these additional resources been available to finance investment rather than armaments, domestic savings would have been a respectable 12–14 per cent of GDP rather than negative. The challenge to the regime by the Contras thus severely aggravated the economic situation, but it must be stressed that poor policies and the consequent poor performance of the economy undermined support for the government and made it much easier for the Contras and their foreign backers to challenge the revolutionary government. The war, in a sense, was partly endogenous: a political consequence of the economic policies that were pursued.

I do not seek to minimize the effects of the civil war on the economy, or to absolve the United States of responsibility for conducting a campaign of economic sabotage and financing the military adventures of the Contras. No one who lived through the era of the Vietnam War can have any illusions about the devastating consequences of external intervention on poor countries struggling for development. My point is a more limited one, and undoubtedly highly controversial: namely, that the misguided economic policies followed by the post-revolution government in Nicaragua helped to make effective and sustained opposition by the Contras possible. It is also likely, incidentally, that the opposition by the Contras accounts in part for changes in policy introduced in 1983.

The modified policies adopted in 1983 included price and credit policies less unfavourable to peasant producers, diminished emphasis on state farms (which actually declined to 13 per cent of the arable land) and greater emphasis on redistribution of land to cooperatives and individual households, and more favourable treatment of urban trading and industrial cooperatives. Thus some of the bias against small and poor producers was removed.

Considering the period as a whole from 1980 to 1986, there can be no doubt that economic performance left a great deal to be desired. General government expenditure (presumably including spending on armaments) increased 20.6 per cent a year in constant price terms. Private consumption in contrast declined 9 per cent a year or by 12.4

per cent per year per head of the population. Gross investment increased only 0.2 per cent a year, net investment almost certainly was negative and the growth of investment per capita was heavily negative.

Food production per head was 24 per cent lower in 1986 than in 1979. Real earnings per employee in manufacturing fell 9.2 per cent a year (1980–85). Output per head declined in agriculture, industry and in services, so that the aggregate rate of growth of GDP per capita during the period 1980 to 1986 was minus 3.2 per cent a year. The high promise and good intentions of the Sandinista revolution evidently remain unfulfilled.

The revolutionary government tried to do too much at once. It was too ambitious, indeed reckless. It attempted simultaneously, first of course, to fight a war; second, to take over responsibility for maintaining a high rate of investment; while third, shifting consumption in favour of state-supplied basic goods and services for the poor. The resources the state could command clearly were inadequate to achieve these three objectives simultaneously and, even with substantial foreign assistance, two of the objectives were only partially achieved. The Contras have been defeated on the ground and in the international political arena[2] and thus the first objective has been largely attained, although it is not impossible that at some point the United States will renew its military support for the Contras. Gross investment has remained quite high, but the efficiency of investment has been terribly low and hence the contribution to output has been meagre. Consumption was shifted from the private to the public sector, but the initial gains to the poor were soon eroded and thereafter living standards have fallen precipitously.

The specific economic policies adopted were in practice anti-peasant, anti-trader and anti-private, a common but unholy trinity in many socialist countries. Viewed another way, economic policies were pro-urban, pro-state and pro-large scale production. The results, sadly, were negative growth rates of production per head, a decline in exports and an acute shortage of foreign exchange, a collapse of domestic savings, soaring inflation, a precipitous fall in private household consumption and increasing hardship for all members of society, including of course the poor, the initial beneficiaries of the revolution.

No one, to be sure, would want to turn the clock back and impose again on the people of Nicaragua the repressive agro-export model of the Somoza era, but present policies, for very different reasons, are equally unsatisfactory. Nicaragua's difficulties are not an inevitable consequence of the attempt to effect a transition to socialism; they are a consequence of serious errors, committed admittedly under extraordinarily difficult circumstances. The outcome, however, could have been different as indicated by the experience of Lenin's 'new economic policy' in the Soviet Union, by the rapid economic recovery enjoyed in the immediate post-liberation period in China and by the relatively smooth transition in Algeria from a colonial to a socialist economy. Nicaragua can perhaps learn from the history of other countries that have passed through similar episodes in their national life, and also from Lenin's words of 1921, quoted at the beginning of these observations. Now that peace or something approaching peace appears to be just round the corner, the reconstruction of the country's economic policies has become an urgent task. I wish the people and their government well.

Notes

1. The depression was so severe that during the fifteen years from 1965 to 1980 the average rate of growth of GDP per head was minus 0.5 per cent a year. Output per head rose in agriculture (0.2 per cent a year) and in industry (1.1 per cent), but the decline in output in the services sector (minus 1.7 per cent a year), reflecting in part the expulsion of the peasantry from the land and migration to the cities, was so great that the average for all sectors fell. (Data are from World Bank, 1988. Unless otherwise indicated, most of the data in this paper were obtained from this source.)
2. Moreover, in July 1986, in an action brought against the United States by the government of Nicaragua, the International Court of Justice in the Hague ruled that US aid to the Contras was against international law. The ruling, predictably, was ignored by the United States.

References

Barraclough, Solon (1982), *A Preliminary Analysis of the Nicaraguan Food System* (Geneva: UNRISD).

FitzGerald, E.V.K. (1988), 'State and Economy in Nicaragua', *IDS Bulletin*, Vol. 19, No. 3 (July).

Irvin, George and Edwin Croes (1988), 'Nicaragua: The Accumulation Trap', *IDS Bulletin*, Vol. 19, No. 3 (July).

World Bank (1988), *World Development Report 1988* (New York: Oxford University Press).

Appendix: Economic Policy in Nicaragua: A Response to the Debate*

A debate on economic policy in Nicaragua is important. We need to know what went wrong not only for the sake of the long suffering people of Nicaragua but also for the sake of social transformations to come in other parts of Latin America. The experiences of the ten years of Sandinista government have much to tell us and we must try to learn from them. I therefore welcome the contributions from John Weeks,[1] Katherine Gonzalez[2] and Joseph Ricciardi.[3]

I differ with much that John Weeks says, and our differences concern many of the central issues, so my response will focus on his remarks, and I will refer only in passing to the views of Gonzalez and Ricciardi. John Weeks begins by overstating the difficulties the Sandinistas confronted after deposing Somoza and he ends by understating the serious consequences of the policies they introduced. In between he thrashes about, blaming everyone for what happened except the government that actually was in power.

Initial Conditions

John Weeks challenges my assertion that the Sandinista revolution was accomplished with relatively little difficulty and counters by noting that in Nicaragua the cost in terms of lives was approximately 10 000 people or 1 per cent of the adult population. Horrible though that is, it does not compare with the death, torture and mutilation that accompanied the revolutionary struggles in such places as Algeria, Vietnam or Mozambique. In Algeria, for instance, one million people are thought to have died during the war against the French, or 10 per cent of the Muslim population.[4] Loss of life, torture, economic dislocation and property damage were far greater than in Nicaragua. Conditions in Vietnam and Mozambique were, of course, even more horrific.

It seems churlish to quarrel over the human and material costs of the Sandinista revolution, since loss of life – be it 1 per cent or 10 per cent of the population – is not something to be added or multiplied as if people were mere objects. One can overlook Weeks' hyperbole in describing the hardships faced by the Sandinistas, but revolution is a serious business and one ought to try to get the facts straight. The purpose of my comparison of Nicaragua with other revolutions was to suggest that the initial conditions in Nicaragua were not less favourable than in other countries where revolutionary regimes have come to power. Weeks does not refute this point.

The thrust of John Weeks' paper, however, is that whatever problems existed in Nicaragua were caused by the United States and are not to be understood as a consequence of government policy or action. The Sandinistas are blameless for what happened; indeed, to suggest otherwise, he says, is to blame the victim. The full responsibility for what happened should fall on the United States. He attempts to sustain this thesis indirectly by uncovering 'three fallacies' in my analysis and then at the end throwing in a fourth fallacy for good

---

* First published in *Against the Current*, No. 26 (May/June 1990). This was written in response to three comments by John Weeks, Katherine Gonzalez and Joseph Ricciardi on the essay reproduced in Chapter 9.

measure. He argues that the Sandinista government had no control over the economy (my first fallacy), there was no possibility of developing a mixed economy (second fallacy) and in any case the government could not agree on a coherent economic strategy (third fallacy).

Control of the Economy

I argue that after the revolution the Sandinistas were left in control of the economy. The state, including the state enterprises, accounted for about 40 per cent of the country's total output, including much land (20%), manufacturing capacity (33%), the agro-processing facilities (50%) and the banking system (100%). John Weeks evidently believes that direct ownership and control by the state of 40 per cent of total output is not enough. He says, 'the Sandinistas lacked effective control over the economy because they were minority holders in the productive sectors'.[5]

Ownership of the banking system and foreign trade enterprises, according to him, gives the government 'precious little' control. Apparently what mattered in Nicaragua was the fact that in 'productive sectors' such as export crops and livestock the government owned only 18 and 10 per cent of the assets, respectively. He might have added that the government didn't own the fish in the sea either, although it does own the entire fishing industry. Weeks appears to think that the cause of the economic problems of Nicaragua is insufficient state ownership of assets and output. It is not enough to possess the commanding heights of the economy, the government must own the foothills and plains as well. If this doctrine is correct there is little hope for social transformation anywhere in Latin America for the foreseeable future. Fortunately, however, the Weeks doctrine is nonsense. Richard III may have lost his kingdom for a horse, but it is impossible to believe the Sandinista revolution was ruined because the state didn't own a majority of the cows and pigs.

Joseph Ricciardi puts his finger on the problem when he observes that the 'vicious cycle of distortions', i.e., price controls, interest rate subsidies, hugely overvalued exchange rates, etc., created a situation where 'the Sandinistas had effectively lost control over the economy'.[6] Note that Ricciardi says that the government lost control over the economy, not that they never had control.

A Workable Mixed Economy

My second fallacy, according to John Weeks, is to believe that in principle there was a mixed economy strategy that could have worked. The Sandinistas claimed their policy was to create a mixed economy. Joseph Ricciardi argues persuasively that there was in fact a mixed economy in Nicaragua, although it operated largely to the benefit of the private agro-export producers and not to the benefit of the country's workers and peasants. I argued that the government could instead have built a mixed economy around small peasant farmers and small urban traders and businessmen. John Weeks, however, will have none of this. He asserts that my analysis is wrong because the power of what was left of the old Nicaraguan elite after the destruction of the Somoza regime was so great and the hostility of the elite so implacable that a mixed economy was not viable. Presumably he believed it was all or nothing: either the elimination of the private sector in its entirety or unreconstructed *laissez faire* capitalism.

It is rather odd to argue that the Sandinista revolution was strong enough to destroy the Somoza elite but not strong enough to tame the remaining elites, and that this explains the failure of economic policy. The alternative explanation that I put forward is that the policies themselves were misconceived. They were anti-rural, anti-small scale production and anti-private; they were pro-urban, pro-large scale production and pro-state. Katherine Gonzalez brings some of these points out clearly in her contribution. She notes that government policy placed an emphasis on the 'modern' sectors of the economy, i.e. that it favoured large scale production. Indeed 'large private producers, who had opposed investing from the very beginning of the revolution, had early been offered concessions by the government'.[7] In rural areas, small and medium farmers, who supported the Sandinistas during the revolution, 'received less in the way of incentives than did the reactionary large cotton growers'.[8]

The government's attitude towards the peasantry is reflected in its land policies. Only 35 per cent of the agricultural land was to be held as individual farms; 65 per cent was to be held either as state farms (25%) or cooperatives (40%). In practice, before 1985, when the policy was changed, only 10 per cent of the land actually distributed was turned over to individual peasant farmers; 90 per cent was allocated to cooperative farms. Gonzalez makes it clear that where the population received land under the agrarian reform, they supported the government, but 'peasants without land would not support the revolution and had in fact joined the counter-revolution in small but significant numbers'.[9]

The Sandinistas alienated some of their natural allies and threw them into the arms of the Contras. It is indeed true, as Weeks says, that 'it is quite amazing the extent to which the Sandinistas accommodated large-scale private interests'.[10] It is equally amazing the extent to which the Sandinistas failed to respond to the interests of small scale private producers, be they individual peasant farmers or small urban traders and business people. That is the moral of this particular part of the story.

The Contra war was not just 'an invasion by a foreign power', as Weeks appears to believe.[11] It was much more complicated than that. In fact I believe the war was partly endogenous, sustained by the rising discontent of large sections of the population over the sharp decline in their standard of living. Weeks dismisses this argument, saying the contribution of economic mismanagement was 'minor indeed' and that the counter-revolutionaries only 'achieved limited popular support'.[12] The overwhelming defeat of the Sandinista government in the February elections shows just how much wishful thinking there was in Weeks' contention. It is now clear beyond a shadow of doubt that the majority of the people did not support the government and, when given a choice, were prepared to vote for a poorly organized, deeply divided opposition coalition.

Was there a Coherent Economic Strategy?

Weeks accuses me of believing the Sandinistas had a coherent economic strategy. This is the third fallacy in my argument. At one level it is absurd to claim the Sandinistas had a coherent strategy. Obviously it was wildly incoherent. That is why the economy is in such a mess. Such coherence as there was only emerges *ex post* when one tries to make sense of what was going on. The Sandinista strategy that I identified was very simple: to win the war, to use the state to generate high rates of investment and growth, and to increase the supply of state-provided services to the poor.

Implementation of these seemingly simple objectives, however, was poor and the result was an economic crisis of the first order. Joseph Ricciardi appears to accept much of my argument and correctly attributes the hyperinflation of 1988 to excessive government spending. He goes on to say, however, that 'much of this excess was simply beyond political control'.[13] Can this be true? Ricciardi's assertion is highly deterministic and for that reason I find it to be unpersuasive. Surely things might have been done differently. Above all the Sandinistas might not have promised more than they could deliver or attempted to do the impossible.

The neglect of savings was in my view a major mistake. Ricciardi misinterprets me when he writes that 'for Griffin, the Sandinistas' fatal error was to alienate the private sector'.[14] What I actually said was that while the state assumed 'responsibility for maintaining a high level of investment, it appeared to take no responsibility for generating the high level of savings necessary to finance that investment. This was a fatal error'.[15] In 1988 central government savings were *minus* 16.7 per cent of GDP.

The huge subsidies, negative real rates of interest and privileged foreign exchange rates offered by the state were highly damaging policies. They favoured large private capital and discriminated against small private capital; they created a fiscal crisis; they reduced both the volume and efficiency of investment and thereby lowered the rate of growth; they harmed employment and the interests of the poor in general. In short, the economic strategy was a disaster, but it was not 'beyond political control'; it was not, as Weeks claims, a conflict within the leadership that 'could not be resolved'.[16] This is rationalization after the event and an attempt at exculpation. The government was responsible for its policies and for their consequences and one should not try to pretend otherwise.

The attempt at exculpation is carried a step further by John Weeks when he denies that the Sandinistas transformed Nicaragua into a socialist country. Indeed he views my observation that the Sandinistas tried to launch a socialist strategy of development as a fourth fallacy in the analysis. There are, of course, several definitions of socialism, but many people would perhaps agree that a country that relied on central planning to allocate resources, that pursued an objective of social and economic equality and that had under public ownership a high proportion of the means of production was indeed socialist. Whatever else Nicaragua was, it certainly wasn't capitalist. And it's no good, following Ricciardi, to describe Nicaragua as a dependent capitalist country. It was essentially a socialist economy, albeit the leadership contained a large populist and romantic component. One cannot avoid the sad conclusion that an opportunity was missed and that socialism in Nicaragua failed. John Weeks is quite wrong to say that to judge the Sandinista government 'against a yardstick of socialism . . . is both unfair and ahistorical'.[17] Again I would say that socialism, like revolution, is a serious business and we should not try to sweep every failure under the carpet by claiming it wasn't really socialism but 'just a phase in national liberation'.[18]

What's a Little Hyperinflation among Friends?

One must credit Weeks with having nerve even if not good sense. He claims to be surprised that Nicaragua's economic performance 'has not been worse' and asserts that 'the "chaos" . . . is largely limited to inflation and the balance of payments'.[19] These views are so extraordinary that it is hard to know where to begin.

Let's start with inflation. Between 1980 and 1987 the average rate of inflation in Nicaragua was 86.6 per cent a year and accelerating rapidly. In 1988 hyperinflation set in and the rate of price increase soared to 11 500 per cent. At the peak of hyperinflation prices rose perhaps at an annual rate of 30 000 per cent a year and the government had no alternative but to abandon its policies and introduce in January 1989 severe and painful measures to stabilize the economy. Indeed by then the economy had largely become demonetized.

The balance of payments was equally chaotic. An authoritative report comments that Nicaragua's exchange rate policy resulted in 'one of the most impressive cases of overvaluation in the economic history of Latin America or indeed the world'.[20] The trade deficit was nearly one-third of GDP, and imports were nearly four times larger than exports.

Inflation and the balance of payments were certainly chaotic, but Weeks is wrong to claim that the chaos was 'largely limited' to these two aspects of the economy. Per capita GDP in 1988 was less than half what it had been in 1976. Average consumption per head over the same period fell more than 70 per cent. Real wages between 1981 and 1988 fell more than 90 per cent. By then, relatively few people worked for wages. The workers abandoned wage employment and fled to the informal sector in an attempt to eke out a living as best they could. Poverty and inequality increased dramatically. Contrary to Weeks, it is hard to imagine, short of a severe famine, that economic performance could have been worse. It is one thing to underline the destructive role played by the United States – the financing of the Contras, the efforts to sabotage the economy, the trade embargo and the successful attempt to buy an election victory – but it is quite another thing to claim that Nicaragua's economic problems are due entirely to external intervention. The Sandinista government made many errors in managing the economy and these errors had dreadful consequences for the people of Nicaragua. Unless we face these errors squarely, and learn from them, there is a danger they will be repeated somewhere else in the world the next time a progressive movement comes to power.

Notes

1. John Weeks, 'Observations or Fallacies?', *Against the Current*, No. 23, (November/December 1989).
2. Katherine Gonzalez, 'Nicaragua's Besieged Economy', *Against the Current*, No. 24 (January/February 1990).
3. Joseph Ricciardi, 'The Nicaraguan Mixed Economy: From Revolution to Stabilization', *Against the Current*, No. 25 (March/April 1990).
4. See Alistair Horne, *A Savage War of Peace: Algeria 1954–1962* (London:

Macmillan, 1977). I worked in Algeria in the Planning Commission in 1963–64 and saw for myself the damage caused by the war as well as the consequences for the population of widespread torture.

5. Weeks, 'Observations', p. 34.
6. Ricciardi, 'The Nigaragua's Mixed Economy', p. 41.
7. Gonzalez, 'Nicaragua's Beseiged Economy', p. 43.
8. *Ibid.*
9. *Ibid.*, p. 44.
10. Weeks, 'Observations', p. 35.
11. *Ibid.*, p. 34.
12. *Ibid.*
13. Ricciardi, 'The Nicaraguan Mixed Economy', p. 39.
14. *Ibid.*
15. Keith Griffin, 'Observations on Economic Policy', *Against the Current*, No. 23 (November/December 1989), p. 32; reprinted in Chapter 10 above.
16. Weeks, 'Observations', p. 35.
17. *Ibid.*
18. *Ibid.*
19. *Ibid.*
20. Lance Taylor, R. Aguilar, S. Vylder and J. Ocampo, *The Transition from Economic Chaos toward Sustainable Growth* (Stockholm: SIDA, May 1989), p. 39.

Part III

The Transition in Central Asia: The Case of Uzbekistan

10 Development, Culture and Social Policy in Uzbekistan

The terms 'social development' and 'economic development' are becoming obsolete. Although the 'social' has long been separated from the 'economic', recent thinking and research challenges this sharp dichotomy as conceptually flawed and as likely to lead to misconceived policy formulation. The two terms gradually are being replaced by the single term 'human development', which embraces both social and economic issues and emphasizes their interlinkages. Throughout this study, human development will be substituted for social development and development policy will be substituted for social policy.

The shift in terminology is important and it is useful to consider briefly what lies behind it. Human development is a new and distinct way of thinking about development objectives and development policies. As its name suggests, human development places emphasis on human beings, women and men, as both the object of the development effort and agent of development. Earlier thinking about development placed an emphasis on the production of commodities as the central objective, and particularly on the aggregate rate of growth of material product per capita (in the centrally planned economies) or domestic product per capita (in the market economies). Moreover, the means for attaining this central objective of the growth per capita of commodity production was the accumulation of physical capital. That is, under the old way of thinking, growth was the end; investment was the means.

Of course the ultimate objective never was the production of commodities for their own sake; the ultimate objective always was the alleviation of poverty, greater choice and an increase in well-being for the population as a whole. None the less, there was thought to be a close connection between increased output of goods and services, reduced poverty and greater human well-being, and hence a short term preoccupation with the tactics of accelerating growth was believed to lead in the long run to achievement of the strategic objective of human betterment.

231

This conventional view began to be challenged in academic circles in the 1960s when a number of analysts tried to shift the emphasis to the direct alleviation of poverty combined with measures to improve the distribution of income. The challenge to orthodoxy was extended by the International Labour Organization in the early 1970s when in a series of influential reports a case was made for making the creation of productive employment the central objective of development policy. The next step in the international arena, again led by the International Labour Organization, was to go beyond employment and focus on the satisfaction of basic human needs, i.e., nutrition, shelter, adequate clothing, basic health and education, etc. This strategy was endorsed by the international community in 1976 at the World Employment Conference held in Geneva.

Meanwhile, the World Bank in Washington at first advocated a modification of the conventional view whereby growth would be combined with a marginal redistribution of income, and for a while 'redistribution from growth', as the strategy was called, represented the consensus view. The consensus, however, was quickly overtaken in the late 1970s by the basic needs approach and for a brief period the World Bank became an active supporter.

FROM BASIC NEEDS TO HUMAN DEVELOPMENT

Current thinking has moved beyond basic needs to human development. Academics had for some time been advocating a change in perspective, but it was not until the economic crisis of the 1980s that these new ideas began to be accepted by the international community as a whole. An early sign of things to come was the publication by UNICEF of an influential report on *Adjustment with a Human Face*.[1] The volume was concerned not with the economic adjustments now facing the former centrally planned economies but rather adjustments facing developing market economy countries, particularly the highly indebted economies in Latin America and sub-Saharan Africa. Even so, the analysis contained in the volume is relevant to Uzbekistan today.

The UNICEF study was followed in 1988 by the report of the United Nations Committee for Development Planning, in which human development was advocated not as a short term remedy for coping with the debt crisis and the need to change the composition of output in response to external shocks, but as the foundation for long run advances in human well-being. A decisive step was taken the next year, in 1989, when human development became the keystone in the United Nations International Development Strategy for the 1990s. The following year (1990) the UNDP, in a radical departure from its previous policy, made human development the organizing theme of its work and published the first of the annual *Human Development Reports*. The sixth report will be published in August 1995 just before the Women's Conference in Beijing. In addition, 21 countries are in various stages of preparing national human development reports, including of course Uzbekistan. Finally, at the Social Summit in Copenhagen in March 1995 a range of human development issues was discussed at the global level under the headings of poverty, employment and social integration.

HUMAN DEVELOPMENT AS AN OBJECTIVE

Human development is both a means and an end in itself. Let us begin by considering human development as an objective. Human development represents a shift from a commodity-centred strategy of development to a people-centred strategy. The objective of human development is to fulfil the potential of people by enlarging their capabilities and this necessarily implies empowerment of people, enabling them to participate actively in their own development.

Amartya Sen, the distinguished Indian economist, has argued persuasively that our objective should be to increase the capabilities of people to lead full, productive, satisfying lives. A larger volume of output per head may of course increase the capabilities of people, but increased output should be seen for what it is, namely, an intermediate product that under appropriate circumstances can enhance human well-being. Our ultimate concern is not output as such but the ability of people to lead a long life, to enjoy good health, to have access to the world's stock of knowledge and information, to participate in the cultural life of their community, to have sufficient income to buy food, clothing and shelter, to participate in the decisions that directly affect their lives and their community, and so on. These are the things that matter – increasing the capabilities of people – and the enhancement of capabilities, not the enlargement of domestic (or material) product, should be the objective of development policy.

This sharp focusing of the objective on capabilities is the great contribution of Amartya Sen to the human development strategy.[2] This change of focus from a commodity-centred to a people-centred view of development has enormous implications for how we perceive development and how governments should think about policies for development. The level of development in Uzbekistan, for instance, looks very different when one focuses on life expectancy, literacy and cultural achievements as compared to focusing on GDP per capita. Uzbekistan's human development, as compared to other countries, is relatively higher than its material output of goods and services. Similarly, 'social policy' seen from a human development perspective is concerned with enhancing human capabilities, be they the capabilities of the unemployed, the handicapped, the elderly or expecting mothers. That is, social policy is a central part of development policy. From a commodity-centred perspective, however, social policy is a marginal issue, being concerned largely with those who are not contributing or who cannot contribute directly to increasing material output. From this out-of-date perspective social expenditure should be kept to a minimum so that resources can be made available for 'real' development of the forces of production.

HUMAN DEVELOPMENT AS A MEANS

Just as there has been a refocusing of the objective of development, so too there has been a change of emphasis on how best to achieve development. Here the contribution of Theodore Schultz has been vital.[3]

Schultz introduced to economics the notion of human capital as a factor of production equally as important as natural capital (water, land, forests) and physical capital (plant and equipment). This simple idea proved to be enormously important and led economists to reconsider what is meant by investment, and what types of expenditure – apart from the accumulation of physical capital – might raise output and the productivity of labour and increase human well-being. There was an explosion of research concerned with estimating the costs and benefits of expenditure on human capital: expenditure on such things as primary, secondary and tertiary education; formal and informal training; nutrition programmes; primary health care; pre- and post-natal and infant care programmes; and pure and applied research.

The human development strategy builds on this research and it is this which makes the strategy distinctive. The first distinctive feature of the human development strategy is precisely the emphasis placed on human capital formation. The justification for this is that the returns on investing in people (in terms of increased material output) are in general as high as if not higher than the returns to investment in physical and natural capital. This fact had been overlooked in previous work for two reasons. First, in the past the benefits of investing in human capital were greatly underestimated, in part because most expenditure on education was thought to be 'unproductive' and in part because the positive externalities associated with education (on the propensity to innovate, on fertility, on attitudes towards risk and savings, for instance) were not understood. Second, the costs of investing in physical and natural capital were understated, in part because negative externalities (e.g., pollution of water and air and their detrimental effects on health) were ignored. The understatement of the benefits of investment in human capital lowered the estimated rate of return while the understatement of the cost of investment in physical and natural capital raised the estimated rate of return. As a result, there was a strong bias against human capital expenditure in favour of expenditures on physical and natural capital. The human development strategy corrects this bias.

Another distinctive feature of a human development strategy arises from the fact that in some cases investment in human capital can economize on the use of physical capital and the exploitation of natural resources. That is, brains sometimes can be a substitute for expensive machinery and scarce natural resources. Hence a well conceived human development strategy should be environmentally friendly and contribute to sustainable development. In Uzbekistan, for instance, if more thought had been devoted to designing efficient water management and cultivation systems, some of the money spent on irrigation, fertilizer and pesticides could have been saved and the environmental disaster of the Aral Sea could have been avoided or at least lessened.

Third, the benefits of investing in people are in general more evenly spread than the benefits from investing in physical and natural capital. This is especially true in a market economy where the ownership of financial and physical assets tends to be highly concentrated. In such a context, greater emphasis on human capital formation should result in a more equal distribution of income, wealth and well-being than would otherwise be the case. In socialist countries the distribution of income tends to be relatively equal. One reason for this is that the means of production are collectively owned and hence income from physical and natural capital accrues to the state and collective institutions rather than to individuals and private corporations. But an additional reason is that in socialist countries there was traditionally a strong emphasis on expenditure on education, health, nutrition and child care programmes, i.e., on human capital, and this helped to raise the productivity of labour and incomes across the entire population.

A fourth distinctive feature of a human development strategy is the importance placed on complementarities among the various types of human capital expenditure. For example, there are complementarities among primary health care, the efficiency with which the body transforms calories into improved nutrition, the ability of children to learn and attendance at school. Similarly, there are complementarities among expenditures on improving the health of women, the amount of education women receive, their fertility and their life expectancy. Thus when it comes to human capital formation, the whole is greater than the sum of its parts.

COMPONENTS OF A STRATEGY

A strategy for human development or, if one prefers, social development can be divided into three components:

(a) the structure of incentives;
(b) the composition of public expenditure;
(c) structural reforms.

We shall have quite a lot to say about each of these components in the chapters that follow, but a few general points are perhaps worth making here.

The Structure of Incentives

The structure of incentives refers not only to the set of relative prices that prevails in a market economy but also to the degree to which people have access to markets, the existence of barriers to entry (and exit) and the extent and nature of discrimination. In many countries, including countries in transition to a market economy, the structure of incentives in this broad sense is in conflict with the objectives of human development. There is much more to creating a market economy than price liberalization.

The human development approach is much concerned with creating markets where they do not exist (e.g., in creating a properly functioning credit market in Uzbekistan), with stimulating competition and regulating monopolies where competition is weak or non-existent (e.g., when privatization of state owned enterprises results in the creation of private monopolies) and with correcting market failures, particularly failures in factor markets. As we have seen, if left to its own devices, the signals generated by an unrestricted market system would lead to persistent underinvestment in the stock of human capital.

Labour markets often are far from efficient. They are fragmented, segmented into non-competing groups and permeated with discriminatory elements, particularly against women. There is thus a strong case in general for governments to become actively involved in improving the functioning of labour markets. This is especially true in countries going through a transition to a market-oriented economy where labour previously was allocated through a planning mechanism and a labour market as such hardly existed.

The same point is true of financial and capital markets, and of the market for land and other forms of natural capital. And again, this is especially true in transitional economies where such markets did not exist or were very underdeveloped. Even in fully developed market economies, however, market failures often arise. Environmental externalities are an obvious example since negative externalities of many sorts have now become a major policy concern worldwide. A decision to place greater reliance on the market mechanism, in other words, does not imply a policy of *laissez faire*; on the contrary, a human development strategy may well require considerable intervention by government. The policy issues are when to intervene and how best to do so.

The policy issues, and the public action that follows from policy, extend beyond the logic of markets and the possibility of market failure. As Drèze and Sen rightly say, 'Incentives are, in fact, central to the logic of public action.' And they go on to elaborate:

> But the incentives that must be considered are not only those that offer profits in the market, but also those that motivate governments to implement well-planned public policies, induce families to reject intra-household discrimination, encourage political parties and the news media to make reasonable demands, and inspire the public at large to co-operate, criticize and co-ordinate.[4]

The Composition of Government Expenditure

Implementing a human development strategy does not necessarily imply a smaller state, but it almost always does imply a change in the composition of government spending. In the specific case of Uzbekistan, the strategy we advocate does require some shrinkage in the range of state activities and the creation of space in which a dynamic private sector can emerge. Equally important, however, is the pattern of public expenditure and the efficiency of delivery of services. Three general principles can be enumerated.

First, the percentage of the state budget earmarked for activities which do not contribute to human development should be reduced to a minimum. This includes spending on the military and internal security, subsidies for some state enterprises, provision of scarce inputs such as water at prices which do not cover costs, excessively large bureaucracies and cumbersome administrative procedures and formalities, etc.

Second, within the broad category of human development spending, there should be a reallocation towards those activities which benefit the largest number of people. This includes policies to redress imbalances between rural and urban areas, shifts in the composition of educational expenditure to favour primary and secondary education relative to tertiary education, reallocation of health expenditure to favour the training of nurses rather than doctors, and so on. There are a large number of areas where substantial improvements in efficiency and equity can be achieved merely by changing the composition of public spending within existing sectors.

Third, a human development strategy must walk a fine line between selectivity in public expenditure and the provision of universal services. The socialist system favoured universal services and non-discrimination, and the results in Uzbekistan and elsewhere have been impressive. The conventional wisdom today, in contrast, is that public expenditure should be carefully targeted on selected (and preferably not numerous) beneficiaries. This view, however, should be challenged on several grounds: targeting often is not possible; selectivity (and hence exclusion) entails high enforcement costs; and discriminatory expenditure programmes undermine national solidarity, participation and commitment. Uzbekistan would be well advised to proceed cautiously in this area.

Structural Reforms

It is widely believed that the transition from a centrally planned to a market guided economy can best be effected by (i) liberalizing all prices, (ii) reducing the size of the public sector and (iii) privatizing all state owned enterprises. Moreover, these measures, it is claimed, should be introduced simultaneously in order to complete the transition as quickly as possible. This 'big bang' or 'shock therapy' view is highly questionable, and we shall consider the arguments in some detail in the next chapter, but before doing so it is useful to say a few words here about structural change.

Improvements in incentives and changes in the composition of government spending clearly are necessary to promote human development and meet social policy objectives, but these two reforms alone will not suffice: it also will be necessary to reinforce price and spending reforms by structural reforms and institutional changes. A well functioning market economy requires more than well functioning markets, it also requires coherent macroeconomic and employment policies, an equitable distribution of productive assets, institutions which provide a minimum of economic security and a social safety net to prevent people from falling into severe poverty, and programmes to ensure adequate nutrition and food security for the entire population.

In Chapters 11 and 12 we shall discuss a number of possible structural reforms which we regard as essential for a successful transition to a more market-oriented economy. Here we single out only two such reforms which have far-reaching implications, namely, a guaranteed employment scheme (as a partial replacement of transfer payments) and a land reform (which can help to ensure prosperity and equality in rural areas). We regard these reforms as far more important than the privatization of state owned industrial enterprises and consequently believe that in the sequence of reforms, employment and land reforms should have higher priority than the reform of property rights in industry.

CULTURE AND DEVELOPMENT

It is perhaps not surprising that in a review of social policy – and more generally of human development strategy – the notion of culture should be prominent. To avoid misunderstanding, however, it is important to specify what is meant when we use the complicated word 'culture' in this context.

Culture should be seen as an overarching concept which embraces both human development and environmentally sustainable development and reconciles the claims of each. As has been explained, the notion of human development increasingly is replacing older notions of economic development and social development. This has led to a shift of focus from a commodity-centred view of development (GDP and the like) to a capabilities-centred view of development (which puts people first). Human development concentrates on the individual human being, i.e., on the single person, and regards people as simultaneously the object of development and the instruments of development. People, however, are not isolated atoms; they work together, cooperate, compete and interact in a multiplicity of ways. It is in fact culture which connects people to one another and makes development of the individual possible. Similarly, it is culture which defines how people relate to nature, the earth and the cosmos and through which we express our attitudes and beliefs towards other forms of life, both plant and animal. It is in this sense that all forms of development, including of course human development, ultimately are determined by cultural variables.

If by 'culture' one means 'ways of living', and if by 'development' one means the 'enlargement of human capabilities', then an analysis of culture and development can be conceptualized as a study of how different ways of living affect the enlargement of human capabilities.[5] A country's culture is not of course static or changeless. On the contrary, it is in a constant state of flux, influencing and being influenced by other cultures, possibly through a process of voluntary exchange and possibly as an outcome of conflict, force and suppression. A country's culture therefore reflects its history and institutions, its social movements and class struggles, and the configurations of political power, internally and in the world at large. Moreover, a country need not contain only one culture. Indeed many countries, perhaps most, and certainly an increasing number of countries are multi-cultural, multi-national, multi-ethnic and contain a multiplicity of languages, religions and 'ways of living'. Uzbekistan undoubtedly is a multi-cultural country which potentially can reap great advantage from its pluralism, and yet also runs a danger of cultural conflict. It is here that government policy is important. Governments cannot determine a people's culture but they can influence it for better or worse and in so doing affect the path of development.

The basic policy principle should be the fostering of respect for all cultures. Respect goes beyond mere tolerance and implies a positive attitude to other people and their culture. Social peace is necessary for human development to occur and social peace, in turn, requires that differences between two cultures be regarded not as something alien and unacceptable or hateful but as experiments in ways of living that contain valuable lessons or information for us all.

More is at stake here than attitudes. There is also the question of power. Cultural domination or hegemony often is based on the 'othering' of subordinate groups. The distinction between 'us' and 'them', and the significance attached to distinctions, is socially determined and distinctions frequently are drawn in order for one group to exercise power over another or to justify to itself the exercise of power. Thus, distinctions based on 'race', 'ethnicity' or 'nationality' are artificial, having no basis in fundamental biological differences, and a policy based on mutual respect of all cultures thus rests on a large body of scientific evidence.

In a world which has become familiar with 'ethnic cleansing', religious fanaticism and social prejudice, the obvious question is how one can replace hatred by respect. Policy makers cannot legislate respect, and neither can they coerce people into behaving in a respectful manner, but they can enshrine cultural freedom as one of the pillars on which the state is founded.

Cultural freedom is rather special; it is not quite like other freedoms. First, most freedoms refer to the individual – freedom to speak one's mind, to go where one wishes, to worship one's god, to write what one likes. Cultural freedom, in contrast, is a collective freedom. It refers to the right of a group of people to adopt a way of life of their choice. Second, cultural freedom is a guarantee of freedom as a whole. It protects not only the collectivity but also the rights of every individual within the collectivity. Individual rights evidently can exist independently of collective rights, but the existence of collective rights, of cultural freedom, provides additional protection for individual freedom. Lastly, cultural freedom, by protecting alternative ways of living, encourages creativity, experimentation and diversity, i.e., the very things that are essential for human development. Indeed, it is the diversity of multi-cultural societies, and the creativity to which diversity gives rise, that makes such societies innovative and dynamic over the long run.

Thus the links between culture and development are close. Space does not allow us to explore all of the linkages in Uzbekistan, but four topics have been selected for brief comment: the nationality question, language, religion and the revival of Islam, and political culture.

The Nationality Question

Uzbekistan is home to an ancient culture and a new state. Having become independent in 1991, the achievement of statehood did not represent the fulfilment of long held nationalist aspirations, and neither was it inspired by over a century of colonial domination, first by tsarist Russia and then by the USSR. Independence was largely an historical accident, a consequence of the disintegration of the Soviet Union, and it can truthfully be said that Uzbekistan became independent despite itself. Certainly, it did not favour the dissolution of the USSR. Indeed in the referendums held in March 1991 throughout the Soviet Union, more than 90 per cent of the people of Uzbekistan voted in favour of retaining the Union, rejecting independence.

The borders of Uzbekistan, like those of most states, are arbitrary. Indeed for centuries Uzbekistan formed the core of a large region of cultural unity that extended well beyond its present boundaries. In the early Soviet period the cultural unity of Central Asia was preserved by the creation of the Turkestan Soviet Socialist Republic, but in 1924, the Turkestan Soviet Socialist Republic was broken up and five new republics were created: the Uzbek, Turkoman, Kazakh, Kyrgyz and Tajik Soviet Socialist Republics. 'These new borders divided the people into separate ethnic groups which they themselves were reluctant to recognize as such.'[6] That is, the borders created ethnic groups and nationalities, not the other way round, and these divisions were perpetuated when the five Central Asian republics became independent. Where once there was unity, today there is national division and rivalry, at least potentially.

The original decision to break up Turkestan into five republics was motivated not by a wish to give each nationality a separate voice but, on the contrary, by a wish to weaken the ability of the Central Asian peoples to resist Soviet power. The shattering of the unity of Central Asia 'is exactly what Stalin wanted'.[7] Those who inherited power at the time of independence might naturally be inclined to perpetuate the structures through which their power is exercised, but it is those very structures which created the nationalities that now are potential rivals, both within and across borders. In 1989, there was a major clash between Uzbeks and Meskhetian Turks in the Fergana Valley of Uzbekistan, and in 1990 there were gun battles between Uzbeks and Kyrgyz in the Kyrgyz city of Osh. This latter outbreak of violence nearly led to war between the two republics.

One cannot at this stage of history reconstruct Turkestan, and neither can one instantaneously un-create nationalist sentiments, but one can recognize in public policy and political deed that nations are 'imagined communities',[8] that the titular population of Uzbekistan is only one of many 'national' groups and that unity and community within the new state will have to be built on shared common citizenship, not on national or ethnic identity.[9] This common citizenship, in turn, if it is to lead to social harmony, must be based on reciprocity of respect for all cultures.

Language

A people's spoken and written language is perhaps their most important cultural attribute. Here again, social policy has historically been used to subordinate the people of Central Asia to Russian hegemony. Language policy, like the nationalities policy, has been used as an instrument of domination, fragmentation and reintegration into a different political structure. Prior to the communist revolution of 1917, the Arabic script was the only means of common communication in Central Asia and a cultural element which connected the peoples of the region to each other and their history. The use of the Arabic script was forcibly discontinued in 1929 and was replaced by the Latin script. The Latin script, in turn, was replaced by the Cyrillic script in 1940 when renewed efforts were made to integrate the Central Asian republics more closely with Russia. Now, after independence, a decision has been made (in 1993) to reintroduce the Latin script, albeit rather slowly, with a target date of the year 2000.

The changes of script in the first half of this century – from Arabic to Latin and then to Cyrillic – affected directly only a relatively small fraction of the population because the level of adult literacy was low. Today, in contrast, there is virtually universal adult literacy and hence the direct impact of a change in script will be widely felt. Indeed there is a danger that if the transition from the Cyrillic to the Latin alphabet is not handled smoothly, a significant part of the literate population could suddenly become illiterate, with undesirable social consequences. This is not an argument against adopting the Latin script, which has many obvious advantages – cultural, commercial and political – but it is an argument in favour of a gradual transition in which both the Cyrillic and Latin scripts are used; it is also an argument in favour of multi-culturalism and the preservation of both traditions. Respect for all the languages of the region – and their ability to convey knowledge and wisdom, grace and beauty – should form part of the social policy of Uzbekistan.

The people of Uzbekistan are remarkable in that large numbers speak (even if they do not write) more than one language and often several: Uzbek and Russian, other regional languages, and increasingly a European language as well, usually English. The country, in other words, is multi-lingual, and this element of cultural diversity is a great asset which can contribute much to development. Indeed the ability to speak more than one language evidently enhances a person's 'capabilities', and the enhancement of capabilities, we have argued, is what development ultimately is about. Language policy, and specifically the preservation of multi-lingualism, should be an important part of the country's education policy.

The Revival of Islam

Uzbekistan was for centuries one of the world's centres of culture and learning. The heart of that culture was Islam. Indeed the most authoritative Hadith, a compilation and analysis of the Prophet's sayings and a book second in importance only to the Koran, was written in Bukhara by Al Bokhari (809–69), whose mosque and shrine can still be seen just outside Samarkand. And Samarkand itself – how its name resonates across the centuries! – became one of the finest cities in the world when Tamerlane made it his capital in 1369. The Timurid style of architecture influenced the entire Muslim world. Timurid science, particularly under Tamerlane's grandson Ulug Beg, had a global impact and in particular contributed to the renaissance in Europe. Tamerlane's great-grandson, Babar, conquered India and established the magnificent Mughal dynasty that ruled the sub-continent for four hundred years. The epicentre of this explosion of culture and development was the Registan Square, an exquisite complex of mosques and madrasahs (colleges of higher learning) that dominates Samarkand. The epicentre, in other words, was Islamic.

Bukhara, too, the rival of Samarkand, was a great centre of Islamic learning. The city contained 360 mosques and 113 madrasahs, and Bukhara was second only to Mecca as a place of learning for Muslims. All of this is part of Uzbekistan's heritage. It should be regarded as a cultural and even an economic asset which the country can put to good use, not something to be feared as a possible source of intolerance, fanaticism and civil discord.

During the Soviet period, unfortunately, Islam was suppressed, mosques were destroyed and madrasahs were closed. Islam did not die, however; it merely went underground and became part of the resistance to colonialism. The resistance movement took several forms. The Muslim Brotherhood, imported from Egypt, preached militancy and the establishment of an Islamic state. Wahabism, imported from Saudi Arabia, is noted for its puritanical views and its advocacy of revolution. The Jadid movement, and its modern revival, originally influenced by the experience of Turkey, is reformist in spirit and modernizing in intent. Yet the expression of Islam that was most characteristic of Central Asia – and indeed originated in Central Asia – is Sufism. The original message of Sufism is tolerance and moderation, culture and philosophy. Sufism is not political, not puritanical, not fanatical, not fundamentalist – and it is indigenous to Uzbekistan and Central Asia as a whole.

The suppression of Islam during the Soviet period has led to a reaction and there is today a great revival of Islam, including of course Sufism and other forms of Islam. 'The Islamic revival has been quite extraordinary, an unprecedented phenomenon in the history of the Islamic world and a clear rejection of the soviet system.'[10] This revival is more than a religious phenomenon; it has profound cultural and social implications as well. It is understandable that governments – observing the turmoil in Afghanistan, the civil war in Tajikistan, the conflict between Islam and a secular state in Algeria, and the politico-religious turbulence in the Caucasus and parts of the Middle East – would be wary of the revival of Islam and tempted to reintroduce the old Soviet policy of suppression.

This would be a serious error. Islam has been embraced by a significant (but unknown) proportion of the population. It won't go away, even if governments would like it to do so. It is, among other things, a social fact of life – a way of living in Uzbekistan – and should be addressed by social policy. The issue is whether Islam will be confronted, its parties banned, its leaders jailed and its practices prohibited, or will it be treated with respect, its culture recognized as a legitimate way of life and its various practitioners allowed to compete openly in the arena of ideas. The policy choice is whether to drive Islam underground once again (and risk encouraging a militant, revolutionary, intolerant reaction) or welcome it into the mainstream of national life (and risk that it will win the competition of ideas). Given the multiculturalism that characterizes Uzbekistan, it is unlikely that any single idea will come to dominate the polity and society.[11] Given that Sufism is the expression of Islam that is indigenous to the region, even if Islam were to win the competition of ideas, it is likely that a tolerant and moderate form of Islam would emerge.

Political Culture

The Soviet political culture is unacceptable to most people. It is authoritarian and arbitrary. It denies people freedoms that most now regard as universal human rights. It is ruthless, indeed murderous, in its treatment of opposition forces. It is intolerant of dissent in whatever form and as regards the arts, it is obstructionist and obscurantist. In Central Asia, as we have seen, the political culture destroyed the unity of the region and created national and ethnic divisions where none had previously existed. It interfered with the written language, switching from one script to another in pursuit of political objectives. And it attempted to suppress religious feeling and expression, thereby depriving its people of their history and one important source of their development.

Yet the Soviet political culture is the political culture that was inherited at the time of independence. It is one of the 'initial conditions' present at the creation of the new Uzbekistan. This culture is certain to be challenged – by liberal-minded reformers, by the nationalists and by one or more Islamic groups – for it is no more acceptable to the people of Uzbekistan today than it was in the Soviet period. The political culture can be maintained only by force, by repression, by ignoring the will of the people. And if force is used, the legitimacy of the regime itself eventually will be called into question.

The transition that is occurring in Uzbekistan today is much more than a transition from central planning to a market-oriented economy. It is also a social transformation which entails a new relationship between culture and development. Part of this new relationship will be a new relationship between the people and their government, a new political culture. Precisely what the new relationship will be cannot be foreseen, but it is likely to include a more open and transparent system of governance, greater accountability of the government to the people, more open discussion and debate of policy and ideas in general, and genuine competition among groups for power. Democracy in this sense definitely is on the agenda and wise statesmen will control the agenda by taking the initiative and effecting the transformation at an orderly pace. If they do not, they risk being swept away by events they cannot control.

Social policy – or human development policy – thus is concerned with much more than how society treats the poor and the unemployed, the sick and the lame, the young and the old. These issues, and others, will of course be discussed in the two chapters that follow, but the issues raised here touch on the essence of the transition: how an 'imagined community' can be transformed into a vibrant reality.

Notes

1. Giovanni Andrea Cornia, Richard Jolly and Frances Stewart (eds), *Adjustment with a Human Face* (Oxford: Clarendon Press, 1987).
2. See Amartya Sen, 'Development as Capability Expansion', in Keith Griffin

Development, Culture and Social Policy 247

and John Knight (eds), *Human Development and the International Development Strategy for the 1990s* (London: Macmillan, 1990).
3. T.W. Schultz, 'Investment in Human Capital', *American Economic Review*, March 1961.
4. Jean Drèze and Amartya Sen, *Hunger and Public Action* (Oxford: Clarendon Press, 1989), p. 259).
5. UNESCO and the United Nations have jointly created a World Commission on Culture and Development and asked it to prepare a report with recommendations on 'Culture and Development'. The report of the Commission is expected to be ready before the end of 1995.
6. Ahmed Rashid, *The Resurgence of Central Asia: Islam or Nationalism?* (London: Zed Books, 1994), p. 32.
7. *Ibid.* It has been argued by Nazif Shahrani that the destruction of 'traditional Islamic social and cultural identities, loyalties and institutions' was effected by (i) territorial and political fragmentation, (ii) the cultural isolation of the people from their past and from other Turkic and Persian speaking peoples, e.g., by creating an 'iron curtain' and by changes in scripts and alphabets, and (iii) the destruction of religious beliefs and values. (See Nazif Shahrani, 'Central Asia and the Challenge of the Soviet Legacy', *Central Asian Survey*, Vol. 12, No. 2, 1993.)
8. B. Anderson, *Imagined Communities: Reflections on the Origin and Spread of Nationalism* (London: Verso, 1983).
9. For an analysis of multi-culturalism in Russia see Valery Tishkov, 'Nationalities and Conflicting Ethnicity in Post-Communist Russia', UNRISD Discussion Paper No. 50, Geneva, March 1994.
10. Rashid, *The Resurgence of Central Asia*, pp. 243–4.
11. See, e.g., Anthony Hyman, *Political Change in Post-Soviet Central Asia* (London: Royal Institute of International Affairs, 1994).

11 The Macroeconomic Framework and Development Strategy

Uzbekistan began life as an independent country with a huge shock: it lost aid transfers from the Soviet Union equivalent to more than 19 per cent of its GDP.[1] These transfers financed a large part of government expenditure and enabled Uzbekistan to support a wide range of public services and outlays on human capital. The results over the years were impressive. Adult literacy, for women and men combined, was 97.2 per cent. The average number of years of schooling was nine (or even higher), roughly equal for women and men. Life expectancy was high at 69 years and average incomes, while low by the standards of the USSR, were relatively high compared to those of neighbouring Asian countries. Accurate estimates of GNP per capita are difficult to obtain, but as an order of magnitude, $960 seems about right.[2]

In addition to the 'aid' shock, there were serious problems arising from the disruption of existing trading patterns and, in the short run, a deterioration in Uzbekistan's external terms of trade. In 1988, for instance, before the economic collapse and the political disintegration of the Soviet Union began, 'foreign' trade accounted for 39.5 per cent of the country's GDP, of which 85.8 per cent was inter-republican trade.[3] Uzbekistan was dependent on the Soviet Union for imports of petroleum, which were provided at well below world prices. With independence came an increase in the price of imported oil and consequently a worsening of the terms of trade.

There were, however, some offsetting factors. First, foreign aid from non-Soviet sources increased very rapidly and by 1992 capital inflows were equivalent to 8 per cent of GDP.[4] Second, trade volumes between Uzbekistan and the former Soviet Union recovered fairly quickly and a shortage of imported inputs which might have severely disrupted production did not occur. The payments system for trade with the former Soviet Union remains a problem, however, and this has helped to perpetuate a cumbersome set of barter agreements and trade controls. Third, in response to the rise in the relative price of imported petroleum,

248

Uzbekistan has been able to increase the domestic output of petroleum and is now rapidly approaching self-sufficiency. Fourth, prior to independence the output of Uzbekistan's large gold mining industry was simply shipped to the Soviet Union: this can be regarded as an unrequited export or as an omitted element which helped to exaggerate the favourableness of the country's terms of trade. Now that Uzbekistan is independent it is earning about $700 million a year from gold mining, and production is rising rapidly. Finally, the external trade shocks combined with political independence gave Uzbekistan the incentive and the opportunity to seek out new trading partners: to search for cheaper sources of supply of internationally traded goods and services, to explore alternative sources of technology, to obtain (if desired) finance capital from abroad and to develop new export markets on a profitable basis.

Despite these positive aspects of the post-independence economic situation, Uzbekistan was not able to prevent the loss of part of its human capital. There was a considerable emigration of non-Uzbek (presumably Slavic) professionals and technicians that began before independence and continued thereafter. One estimate of net emigration is that it was 1.8 million persons in 1990 and 1.0 million in 1991.[5] Given that the total population is about 22 million people, this represents a loss of nearly 13 per cent in just two years. A second study reports 'a million Russians holding key technical and managerial posts having left by 1993'.[6] Official estimates, however, are much lower, namely, 274 400 between 1990 and 1993. Even this figure represents a significant proportion of the Slavic population. Part of the exodus probably was due to economic factors (namely, actual or anticipated declines in real incomes), but the political and social issues discussed in Chapter 10 undoubtedly also played a part (namely, nationality/ethnic conflict and the fear that multi-lingualism would be replaced by exclusive use of Uzbek, particularly in the schools). The link between culture, human capital and development is in this case exceptionally close.

The overall performance of the economy since independence has been poor, although it has been less bad than that of the average for the countries comprising the Commonwealth of Independent States. The basic data are presented in Table 11.1. The reader is warned, however, that estimates of inflation, changes in output and population growth vary considerably from one source to another, and hence the figures in the table should be regarded as indicating orders of magnitude only.

It is evident from the table that the transition from a centrally planned to a more market-oriented economy has been accompanied by rapid

Table 11.1   Output, prices, population growth and real incomes, 1989–94
(percentage change per annum)

Year	Retail price	Real GDP	Population growth	Real GDP (per capita)
1989	0.7	4.5	2.4	2.1
1990	4.0	6.6	2.2	4.4
1991	105.0	−0.5	2.4	−2.9
1992	528.0	−11.1	2.4	−13.5
1993	851.0	−2.3	2.2	−4.5
1994	746.0	−3.5	2.3	−5.8

Sources: 1991–94: Goskomprognozstat; 1989–90: World Bank, *Uzbekistan Economic Memorandum, Vol. 1: Main Report*, 20 June 1994, Table 1.1, p. 1.

inflation which in fact accelerated between 1989 (when prices were stable) and 1993 (when retail prices increased 851 per cent in one year). The rate of inflation declined in 1994, although retail prices still increased 746 per cent over the year. The rate of increase was falling, however, so that by the end of the year prices were rising at the lower pace of 423 per cent per annum. Encouraged by these results, the IMF and the government aimed to reduce the monthly rate of inflation to 2 per cent by the end of 1995.[7] This is equivalent to an annual rate of about 27 per cent. Unfortunately, however, inflation accelerated again during the first quarter of 1995 to roughly 13 per cent a month. This implies an annual rate of 333 per cent, which if it indeed materializes would be a major setback to the stabilization programme.

Output declined, not perhaps dramatically, but certainly very sharply. In the two years before independence growth on average was about 5.5 per cent a year, but in the few years since independence growth rates have been negative. Over the entire period 1991–94 the cumulative decline in real GDP was 16.6 per cent. Unfortunately, as with inflation, the growth outlook for 1995 appears to be getting worse and it is quite possible that production will fall by an additional 10 per cent this year. If this does in fact occur, it means that output at the end of 1995 will be a quarter less than five years ago.

Consider, finally, what has happened to the real incomes of the people of Uzbekistan. The last column of Table 11.1 contains estimates of the yearly changes in real GDP per head, assuming the population growth rate was as indicated in the third column. As can be seen, real incomes rose on average 3.2 per cent a year in 1989 and 1990, but thereafter they fell, precipitously in 1992 and more moderately in the other three years. The cumulative fall in incomes was 24.4 per cent in just four years. A further sharp decline in average incomes this year could well cause severe hardship in certain sections of the community and possibly result in public manifestations of discontent, especially in urban areas.

It is quite evident that a resumption of growth in output and per capita incomes should be a very high priority. It is possible, even probable, that the national accounts underestimate the level of output and average incomes – informal sector activities are not fully recorded, illegal activities such as drug transporting and production are unrecorded and the very substantial self-provisioning in rural (and urban) areas is not fully recorded – but it is unlikely that the expansion of these three activities has been so rapid that the aggregate growth rates reported in Table 11.1 totally misrepresent the true picture. Uzbekistan undoubtedly confronts a situation of falling living standards and rising poverty, although lack of data makes it impossible to quantify the incidence of poverty, much less trace changes in the incidence of poverty over time.

Macroeconomic policy is made very difficult by the presence simultaneously of very rapid inflation and negative rates of growth. A socially conscious government may be tempted in such circumstances to relax efforts to stabilize prices and devote all its energies to stimulating the economy and 'go for growth'. This temptation should be resisted.

THE IMPORTANCE OF PRICE STABILITY DURING THE TRANSITION

The benefits of a market-oriented economy depend upon the ability of producers and consumers to respond to changes in relative prices. Higher relative prices for some goods and services encourage producers to expand production and consumers to curtail demand. Lower relative prices, by reducing profits, provide an incentive to producers to reduce output and shift resources to other uses; consumers, on the other hand, will have an incentive to alter the pattern of consumption in favour of the now-cheaper products. Provided relative prices accurately reflect social costs and benefits, the reallocation of resources that occurs in response to changes in relative prices should lead to increased efficiency, higher total output and incomes and an improvement in the average standard of living.

Rapid inflation, however, hampers the operation of the price mechanism and makes it much more difficult to achieve the gains which a more market-oriented economy should make possible. This is especially true during a period of price liberalization in an economy that previously relied on administrative measures to allocate resources.[8] There are several reasons for this. First, rapid price inflation – certainly a rate of inflation of 50 per cent per annum or more – weakens price signals and hence reduces the power of the market mechanism to allocate resources efficiently. The reason for this is that when all prices are rising rapidly, it is difficult for producers (and consumers) to detect small changes in relative prices. Yet it is relative prices that matter.

Second, during periods of rapid inflation virtually all prices are rising, but not all prices are rising continuously. Prices change at different times throughout the year, some lagging behind for a while and then spurting ahead with a large price increase. The result is that relative prices change arbitrarily during the course of the year and the changes in relative prices can be very large. This adds to the difficulties producers face when making production and investment decisions. Rapid inflation introduces great uncertainty into the decision making process and this tends to dampen investment and lower the overall rate of growth. In this sense it is not possible in a market economy to ignore rapid inflation and 'go for growth': stabilization is essential.

Third, rapid inflation inevitably is accompanied by arbitrary and hence inequitable changes in the distribution of income. Every change in relative prices entails both a change in the optimal composition of output and a change in the pattern of rewards and the distribution of income. When changes in prices are arbitrary, changes in rewards and incomes are arbitrary. Those on fixed incomes, such as pensioners, obviously suffer severely; but ordinary employed workers also suffer when, for instance, changes in nominal wages lag behind changes in the average price of consumer goods. The same is true of small business persons (and others) who happen to be producing products whose prices temporarily are slow to adjust to changes in the general level of prices. The consequence is that the structure of incomes and the degree of inequality becomes unpredictable and totally irrational.

Finally, because of (i) the feebleness of price signals, (ii) the adverse effects of inflation on investment plans and (iii) arbitrary changes in the distribution of income, sustained high rates of inflation are likely to result in political discontent which undermines support for the reform process as a whole. If average incomes are falling because of negative real growth, if investors are disgruntled because of an uncertain business climate, and if large numbers of households are angered by changes in the distribution of income that are unrelated to work effort, skills, entrepreneurship or considerations of equity, the benefits of reform soon will appear to be far less than the costs. Present sacrifices in favour of future gains will be perceived to be a poor bargain and there is a risk that the entire reform effort will grind to a halt. A reasonable degree of price stability is therefore a necessary condition for success, although price stability alone is hardly sufficient.

STRATEGIC PRICES AND AN EFFICIENT COMPOSITION OF INVESTMENT

Not all prices are equally important. Some prices are strategic in the sense that they influence the overall performance of the economy, and not just the efficiency of resource use in a particular branch of industry. In the case of Uzbekistan we shall concentrate in this chapter on five markets which have a major impact on macroeconomic efficiency and growth: the market for foreign exchange, the market for finance capital, the wage rate for low skilled labour, the price of water and the price of energy. If policy interventions ensure that these five markets function well, the probabilities are high that macroeconomic performance will be satisfactory. Development policy should therefore focus on a limited number of price interventions where public action can be expected to have a high payoff.

The Market for Foreign Exchange

The economy of Uzbekistan is highly dependent on foreign trade. The ratio of exports to GDP was 49.7 per cent in 1993, with the share of exports to the former Soviet Union falling and the share of exports to the rest of the world rising rapidly since 1991. The country relies on imports for foodstuffs and a wide array of basic manufactured consumer goods as well as for capital equipment, current inputs and spare parts. In 1993 the ratio of imports to GDP was 60.2 per cent. It is therefore vitally important that the foreign exchange market function properly. Two issues arise here, namely, price and access.

On the surface the balance of payments position appears to be strong. The trade account, which had a small deficit in 1992 and 1993, now is in balance (and possibly running a small surplus); there are large net capital inflows which cover the current account deficit; and foreign exchange reserves are large and rising. Beneath the surface there are problems, however. First, the official exchange rate has appreciated in real terms, thanks in part to large inflows of foreign aid and foreign private investment and in part to a decline in real incomes which has reduced the demand for imports. The appreciated exchange rate has made it more difficult for Uzbekistan's exports to be competitive in world markets and for domestic industries to compete with imported goods from abroad. Foreign capital inflows, in other words, actually have exacerbated the problems of structural adjustment through their impact on the exchange rate. Uzbekistan might be better off with less foreign aid.

Second, although there is an auction for foreign exchange, the price of foreign exchange actually is controlled by the government and not determined by market forces. The management of the exchange rate is achieved partly by determining the volume of foreign exchange that will be sold at auction and partly by regulating access to the foreign exchange auction. The latter, in effect, determines the demand for foreign exchange in the auction. Third, those denied access to foreign exchange at the official price have no alternative but to resort to the black market. The difference between the official exchange rate (until recently 25 sums per US dollar) and the black market rate (40 sums) is 60 per cent. That is, different users of foreign exchange pay very different prices and thus face very different incentives. It is highly desirable that the dual market for foreign exchange be unified and that access be widened to include everyone who has legitimate reasons for wanting to buy or sell foreign currencies.

Third, contrary to initial appearances, foreign trade still is managed by direct controls rather than by the price mechanism. There are no tariffs on imports but there still are import licences. It would be better in fact to abolish import licences (which create economic rents and consequently opportunities for corrupt practices) and to replace them with a modest tariff (say, a uniform rate of 10 per cent) which would provide some compensation to domestic producers competing against foreign imports for the appreciated exchange rate while generating government revenue that would help to reduce the fiscal deficit. In addition to import licences there are taxes on many exports, notably on above-quota exports of cotton.

Fourth, there also are quantitative controls on exports. On 1 January 1995 the government reduced the number of products subject to export quotas from 26 to 11.[9] This represents a decline of nearly 58 per cent in the number of products to which export restrictions apply.

Unfortunately, however, this gives a misleading impression of the extent of trade liberalization. In fact, several major export products still are regulated in part by quotas, including cotton and natural gas. If one considers not the number of products but the proportion of total exports still subject to quotas, it transpires that the reforms have increased quota-free exports only from 26.9 per cent of the total to 35.4 per cent.[10] While this is not a negligible change, Uzbekistan still has a long way to go before exports can be traded freely.

Given the size and significance of the foreign trade sector in Uzbekistan's economy, it is vital that scarce foreign exchange be allocated to those who can use it most efficiently and that no disincentives be created that discourage people from earning more foreign exchange by expanding production for export. At present it appears that the market for foreign exchange, because of restricted access, discriminates against small businesses, the informal sector and small farmers, i.e., precisely those sectors where the return to investment is likely to be exceptionally high, and where there are promising possibilities for generating employment quickly. At the same time, export quotas are a severe obstacle and limit the amount of foreign exchange available. They should be abolished. It makes no sense to reduce artificially the supply of foreign exchange and then to allocate that foreign exchange inefficiently and inequitably.

Exchange rate policy, seen in this broad framework, is a top priority for market reform. A unified exchange rate, with free access and current account convertibility, is one of the keys to increasing the level of investment, raising the productivity of capital, igniting economic growth and halting the decline in the standard of living.

The Market for Finance Capital

Capitalism is about capital and a modern, market-oriented capitalist economy cannot function properly without an efficient market for finance capital. A strong banking system, carefully regulated by government, whether privately or publicly owned, is an indispensable market institution. One is tempted to say that this is a *sine qua non* for an economy undertaking systemic change. That perhaps would be an exaggeration, but there is little doubt that a weak banking system makes the transition to a market-oriented economy more difficult. Alas, Uzbekistan has a weak banking system.

The role of the banking system in a commercial economy is to serve as a financial intermediary, accepting deposits from those who have monetized savings and allocating credit to investors who have profitable projects which require more funds than they can mobilize from their own resources. If the banking system operates efficiently, it should contribute to a higher level of savings and, more important, to a more productive allocation of investment and hence to a faster rate of growth. (An inefficient pattern of investment is evident from the fact that in 1993, for instance, investment accounted for 23.8 per cent of GDP yet growth was negative.) Once again, as in the market for foreign exchange, the problems of the banking system can be grouped under two headings: price and access.

At the time of independence Uzbekistan inherited three large banks which facilitated financial transactions in agriculture, industry and foreign trade. Since then, 26 new banks have been created, including three that are private, another oriented towards the private sector and a fifth intended to encourage joint ventures with foreign enterprises. Uzbekistan thus has a two-tier banking system with a Central Bank occupying the upper tier, but with functions and responsibilities that are not yet entirely clear. The second tier banks, i.e., the commercial banks, continue to operate in a way similar to that under a central planning regime. Most of their loans are to state enterprises, many of which are in arrears on repayments, and hence the asset portfolios of the banking system include a substantial proportion of non-performing loans. The banking system, in effect, still is used to provide subsidies to cover the operating deficits of state enterprises.

One consequence of these practices is that the banking system is very fragile and, without a continuous injection of credit from the Central Bank, it probably would collapse. That is, it would go bankrupt. A second, equally serious consequence is that large sectors of the economy do not have access, or have only very limited access, to financial capital; they are unable to obtain loans to finance potentially profitable activities. The banking system, in other words, is not performing its crucial function of allocating capital to projects with the highest rate of return. Small and medium sized enterprises are starved of credit, as are private farmers and the informal sector. The results are that (i) finance capital is used to cover losses of state enterprises rather than increase investment, (ii) the expansion of a genuinely private sector is inhibited and restructuring is delayed and (iii) inequities are created, since those who are denied access to credit tend to be relatively small enterprises.

Quite apart from access, there is the question of price, i.e., real rates of interest. Nominal deposit rates are low and negative in real terms. Savers thus have little incentive to deposit funds with the banking system, and while this may not have much effect on aggregate savings – since the elasticity of savings with respect to changes in the real rate of interest may be low – it will affect the form in which savings are held. Low deposit rates of interest will reduce the volume of deposits and make it more difficult for the banking system to perform its intermediation function.

Lending rates have varied but they, too, usually have been negative in real terms. In 1994, for instance, the average lending rate of the Agricultural Bank, the largest in the country, was about 76 per cent a year, whereas retail prices rose 746 per cent that year. Thus those who have access to the credit market obtain finance capital at no cost. This makes it virtually impossible to allocate capital efficiently, and to ensure that resources are used where they will be most productive. It also increases the demand for credit and where, as in Uzbekistan, the monetary authorities are accommodating, this increases inflationary pressure. The market for finance capital, in other words, is functioning poorly. Several reforms are desirable: (i) access to the banking system should be widened considerably; (ii) subsidies to state enterprises should not be channelled via the banking system but done in a transparent manner through the Ministry of Finance; (iii) nominal deposit rates of interest should be raised substantially so that savers receive a real rate of interest on deposits; (iv) lending rates should also be positive in real terms (at least 10 per cent per annum) and these rates should remain broadly constant for periods of time so that businesses can make investment plans with a minimum of uncertainty about conditions in the financial markets.

The Wage Rate

There is considerable slack in the labour market in the form of modest registered open unemployment, a large amount of part-time working, an enormous but unquantified amount of disguised unemployment in the state enterprises and surplus labour in agriculture. Government policies began to respond to this problem in 1992 when, for the first time, provision was made for the payment of unemployment benefits, an employment service was created and funds were set aside to finance training schemes. These programmes, while perhaps desirable, are totally inadequate to meet the scale of the problem and it is evident that a massive effort will have to be made to create more employment opportunities. The question of unemployment compensation will be discussed in Chapter 12.

Our concern here is with the narrow question of wage determination. For most practical purposes there is no functioning labour market in large parts of the economy. Wages are government determined in the public sector – the structure of wages being expressed as multiples of the legal minimum wage – and even in the non-public sector, wages are heavily influenced by public sector wages. In an attempt to control inflation, the government has increased its intervention in the labour market further, thereby neutralizing the effects of supply and demand and moving away from its stated intention of creating a more market-oriented economy. This in itself is a bit surprising.

The government has announced that the 'quarterly increase in the wage bill of non-public enterprises will not be allowed to exceed the targeted increase in prices'. Any excess wage payments 'will be taxed at steep penalty rates'.[11] This is described by government as an incomes policy although it might more accurately be described as a wage reduction policy. The implicit assumption seems to be that inflation in Uzbekistan is caused by cost-push pressures arising in the labour market. This clearly is an incorrect analysis: not only is there a large amount of excess labour in the economy but real wages have been falling (not steadily, but systematically) along with per capita income since independence.

The targets for inflation in 1995 were 4–5 per cent per month by the middle of the year and 2 per cent per month by the end. The actual rates of inflation, as we have seen, were well above this, namely, 17, 16 and 10 per cent per month in the first three months of 1995. Thus the incomes policy, if implemented, would impose a very sharp fall in real wages on ordinary working people. This cannot be good development policy given the current conditions in the country. Presumably the intention of the policy is to provide a strong incentive to enterprises to restrain wage increases, but this can best be done not by imposing a totally arbitrary incomes policy but by making it much more difficult for enterprises to finance wage increases by increased borrowing from the banking system. Banking reforms, not wage taxes, are what is required.

Indeed the government should be moving in the opposite direction, refraining from setting wages by administrative measures and instead allowing market forces to operate. This will necessitate not only banking reforms but also management reforms within the state enterprises, a subject we shall discuss below.

The general strategy should be to squeeze credit further and force loss-making state enterprises to shed their disguised unemployment. If nothing else is done, this would increase open unemployment dramatically, which is socially unacceptable and economically unnecessary. Instead a guaranteed public works employment scheme (discussed below) should be organized to absorb people who would otherwise be unemployed. This public works scheme would concentrate on the construction of income earning physical assets, thereby raising the rate of investment and helping to restore growth. The credit squeeze would reduce the rate of inflation. The disguised unemployed in state enterprises (and in agriculture) would be transformed into construction workers. Part of the finance capital (bank credit) now used to pay the wages of the disguised unemployed in state enterprises could be used to finance the public works programme. There would be no net increase in credit and a net decline in (disguised) unemployment. The rate of inflation would fall and the growth rate would rise.

The Price of Water

Uzbekistan is a semi-arid country: the annual precipitation in Tashkent is only 393 mm. Yet agriculture is by far the most important sector in the economy and water is very scarce. Only 10 per cent of the country's land is arable and 95 per cent of the cultivated land is dependent on irrigation. The major sources of water are two river systems – the Amudarya and the Syrdarya – which flow into the Aral Sea. Because of excessive withdrawals of water from these river systems, the Aral Sea is shrinking rapidly and the volume of water in the sea in 1993 was only 26.2 per cent of what it was in 1960. The shoreline has retreated 60–80 km, the seabed has been exposed and – because of heavy use of chemical fertilizer and pesticides in cotton cultivation – both irrigation water and drinking water have become heavily polluted, with serious consequences for the health of the population.

Water resources, the most precious component of Uzbekistan's stock of natural capital, have been badly managed. Water has been wasted, it has been polluted, it has been allowed to poison the land through salination and, worst of all, it has been allowed to damage the health of the people. No incentives have existed to encourage an efficient use of water. It has been treated as if it were a free good. Indeed, until this year, irrigation water literally was a free good. The government has begun to respond to this deplorable situation and has decided that water charges will be introduced in 1995 to achieve 'at least 50 per cent operating cost recovery'.[12] This is a small step in the right direction, but the objective must be to create a well functioning market in water as soon as possible. The health of the people and the prosperity of the agricultural sector depend upon it.

Several points are relevant here. First, the government has only announced its intention; a system of water charges is not yet in place. The creation of such a system should have high priority. Second, at the moment the intention is to cover only half of the operating costs of the irrigation system. There is no case on efficiency grounds for subsidizing water and the policy should be, as a minimum, to cover the full costs of operation of the system. Moreover, given that the terms of trade will soon turn sharply in favour of agriculture,[13] there is no case on grounds of equity to subsidize water.

Therefore, in future water charges should also cover the capital costs of the system. Incentives should be created to use the existing irrigation system more intensively and to maintain the system in good repair. The physical capital embodied in the irrigation system should not be treated as a free good. Finally, the revenues from water charges can make a useful contribution to the budget, compensating in part for the decline in agricultural quotas and the rise in procurement prices. Agricultural incomes should soon begin to rise significantly and water charges are a good way to tax these rising incomes and help finance essential public services.

The Price of Energy

Uzbekistan has been blessed with an abundance of energy resources in the form of natural gas, oil and coal. During the Soviet period, however, this important part of the country's stock of natural capital was not fully exploited. The natural gas industry was developed, but the petroleum sector remained fairly small, and in fact Uzbekistan imported from the rest of the Soviet Union more than 60 per cent of its petroleum. Now that the country is independent, numerous opportunities to develop the energy sector exist, although there are a number of problems that must be faced during the transition. Our purpose here is merely to call attention to one important issue that arises during the transition to a market guided economy: the question of the price of energy.

One of the characteristics of central planning during the Soviet period was the very low price of energy, including the price of oil. This affected patterns of production and consumption throughout the Soviet bloc, including Uzbekistan. Indeed the amount of energy required to produce one unit of domestic product was much higher in Uzbekistan than, say, in Japan, Western Europe and most other developing countries. This was a consequence of Soviet oil prices being only a fraction of those that prevailed in the world market. Even the United States, which by the standards of developed countries has a very low price of energy (because of low energy taxes), had a higher relative price of oil than Uzbekistan.

At the time, Uzbekistan seemed to benefit from the Soviet pricing and trading arrangements. As a net importer of petroleum, the low prices meant that the country enjoyed favourable terms of trade and a higher standard of living. The rise in import prices at the time of independence worsened Uzbekistan's terms of trade, created balance of payments problems and lowered average incomes. The disadvantages of the pre-independence arrangements, however, outweigh the advantages. First, the country failed to develop fully its natural resources. Second, the country failed to exploit its comparative advantage in the energy sector and generate higher incomes through exports at world prices. Third, after independence the country was left with an inefficient industrial sector that is dependent for its economic viability on the availability of cheap oil.

The task for the future is to reform the energy sector, push ahead quickly with an expansion of production and make certain that the government receives a reasonable share of the rents created by trading at higher world prices. Taxation of a flourishing and rapidly growing energy sector could in a few years contribute much to government revenues. It is equally important that the price of energy in the domestic market should reflect prices in the world market. At present both enterprises and households are subsidized by being supplied with cheap energy, particularly fuel oil. Domestic prices should be raised to world levels so that individual enterprises which consume energy are forced to become competitive and the structure of the industrial sector which then evolves reflects the true costs of production. Energy intensive industries will naturally be favoured in Uzbekistan and there is no need to increase the natural advantage they enjoy by artificially reducing energy prices through subsidies. The energy sector should be a source of development revenue for government, not a source of subsidy for old or new industrial enterprises.

THE RESUMPTION OF GROWTH

Stabilization of the general level of prices and the creation of efficient markets in a few strategic sectors are central elements in a macroeconomic framework designed to achieve a smooth and rapid transition from a centrally planned to a market guided economy. The third element in the macroeconomic framework should be policies to resume growth and create employment opportunities. There are four issues we shall address: (i) creating space for the development and expansion of a small scale, labour intensive private sector, (ii) the transfer of ownership of existing state enterprises to the private sector, (iii) the transformation and expansion of the rural economy and (iv) the organization of a large public works programme to accelerate investment and create jobs.

It is widely believed, particularly in international financial circles, that price stabilization, privatization and market reforms will ensure rapid growth. That is, the spontaneous reaction of producers will bring about a swift increase in production once the institutions of a capitalist economy are in place. This is sometimes described as 'the magic of the market'. A less flamboyant statement of the same idea by the head of the World Bank's regional mission in Central Asia is that 'the supply response to correction of price signals and institutional strengthening can be expected to be strongly positive'.[14]

We are not so optimistic. We do not anticipate that price and institutional reforms alone will bring about 'strongly positive' results. We do not believe in magic. Apart from changes in cropping patterns in agriculture in response to changes in relative prices, we do not believe that supply elasticities are high. The key to a resumption of growth is investment. Restructuring of the economy, i.e., a change in the composition of output, will require massive investments over an extended period of time. The speed of response to price signals depends on the level of investment and the productivity of capital. If the rate of investment is high, and if investment is channelled into highly productive sectors, supply will increase quickly, but if the volume and efficiency of investment are low, supply will respond slowly, even if there is price stabilization and market institutions are in place.

It is therefore important that development policy should concentrate on a relatively few sectors where there is a potential for a rapid increase in output and incomes. One such sector is the small scale private sector, including micro-enterprises and informal sector activities.

Creating Space for the Private Sector

While it often is possible to increase output and incomes in existing enterprises by raising efficiency, the most promising source of growth in Uzbekistan is likely to come from the creation and expansion of new enterprises. The absence of a small scale, labour intensive private sector is a vacuum waiting to be filled. The fact that private initiative was virtually prohibited during the Soviet period – except in the bazaar economy – suggests that there are numerous opportunities for new entrepreneurs and business people, women as well as men, to engage in production and trading activities. There are many obvious possibilities, including the establishment of private restaurants, the development of tourist facilities (decent hotels, comfortable guest houses, transportation services, guides), the revival of a handmade carpet industry, the expansion of light manufacturing and the cotton textile industry (which at present processes only 15 per cent of the country's cotton), the expansion of food processing and other agriculture-related industries, the creation of small construction firms, etc.

Most such activities will be small in scale. They will not require large amounts of capital initially and many new activities – particularly the micro-enterprises – can be self-financed. Small enterprises typically are labour intensive and hence create a lot of employment per unit of output. The gestation period usually is brief, i.e., there is only a short lag between the commencement of investment and the beginning of the flow of output, and consequently the supply response is rapid. Finally, since entry into such activities is easy, competition is intense and prices to consumers low.

Access to foreign exchange and to finance capital often are the most salient constraints to private sector investment and hence our previous discussion of the foreign exchange and capital markets is especially important in this context. Information also is essential so that entrepreneurs can learn where market opportunities and sources of supply exist. A lively business press, good telephone, radio and communications services and unhindered mass media all contribute to the development of a thriving small business sector. Lastly Uzbekistan will have to develop a system of commerical law which protects private property rights and provides legal remedies when there are disputes. This will take time.

The government issued a decree in January 1995 providing equal rights for private and state enterprises, simplifying registration procedures and removing restrictions on the number of employees in private firms. The next step is to enforce the decree and to ensure that the police, tax authorities and local officials do not harass small traders, shopkeepers and other business people but rather encourage and assist them.[15] Space must be created for the emergence of a small scale, labour intensive private sector. This is an important component of 'social policy' or, as we prefer to call it, general development policy. At present it cannot be said that Uzbekistan has shown by its actions that it truly wishes to have a large and dynamic private sector, despite its programme of privatization.

Privatization

One way instantly to create a private sector is to transfer ownership rights of existing state enterprises to non-state entities (cooperatives, workers' organizations, private individuals, partnerships or firms, foreign corporations). There may in some cases be microeconomic efficiency gains from privatization in this sense, but the macroeconomic benefits are somewhat doubtful. We do not share the enthusiasm of the international financial institutions for massive and rapid privatization of state enterprises and are not persuaded by their arguments that privatization is one of the keys to a successful transition.[16] The decisive element, as argued above, is an increase in investment and output. If privatization achieves that, it should be warmly welcomed; if it does not, it should be given a low priority. Let us consider the record of privatization so far in Uzbekistan.[17]

The first of two phases of privatization covers the period 1992–93; the second phase began in January 1994 and continues. Privatization in Uzbekistan covers several different types of property:

(a) housing;
(b) small scale enterprises engaged in trading and the provision of consumer services;
(c) local industries, often medium scale enterprises employing between 150 and 2000 workers;
(d) large enterprises producing for national and international markets employing more than 2000 workers;
(e) land, both urban and rural.

During the first phase emphasis was placed on privatizing the stock of housing and small enterprises. By the end of 1994 over 96 per cent of the housing units had been turned over to the occupants, apparently with little difficulty and at only nominal cost to the buyers. In 1993, for instance, the cost of a dwelling sold was only between 23.9 and 157.9 per cent of the average monthly wage.[18] Given that there are virtually no homeless people in Uzbekistan – everyone has a place to live – the transfer of ownership was neither inequitable nor administratively cumbersome. There may be marginal benefits from privatization, e.g., better incentives to maintain and repair structures, and certainly there can be no strong objection to the programme.

In principle there are also advantages to privatizing small state enterprises, although in practice several problems have arisen. First, few small enterprises were offered for sale to the public and consequently most people had no opportunity to acquire shares in an enterprise or to purchase the business outright. Second, most small enterprises were either given to the staff or sold to them at a price which one presumes was below the market clearing price. That is, assets accumulated in the name of the entire population were simply given away (in whole or in part) to a small minority of the population who happened to have a job in the enterprise. The resulting distribution of capital assets was arbitrary and almost certainly inequitable. As far as one can tell, there has been no resulting upsurge in growth that might justify such arbitrariness. Neither can this transfer of property rights be explained by a desire to experiment with schemes of workers' self-management, since there is no evidence of a serious attempt to promote a system of self-management.

Approximately 600 medium sized state enterprises also were privatized during phase one. Shares were allocated to the staff and the government, with the government usually holding a majority of the shares. To the extent that the government retained ownership, privatization was a misnomer; to the extent that public assets were given away to a privileged group of enterprise employees, privatization was inequitable. Significant gains in efficiency and growth have yet to materialize.

Even more problematical was the privatization of roughly 400 large state enterprises during phase one. As with the other asset distributions, shares were distributed between the government (which retained a majority holding) and the staff of the enterprise. The difference this time is that only the managers were given shares; ordinary workers in the enterprise received nothing. Only the credulous can believe this will encourage growth and only the gullible can think this is equitable. Some might attempt to justify Uzbekistan's experience with privatization on ideological grounds, but it certainly cannot be justified on the grounds that it improves the macroeconomic framework for growth.[19]

In phase two the intention is to privatize virtually all of the remaining large state enterprises. Given the experience so far, it seems a bit odd that this should be given high priority. It would be better, we think, to concentrate on creating space for new private enterprises to emerge (removing all obstacles to their expansion) and to assess seriously the merits and demerits of what has been achieved to date by privatization (examining the effects on growth, efficiency and equity). A period of pause and reflection would be valuable.

Meanwhile, much can be done to improve the efficiency, flexibility and competitiveness of the remaining large state enterprises. Nothing we say should be interpreted as an argument in favour of maintaining the status quo. The state enterprises urgently need to be reformed. They should become more autonomous. Management should be given more freedom to take decisions and then be held responsible for them. Workers should not be guaranteed employment regardless of their performance, and management should have discretion to hire and fire employees as necessary. Financial controls should be relaxed, managers should be instructed to maximize profits and firms allowed to retain profits for reinvestment after payment of taxes. State firms should be exposed to competition, both from imports and by allowing domestic and foreign private producers freely to enter into sectors from which they had previously been excluded. If the large state enterprises are to survive, all of this will have to happen, whether or not the firms are privatized. The mere transfer of legal title is unlikely to achieve much, at least in the short run, whereas genuine reform of the management and operation of state enterprises could result in fairly quick and large returns.

Finally, a brief word about the privatization of agricultural land. In principle a redistribution of collective land in favour of small farmers, either by sale or through long leases, has many attractions, and the experience of China shows that in practice such a redistribution can be highly successful.[20] Provided there are safeguards to maintain collective assets and to exploit economies of scale where they exist (as in many irrigation systems), there is no reason why privatization of agricultural land should not be highly advantageous in Uzbekistan, and we would encourage the government to experiment with alternative programmes of redistribution.

Growth of the Rural Economy

Indeed the prospects in agriculture for achieving rapid growth are very promising. This is a sector – and happily a large and important one – where a rapid supply response is likely, given appropriate policies. Agriculture has been severely squeezed since independence, the resources transferred out of the sector being used by government to offset the termination of Union transfers. Despite the squeeze, agriculture has been remarkably resilient and has performed surprisingly well.

A number of reforms – in institutions, prices and technology – should lead to a rapid growth in output, and several of the reforms already are under way or have been announced. As implied above, we favour the creation of a small farmer system within a communal institutional arrangement. Land reform – or land privatization if that is preferred – is a desirable institutional change which should help to accelerate growth. The planned reduction in delivery quotas and the planned increases in procurement prices will turn the terms of trade in favour of agriculture (specifically cotton and wheat), and this will provide a further incentive to expand output. The introduction of water charges (discussed above), the removal of subsidies on fertilizer and pesticides, and the imposition of land taxes or leasehold charges will create incentives to use scarce inputs more efficiently. Finally, technological improvements in cotton cultivation, which raise yields and improve quality, could increase output and incomes quickly.

Agriculture thus could become a leading sector during the transition period. If this were to occur, the distribution of income among the population would change. The rural population would gain relative to the urban, and unless urban incomes resume their growth (say, through the expansion of small scale enterprises and the mounting of a public works programme), the decline in the urban sector's terms of trade would lower urban incomes absolutely, not just relatively. Poverty in urban areas might then increase. A reduction in rural–urban inequality implies that the Uzbek population (which is predominantly rural) would gain relative to the Slavic/non-Uzbek population (which is predominantly urban). If not handled carefully – if the real incomes of the non-Uzbeks are allowed to fall further – this could result in social tensions and unrest. It might also lead to another wave of emigration of Russians and other Slavs, thereby depriving the country of part of its human capital.

The growth of the rural economy has the potential to raise not only average incomes in Uzbekistan but also the incomes of some of the poorest people in the country, the rural Uzbeks. The growth strategy, however, must be balanced and in particular young people newly entering the labour market must have a reasonable prospect of obtaining a job and earning at least a minimum livelihood. This is what makes a guaranteed employment programme so important.

A Guaranteed Employment Scheme

Under the Soviet system all workers were guaranteed employment. Indeed, work was a duty of every citizen. This system had the advantage of providing everyone with a livelihood and giving everyone a sense of participation in the life of the community. But because workers were employed on farms, in state enterprises and in the public administration even when they were not needed – even when they contributed little or nothing to output – labour was often in surplus or in disguised unemployment. During the transition from a centrally planned system to a more market-oriented economy there is a danger that open unemployment will increase, that the disguised unemployed in state enterprises will be made redundant and that as restructuring occurs, workers will be sent home (possibly on full pay) or offered part-time employment only. A market economy can be ruthless in depriving people of a livelihood, a job and a sense of participation in worthwhile activities. On the other hand, if a market economy functions well, resources will be used efficiently and average incomes are likely to be higher than otherwise.

A socially minded government, concerned about the well-being of the people, might reasonably be hesitant to move ahead quickly with market reforms for fear that large scale unemployment would ensue. While the fear is legitimate, the hesitancy is not. It is possible within a market-oriented economy to guarantee employment at the minimum wage to everyone seeking work. Moreover, an employment guarantee scheme can contribute to growth by using surplus labour to undertake income generating capital construction projects in both rural and urban areas.[21] Such projects can add to the country's infrastructure (roads, bridges, airports), repair urban structures and facilities, build schools and clinics, undertake on-farm improvements (repair and maintain irrigation facilities, plant orchards, reforest hillsides) and in a large number of ways add to the country's stock of physical capital.

The returns on properly designed and managed public works projects can be high. The gestation period is short. They provide a great deal of employment. Above all, public works projects enable the country to transform otherwise idle labour into capital formation and growth. A guaranteed employment programme can be a major component of a strategy designed to encourage a resumption of growth and, as explained above, this need not be inflationary.

SUMMARY

The current macroeconomic framework has yielded disappointing results. Price stabilization remains elusive. Growth rates have been negative. Average incomes have declined. There has been large scale emigration of skilled and professional labour.

Evidently some adjustment of macroeconomic development policy is needed. We recommend, first, continued, indeed augmented, efforts to reduce the overall rate of inflation. Second, we recommend that efforts be concentrated on improving the price mechanism in five strategic areas, namely, (i) the market for foreign exchange, (ii) the market for finance capital, (iii) the wage rate for low skilled labour, (iv) the market for water, and (v) the market for energy.

It is vital to the success of the reform process that aggregate economic growth be resumed quickly and that the benefits of growth be widely distributed among the working population. We recommend, third, that efforts be concentrated on creating space for the emergence of a large, labour intensive, small scale private sector. There are many obstacles to the rapid growth of small and medium sized enterprises and the removal of these obstacles should be given very high priority. Next, we recommend that there be a temporary pause in the privatization of large scale state industrial enterprises while an evaluation is conducted of the effects of phase one of the privatization programme on growth, efficiency and equity. There should be a shift of emphasis from privatization to increasing the efficiency of public sector industrial enterprises. We do not believe that further privatizations merit high priority at this time, given the other tasks faced by the government. Fourth, we believe that the transformation and expansion of the rural economy represents an opportunity for rapid economic and social gains and we recommend that rural development be given high priority. Finally, we recommend that a large scale public works programme be organized partly to provide employment and partly to accelerate capital formation. There is considerable slack in the labour market in the form of (i) disguised unemployment in state enterprises and the recently privatized enterprises, (ii) part-time employment, (iii) a modest amount of registered open unemployment and (iv) surplus labour in agriculture. A scheme to guarantee everyone a job would be socially and politically attractive while providing considerable economic benefit.

The macroeconomic framework we recommend thus rests on three pillars: price stabilization achieved through tight credit conditions, market reforms in a selected number of strategic areas and accelerated growth. These three pillars are equally important. A failure in any one area is likely seriously to weaken the entire edifice. Hence the importance of getting priorities right.

Notes

1. World Bank, *Uzbekistan: Adjusting Social Protection* (Washington, DC, 20 December 1994), p. 2. The ratio of union transfers to GDP rose steadily in the years before independence and then fell abruptly to zero. The average transfer during the 1980s was much less than 19 per cent.
2. The range of estimates of GNP per capita is exceptionally wide. At the top end is an estimate for 1991 of $2790 in PPP terms (UNDP, *Human Development Report 1994*, New York: Oxford University Press, 1994). At the bottom end is an estimate for end 1994 of about 2100 sum, which would be less than $100 when converted at the official exchange rate that prevailed at the end of the year. Note that the official exchange rate was 25 sum = US$1 until late March 1995, whereas the black market rate was 40 sum = US$1. In late March the official rate was devalued to 26.1 sum to the dollar.
3. Michael Kaser and Santosh Mehrotra, *The Central Asian Economies after Independence* (London: Royal Institute of International Affairs, 1992), p. 64.
4. World Bank, *World Development Report 1994* (New York: Oxford University Press, 1994).
5. Kaser and Mehrota, *Central Asian Economies*, p. 27.
6. Ahmed Rashid, *The Resurgence of Central Asia: Islam or Nationalism?* (London: Zed Books, 1994), p. 95.
7. IMF, 'Note for the 1 March 1995, Consultative Group Meeting', Tashkent, mimeo, n.d., p. 4.
8. Keith Griffin and Azizur Rahman Khan, 'The Transition to Market Guided Economies: Lessons for Russia and Eastern Europe from the Chinese Experience', in Bernd Magnus and Stephen Cullenberg (eds), *Whither Marxism? Global Crises in International Perspective* (New York and London: Routledge, 1995).
9. Government of Uzbekistan, 'Statement on Economic Reform', a document prepared for the Consultative Group Meeting for Uzbekistan in Paris on 1 March 1995, Tashkent, February 1995.
10. Data supplied by the IMF.
11. Government of Uzbekistan, *'Statement'*.
12. Ibid.
13. See UNDP, *Social Policy and Economic Transformation in Uzbekistan* (Tashkent, April 1995), Ch. 4.
14. Parvez Hasan, 'Economic Reform, External Finance Requirements and World Bank's Role in Uzbekistan', remarks made at an international conference in London on 'Doing Business in Uzbekistan', 25–6 October 1994.
15. See Simon White and Jesper Petterson, *A Report on the Legal and Regu-*

latory Environment Affecting Small and Medium Enterprises (SMEs) in Uzbekistan (Tashkent: UNDP, March 1995).
16. See, for example, World Bank, *Uzbekistan: An Agenda for Economic Reform* (Washington, DC, 1993), Ch. 6.
17. For an analysis of similar problems of privatization in Mongolia, see Keith Griffin (ed.), *Poverty and the Transition to a Market Economy in Mongolia* (London: Macmillan, 1995), Ch. 1.
18. IMF, *Uzbekistan Economic Review* (Washington, DC, March 1994), Table 21, p. 59.
19. Not even the World Bank, an enthusiastic advocate of privatization, makes such claims. See World Bank, *Uzbekistan: Status Report on Structural Reforms*, a report to the Consultative Group Meeting, Paris, 1 March 1995, pp. 4–6.
20. See, e.g., Keith Griffin (ed.), *Institutional Reform and Economic Development in the Chinese Countryside* (London: Macmillan, 1984).
21. See, e.g., Keith Griffin and Terry McKinley, *Implementing a Human Development Strategy* (London: Macmillan, 1994), Ch. 5.

12 Social Protection

In Chapter 10 we emphasized that social policy is indistinguishable from development policy in general. In Chapter 11 we stressed the importance of reversing the decline in average living standards and achieving sustained growth. The need to generate employment and ensure that the benefits of growth are widely distributed is another theme, as is the potential of rural development to contribute rapidly to a rise in income.

Development policies concerned with protecting people from the vicissitudes of life are the subject of this chapter. That is, this chapter is concerned with what many people conventionally regard as the core of 'social policy': the need to protect people from the infirmities of old age, from congenital or acquired physical or mental handicaps, from the loss of employment and from unexpected shocks to income arising from droughts, pests, storms and so on. These are undoubtedly important issues, philosophically and practically, for the way we treat the less fortunate members of society tells us much about our values and attitudes, our vision of the just society and our conception of the rights and duties of citizenship.

As is clear from the two preceding chapters, however, social protection should be viewed through a wide-angled lens. Virtually all development policies have an impact both on the number of people who need social protection and on the types of vicissitudes of life they are likely to confront. If growth is rapid, if employment opportunities are widely available, if income is distributed relatively evenly, then problems of open unemployment and poverty are likely to be small and easily managed. Similarly, if the system of education and training is comprehensive and of high quality, workers will be flexible, adapt readily to changing conditions in the labour market and, everything else being equal, less likely to become unemployed. If the quality of the health system is high, and if everyone is provided with basic health services and adequate nutrition, the ability of children to learn will be improved, days lost from work because of illness will be reduced, the average productivity of labour per working day will be increased and human development in general will be promoted. Under such circumstances, policies aimed at providing social protection for specific groups in the community can be relatively modest in scope and the claims on public revenues to finance them need not be burdensome. On the other hand, if growth rates are negative, poverty is widespread and increasing, the health service is deteriorating and the educational system is declining in quality, the need for social protection will increase dramatically and almost certainly exceed the financial capabilities of government. To prevent this happening, development policy must be carefully designed to ensure that during the transition to a more market-oriented economy average living standards improve so that social protection policies can focus on 'residual' distress, i.e., on those who, for various reasons, are unable to participate in the labour force or who suffer severe hardship because of the restructuring of output and the reallocation of resources that inevitably accompanies the transition.

POVERTY

There is no system in Uzbekistan for collecting data on a regular basis on household income and expenditure. It is therefore impossible to measure the degree of inequality in the distribution of income or to construct estimates of the extent and location of poverty, the incidence of poverty among the different nationalities or to prepare a social profile of the characteristics of the poor. As a result it is exceptionally difficult to design policies which benefit the poor exclusively or even predominantly. Distributive policies in Uzbekistan have to be based on anecdotal evidence, informal guesses and common sense rather than on reliable statistical information.

There is some evidence from the pre-independence period that the distribution of income was unusually equal (compared to other developing countries) and that the degree of inequality actually was falling. Between 1970 and 1986 the Gini coefficient fell from 0.299 to 0.246, or by 17.7 per cent. Over the same period the share of income of the poorest 40 per cent of the income earning population rose from 17.5 to 21.8 per cent of the total.[1] Given the average level of income in Uzbekistan in the 1980s and the low degree of inequality, the level of poverty at the time of independence must have been low. Since then, inequality almost certainly has increased and average incomes have fallen but, even so, there is no visible evidence of widespread poverty. There is no squalor; calorie intake is high; people are well dressed; there is no homelessness; begging on the streets is unusual.

Poverty undoubtedly has increased but the proportion of the population living in poverty is low and the depth of poverty – measured by the average income of the poor – is not great. It is known that there are considerable differences in living standards between urban and rural areas. It is also evident that there is great regional variation, with Karakalpakstan being well below the average. Equally evident is the fact that on average European households are more prosperous than Uzbek and other households of Central Asian origin. Beyond this, there is considerable uncertainty. Fortunately, however, a remedy for our ignorance is in sight. Starting in April 1995, Goskomprognozstat, with assistance from the World Bank, will conduct an *ad hoc* survey of 20 000 households in order to obtain baseline data on the distribution of income. The results of the survey, unfortunately, will not be available for 12–14 months. Meanwhile, poverty is increasing and some public action is essential.

The government has responded in an imaginative way by allocating funds to assist 'needy families' and entrusting the distribution of these funds to neighbourhood committees called *mahallas*. The *mahallas* in effect are the front line in the system of social protection. The system has been in existence only since the fourth quarter of 1994 and it is too early to tell how well it works, but it is certainly an interesting experiment and worth monitoring closely. There are about 12 000 *mahallas* in the country and the government guesses that there are about 500 000 needy families, or between 40 and 50 on average in each neighbourhood. The budgetary allocation is very small – only 1.5 per cent of the total government budget – but if the programme is a success, it should be possible to increase the allocation in future, if necessary at the expense of other social programmes such as child allowances.

The *mahalla* committee not only distributes the funds, it also decides who is poor (and therefore deserving of support) and who is not. It is this latter function that makes this poverty alleviation programme so distinctive. Central and local government, unable themselves to target the poor, have turned the task over to the neighbourhood committees, relying on local knowledge to substitute for statistical data. The system has obvious advantages: it is highly decentralized, unbureaucratic and flexible, and thus cheap to administer. There are also some obvious possible disadvantages: if there is a great deal of geographical mobility in future, local knowledge may become seriously incomplete; the standards used to assess poverty and needs may vary markedly from one *mahalla* to another; and within a given *mahalla* people may be treated unequally, perhaps because of discrimination on the basis of nationality, religion or language. Hence it is important to monitor the programme without interfering with local discretion, and then adjust the scheme to correct any weaknesses that are found. Meanwhile, studies at central government level should be undertaken in order to establish guidelines to assist the work of the *mahalla* committees. The purpose of the guidelines should be to estimate poverty thresholds – in terms of capabilities as well as incomes – to ensure that it is the needy who in fact receive most of the assistance.

The national allocation for needy families in late 1994 was 122 million sums per month. Planning figures were based on the assumption that each needy family would receive the equivalent of 1.5 to 3 minimum wages. In April 1995 prices this implies a monthly benefit between 225 and 450 sums per family.

Field observations in Fergana suggest the planning assumptions are broadly correct. The *mahalla* committee in the neighbourhood visited consisted of a Chairman and Vice-Chairman (whose salaries were paid by local government) and 15 persons selected from the community (who were unpaid volunteers). Elections to the committee were to be held every 30 months. The neighbourhood consisted of 1110 families (or 4300 persons), a number sufficiently small for every family to be known well by at least a few members of the committee. In identifying the poor a number of considerations were taken into account: the number of children in the family, housing conditions, physical health or handicaps, the income of elderly pensioners, and so on. Using these criteria, 118 families were identified as needy, or over 10 per cent of the total. The amount of assistance given to each family each month was reported to be 200–300 sums, all of which was in cash.

The *mahalla* committee received its funds for needy families not from the central government but from local government. In Fergana there are 46 *mahallas* and local government officials allocated their funds among these *mahallas* partly on the basis of population size and partly on the basis of their assessment of the likely number of needy families. The local government's budget for needy families was about 4 million sums per quarter, or approximately 87 000 sums on average for each *mahalla*. The quarterly budget for the *mahalla* committee visited was actually 72 000 sums, implying either a slightly smaller or slightly less poor neighbourhood than the average. (Note, too, that this budget divided among the 118 needy families implies a monthly benefit of 203 sums per family.)

It would be premature to claim that the *mahalla* system is an effective institutional arrangement for assisting vulnerable groups and the disadvantaged – and certainly many of the national non-governmental organizations favour targeted funds aimed at their constituents – but the use of discretionary funds in the way described above is a valuable social experiment that may yield many useful lessons. Those who advocate empowerment of local people and the devolution of authority, as we do, should welcome this initiative. International agencies and foreign governments that wish to channel their aid directly to the poor now have a vehicle that can be used to achieve their objective.

UNEMPLOYMENT COMPENSATION

There is very little registered unemployment in Uzbekistan: less than 1 per cent of the labour force.[2] There is, however, a great deal of underutilized labour in various forms. Many people, particularly in the urban areas, have part-time jobs. Some have been temporarily laid off and sent home on full pay. There is considerable seasonal unemployment, especially among women in the rural areas. More important, there is a huge amount of surplus labour in agriculture.[3] Agriculture has increased the size of its labour force at a time when agricultural output has declined; in effect, the sector has acted as the residual source of employment. In the industrial sector, the state enterprises have large amounts of disguised unemployment, i.e., workers who are not needed for production but who nevertheless remain on the payroll for social reasons, to provide them with a source of income. The same situation exists in the privatized firms, since they are not allowed to dismiss workers for three years after privatization. There is hence enormous slack in the labour market which is prevented from becoming visible unemployment by peculiar institutional features in industry and agriculture. Uzbekistan is in fact operating a gigantic unemployment compensation scheme to provide social protection to workers who otherwise would be without a job and a source of livelihood. In agriculture, unemployment compensation is 'financed' by reducing the average productivity of labour, lowering real incomes and sharing poverty. It is a form of agricultural involution. In industry, unemployment compensation is financed by the banking system. Enterprises borrow money to cover their losses – losses which arise in large part because they must pay wages to large numbers of unnecessary workers. The result is rapid inflation, heavy indebtedness of the large enterprises and the gradual destruction of the financial viability of the industrial sector. The present system of 'disguised unemployment compensation' cannot continue indefinitely; something better will have to be devised.

One alternative is to allow enterprises, whether factories or farms, to shed their surplus labour – to transform disguised unemployment into open unemployment – and to compensate jobless workers so that they can continue to subsist. The payment of unemployment benefits would have to be financed by the government and would be inflationary. Offsetting this, however, would be a substantially reduced need of large enterprises for credit. A 'hard budget constraint' for large state and privatized firms would become credible for the first time.

There is in fact an explicit unemployment compensation scheme for the small number of registered unemployed workers.[4] The rules are complex, registration is not easy and the benefits are low. Indeed 'most benefit recipients get not more than the minimum wage'.[5] The implication is that registered unemployed workers receive less in benefits than they previously earned on a job. On the other hand, the 'disguised unemployment compensation' scheme is resulting in falling real earnings. Indeed the 'incomes policy' recently introduced – which we have called a wage reduction policy[6] – is clearly intended to allow real wages to fall by adjusting nominal wages less rapidly than the likely rate of inflation. One way or another, wages and incomes will have to decline as long as aggregate GNP continues to fall.

If the government wishes to move towards a system of open unemployment combined with unemployment benefits equivalent to the minimum wage, it certainly can do so. Indeed it would be superior to the present system of 'disguised unemployment compensation'. There is, however, an even better alternative.

During a period of systemic transformation and movement towards a market economy, when there is a pressing need to achieve a positive rate of growth, it seems foolish to pay workers unemployment benefits so that they can subsist in enforced idleness when they could instead be put to work, at a low wage, constructing income earning assets. That is the purpose of the employment guarantee scheme we have recommended.[7] That is, instead of paying the openly unemployed a minimum wage, pay the same people a minimum wage and give them a job which increases output, investment and growth.

The guaranteed employment scheme would be financed in the same way as an unemployment compensation scheme, namely, by the government. To the extent that government expenditure increased, the scheme would be inflationary. There are, however, two offsetting factors. First, the supply of credit through the banking system to large state and privatized enterprises would be reduced since there would no longer be a need to finance their deficits to enable them to make wage payments to the disguised unemployed. Net credit creation would decline, even if deficit financing were used by the government to fund the scheme, because those employed on public works projects would be paid only the minimum wage and not the (at present) higher wage paid by large enterprises. Thus, on the financial side, the guaranteed employment programme would be anti-inflationary. Second, to the extent that the public works programme increases investment in income generating assets, real output should increase. This increase in aggregate supply also would have an anti-inflationary impact and, of course, a growth accelerating impact.

Thus a policy designed to provide social protection to those who would otherwise be unemployed can help to rebalance the economy, reducing inflationary pressures while increasing investment and growth.

PENSIONS

Economic security for the elderly has long been a priority in Uzbekistan. No society, however low its per capita income may be, is so poor that it cannot afford to make some provision for those who no longer are able to engage in productive employment.[8] Uzbekistan, in fact, has a very generous pension system – far more generous than in most developing countries – and it is important to consider whether the system needs to be modified in light of the present circumstances of the country.

Under the present system, men who have worked at least 25 years are entitled to retire at the age of 60 and women who have worked at least 20 years are entitled to retire at the age of 55. Those classified as being employed in 'moderately dangerous' occupations may retire five years earlier than the norm and those classified as being employed in 'very dangerous' occupations may retire 10 years early. Thus in principle some men are entitled to retire at 50 and some women at 45.

At present there are about 2.5 million pensioners. Over 13 per cent of those on a pension are continuing to work.[9] Two possibilities for reform of the pension system immediately suggest themselves. First, the average age of retirement should be raised. Second, women and men should be treated equally. We recommend that the age of retirement should be 65 for both women and men. A third possible reform, about which we are less certain, is that provision for early retirement for employees in dangerous occupations should be abolished. Public policy should instead concentrate on improving occupational health and safety – making jobs less dangerous – rather than compensating people for exposure to risks of life and limb by allowing them to retire at 45 and 50, for women and men respectively. Even after health and safety standards are improved, some occupations will of course continue to be more dangerous than others. The correct way to address this problem, we believe, is through compensating wage payments, not early retirement.

The level of pensions also is remarkably generous. The maximum pension is equal to 75 per cent of previous earnings, although of course not everyone draws the maximum pension and the pension is not formally indexed. Once again, a case can be made for reform by reducing the average level of benefits. One possibility would be to prevent people from drawing a full pension if they continue to work after retirement. This, however, creates a disincentive to work which we regard as undesirable. The elderly should be allowed to supplement their pensions by working if they wish and they should incur no penalty by doing so. Some might argue that, given the large amount of surplus labour in the economy, it is in the wider social interest to discourage retirees from seeking paid employment. We disagree. Surplus labour can readily be absorbed and productively used in the employment guarantee scheme we have proposed, and it can hardly be in the public interest to discriminate against the elderly.

The alternative we recommend, similar to the suggestion made by the World Bank,[10] is that a minimum or basic pension be provided to everyone as a right, and that the minimum pension be adjusted regularly to compensate for inflation. That is, the elderly should be entitled to a low but constant real income that provides a minimum degree of economic security. Pension supplements above the basic level can be varied from time to time depending on general economic conditions and the financial position of the government.

Such a policy would combine equity (a fixed minimum real pension for all) with fiscal prudence. Uzbekistan cannot afford to continue to spend 11.4 per cent of its GDP on pensions, as it did in 1993.[11] Some reallocation of public expenditure towards poverty alleviation and employment creation programmes would provide a greater degree of social protection and hence would be in the public interest.

PROTECTION OF WOMEN AND CHILDREN

The population of Uzbekistan is young: 43 per cent of the population is less than 16 years old. Furthermore, over half the population is female and life expectancy of women (72 years) exceeds that of men

(66 years) by six years. The population growth rate continues to be high (2.7 per cent per annum), although it has fallen from the mid-1980s, when it was more than 3 per cent a year. The birth rate declined by nearly 13 per cent between the peak in 1986 and 1992, but it is still rather high compared to many other countries: 33.1 per thousand in 1992 on average and 38 per thousand in the rural areas.

The social protection of women and children should begin with a well-funded family planning programme. Compared to other health programmes, family planning is inexpensive and represents a good return on expenditure. It should be a central element in a human development strategy which aims to protect the health of the mother and ensure the survival of infants.

During the Soviet period the structure of incentives was strongly pro-natalist. The cost to the family of an additional child was negligible; most costs were borne by the state. Pre- and post-natal services were free; hospital deliveries were free; food was subsidized; education was free; basic health services were free; and children were guaranteed a job on a *kolkhoz* (collective farm) or in a state enterprise when they left school. All that is now changing as Uzbekistan moves towards a more market-oriented economy. More responsibility will be placed on the family, the number of services provided by the state will decline and their cost to the individual will rise. This will change the structure of incentives and the desired size of family will fall, and probably already has begun to do so. The state should assist this process by helping families to control the number of children that are born and by enabling women to regulate the interval between births, both in the interest of the mother and of her other children.

There clearly is a demand for family planning services. The Ministry of Health supplies intra-uterine devices free of charge and claims that 40 per cent of women use them. Even if this exaggerates the effectiveness of the programme in reducing fertility, it shows that there is at least a latent demand for contraceptives. The Ministry should launch a public information campaign to reduce ignorance about family planning methods and at the same time it should give women more choice by increasing the number of types of contraception available. This will increase costs but still will be cheap at the price. Moreover, external assistance may be available to help finance a well-designed, comprehensive programme in reproductive health.

Other public health measures are desirable to protect mothers and children, e.g., an expanded programme of immunization and a more efficient programme to control diarrhoeal diseases and pneumonia. Perhaps the highest priority, however, is measures to reduce the extraordinarily high incidence of anaemia among women and children. Anaemia probably is due to nutritional deficiencies and in particular to an inadequate intake of one or more micronutrients. More research, followed by public action, is needed urgently. The NGOs we have consulted feel very strongly about this and the government ought to respond.

SUMMARY

In this chapter we have concentrated on just four areas of social protection which we regard as central. These are (i) measures to relieve poverty, (ii) a programme to provide productive employment for workers who otherwise would be unemployed, (iii) a pension scheme to ensure the elderly enjoy a minimum level of economic security and (iv) programmes to provide protection to women and children.

We have deliberately kept the list short in order to highlight priorities. If Uzbekistan can alleviate the worst forms of poverty, guarantee a job to everyone who desires one, and provide security to everyone in their old age it will have created a foundation of social protection that should enable it to effect the transition from a centrally planned to a social market economy without creating intolerable hardship and distress. If, in addition, Uzbekistan can establish a good family planning service and provide other measures to protect the well-being of women and children, it will ensure that the next generation inherits a country of which they can be proud.

Notes

1. Michael Kaser and Santosh Mehrotra, *The Central Asian Economies After Independence* (London: Royal Institute of International Affairs, 1992), p. 35.
2. See UNDP, *Social Policy and Economic Transformation in Uzbekistan* (Tashkent, April 1995), Ch. 3.
3. Ibid., Ch. 4.
4. For details of the scheme see World Bank, *Uzbekistan: Adjusting Social Protection* (Washington, DC, 20 December 1994), pp. 28–31.
5. Ibid., p. 28.
6. See Chapter 11.
7. See Chapter 11 and UNDP, *Social Policy* , Ch. 3.
8. See Keith Griffin and Terry McKinley, *Implementing a Human Development*

Strategy (London: Macmillan, 1994), pp. 90–5, and Ehtisham Ahmad, Jean Drèze and Amartya Sen (eds), *Social Security in Developing Countries* (Oxford: Clarendon Press, 1991).
9. World Bank, *Uzbekistan*, Table 5.1, p. 58.
10. Ibid., Ch. 5.
11. Ibid., p. 61.

Index